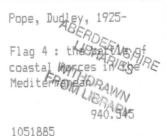

D1423934

1051885

Also by Dudley Pope

NON-FICTION

The Battle of the River Plate
73 North
Life in Nelson's Navy
England Expects
At 12 Mr Byng was Shot
The Black Ship
Guns
The Great Gamble
Harry Morgan's Way
The Devil Himself

FICTION

The *Ramage* Series

Ramage
Ramage and the Drum Beat
Ramage and the Freebooters
Governor Ramage RN
Ramage's Prize
Ramage and the Guillotine
Ramage's Diamond
Ramage's Mutiny
Ramage and the Rebels
The Ramage Touch
Ramage's Signal
Ramage and the Renegades
Ramage's Devil
Ramage's Trial
Ramage's Challenge
Ramage at Trafalgar
Ramage and the Saracens
Ramage and the Dido

The *Yorke* Series

Convoy
Decoy
Admiral
Galleon
Corsair

FLAG 4

THE BATTLE OF COASTAL FORCES
IN THE MEDITERRANEAN

by

DUDLEY POPE

CHATHAM PUBLISHING

LONDON

Published in 1998 by
Chatham Publishing,
1 & 2 Faulkner's Alley, Cowcross Street
London EC1M 6DD

Chatham Publishing is an imprint of
Gerald Duckworth & Co Ltd

First published in 1954
by William Kimber and Co Limited

ISBN 1 86176 067 1

Printed and bound in Great Britain by
The Cromwell Press, Trowbridge, Wilts

CONTENTS

ILLUSTRATIONS

To
K. P. P.

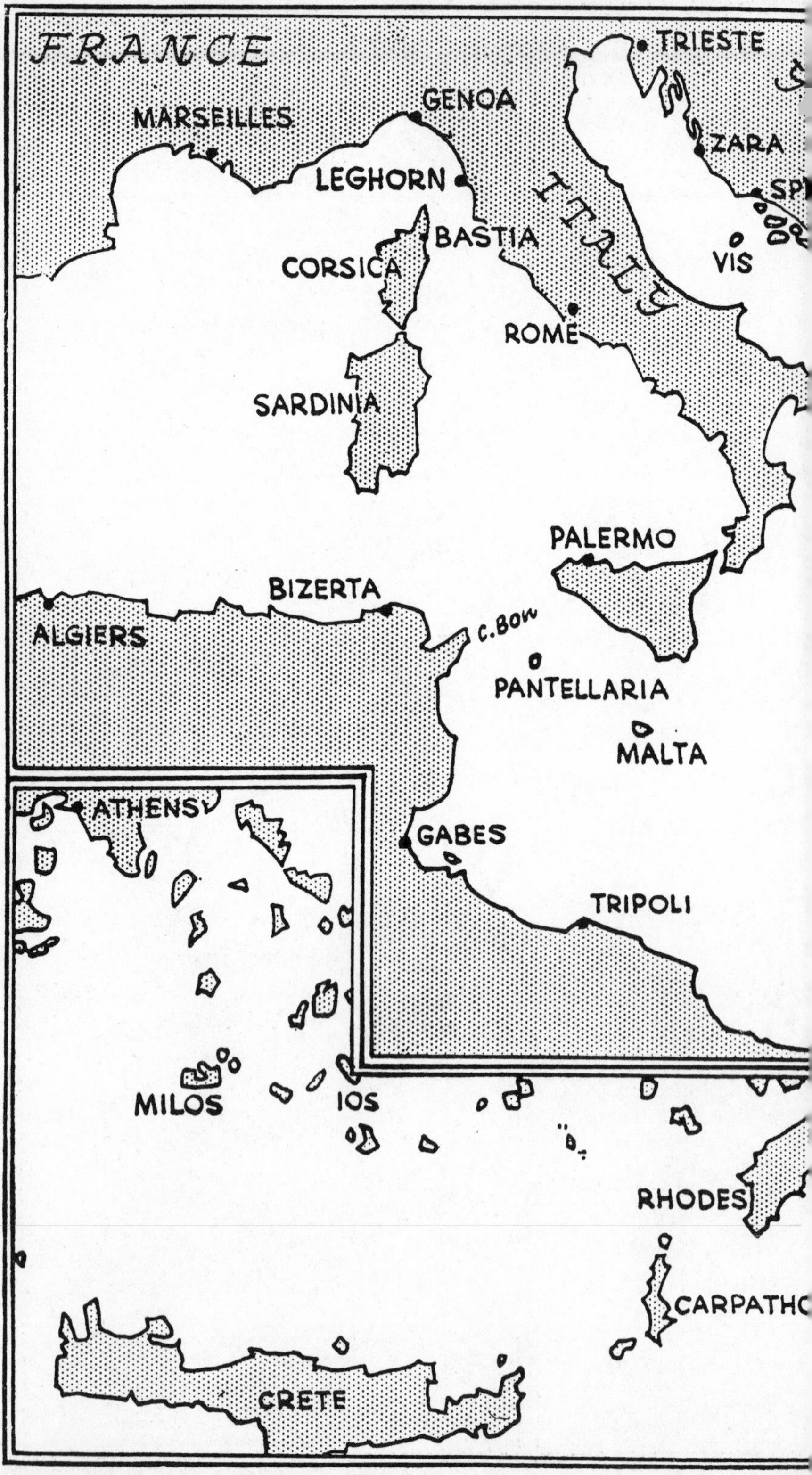
FRANCE
TRIESTE
GENOA
MARSEILLES
ZARA
LEGHORN
ITALY
BASTIA
CORSICA
VIS
ROME
SARDINIA
PALERMO
BIZERTA
ALGIERS
C. Bon
PANTELLARIA
MALTA
ATHENS
GABES
TRIPOLI
MILOS
IOS
RHODES
CRETE

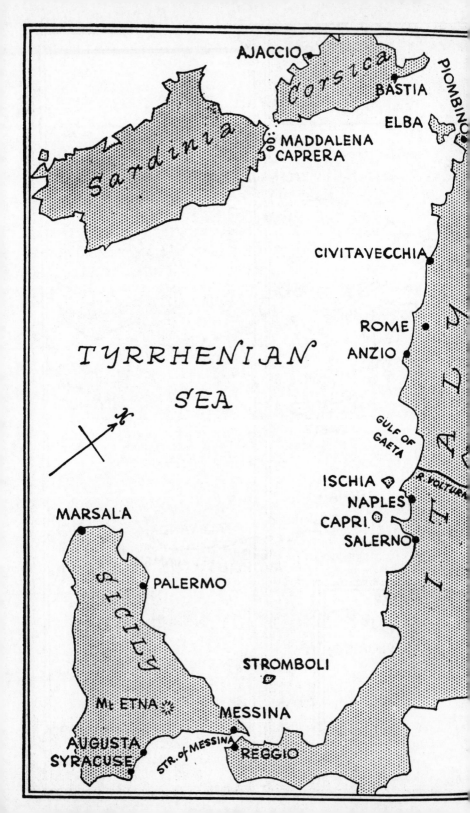

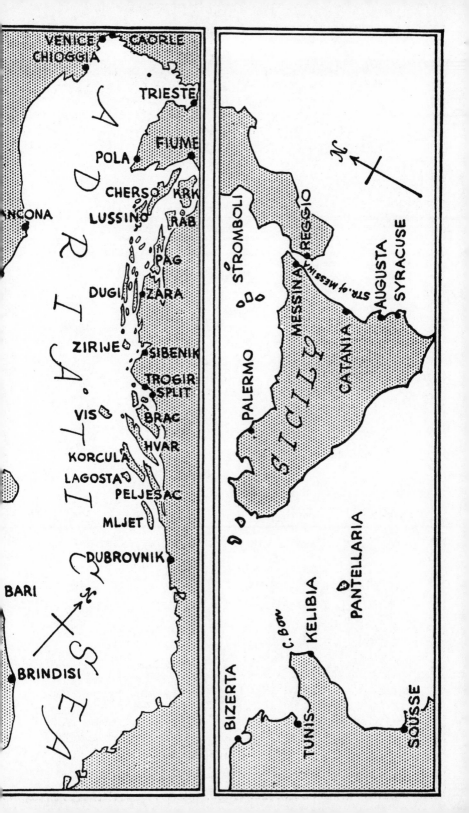

AUTHOR'S PREFACE

WHEN you have finished reading this book you may wonder why the almost incredible story of Coastal Forces in the Mediterranean during the Second World War was not written before this.

I do not know, but I have written this narrative because it was essential that the events were recorded before the details faded in the memories of the officers and men concerned.

Since I had only a limited amount of space at my disposal, I have concentrated on the actions, tactics and strategy of Coastal Forces rather than on the men. For this reason, and also because the people concerned live in many countries, it has been impossible to make the story as personalised as I would have liked.

Although this is not an official history, I have been most fortunate in having the whole-hearted co-operation of the Admiralty and many of the officers commanding flotillas and boats.

At the outset there were two ways of writing this book: either as an almost day-to-day account of the work of individual boats, with little or no reference to the rest of the war; or a broader account with a brief outline of the rest of the Mediterranean war at sea woven into the narrative.

After hearing many opinions, both lay and expert, I decided on the latter course because, while the war at home was more fully reported at the time, the Mediterranean war at sea was rather scantily reported in communiqués and newspapers. The necessities of censorship had a great deal to do with this; and fortunately the Admiralty censors have dealt lightly with my manuscript.

This book tries to answer the question of why the Allies—and the Axis—fought so hard for what was, in effect, large expanses of sand and water. Because I did not serve in this theatre, and because to my mind it is not necessary in a story such as this, I have made no attempt to give physical descriptions of places. I trust readers will consult the maps.

Because of the limited space available, more than a third of the original MS. had to be cut. This resulted in the necessity to omit details of gallant and cleverly-fought actions which, although interesting, were similar to ones previously told in this book.

There has been a good deal of difficulty in gathering details because, for instance, the Canadian officers of certain flotillas naturally returned home at the end of the war. This has meant I have mentioned the British officers in those flotillas because they were equally able to tell the story and were accessible.

Many people have spent a lot of their valuable time helping me assemble details of actions, and I must thank the following people:

Admiral of the Fleet Sir Rhoderick R. McGrigor, G.C.B., D.S.O., First Sea Lord and Chief of Naval Staff, for the Foreword he has written; the Board of Admiralty for permission and facilities to see a large number of documents concerning the Royal Navy in the war; the Historical Section, Admiralty, and in particular Cdr. G. A. Titterton, R.N. (Retd.), the Mediterranean Narrator, and Mr. G. H. Hurford, F.R.Hist.S., Miss E. M. Curry and Miss D. Johnson, of the Information Room; and Cdr. M. G. Saunders, R.N. (Retd.), of the Foreign Documents Section, for much valuable information concerning German reports.

The Chief of Naval Information, Capt. A. W. Clarke, C.B.E., D.S.O., R.N. (Retd.), and the following members of his department: Mr. H. G. O. Cross, M.B.E., the Deputy Director; Mr. E. Thompson and Mr. Mervyn Ellis, of the Scrutiny Section; Mrs. Edwards, of the Library; and Mr. W. Parry, of the Photographic Library.

Officers who served with Coastal Forces in the Mediterranean have given me a great deal of help, and I would like to thank in particular Lt.-Cdr. T. J. Bligh, D.S.O., O.B.E., D.S.C.* who has provided me with some excellent material, both in writing and verbally; and I have had a lot of assistance from Cdr. R. A. Allan, D.S.O., O.B.E., M.P.; Capt. Morgan Giles, D.S.O., O.B.E., G.M., R.N.; Capt. A. E. P. Welman, D.S.O.*, D.S.C.*, R.N. (Retd.); Cdr. D. Jermain, D.S.C., R.N.; Cdr. C. W. S. Dreyer, D.S.O., D.S.C.*, R.N.; Lt.-Cdr. C. Jerram, D.S.O., D.S.C.*; Lt.-Cdr. J. Montgomerie, D.S.C.; Lt.-Cdr. M. Solomon, D.S.C.; Lt.-Cdr. Edelsten-Pope, R.A.N.R.; Lt.-Cdr. Brian Close, D.S.C., R.A.N.R.; Lt.-Cdr. G. W. Stead; Lt. D. H. Brown, D.S.C.; Lt. R. Aitchison, D.S.C.; Lt. H. Prince; Lt. P. D. Barlow, D.S.C.; Lt. J. Collins, M.B.E., D.S.C., and Lt.-Cdr. Basil Bourne, D.S.C.

My thanks are due to Lt.-Cdr. J. Ivester Lloyd, D.S.C., and Lt. L. Reynolds, who very generously put written material and photographs at my disposal; Lt. A. T. Robinson, D.S.C., who provided several of the photographs used in this book; the Yugoslav Ambassador; and

Rear-Admiral Charles L. Andrews, Jr., U.S.N. (Retd.). I have had much technical help and advice from Cdr. Peter Du Cane, O.B.E., R.N. (Retd.), managing director of Vosper Ltd., and from Lt.-Cdr. (E) R. P. Pratt. Brigadier Tom Churchill, C.B.E., M.C., was of great help concerning the Army side of Adriatic operations.

To Cassell & Co., publishers of *The Second World War*, and Hutchinson & Co., Ltd., publishers of *A Sailor's Odyssey*, my thanks are due for permission to publish extracts from the books written by Sir Winston Churchill and Admiral of the Fleet Viscount Cunningham.

My colleague Mr. Jack Ramsay painted the excellent dust jacket and drew the maps; and my sailing companion, Mr. Colin Mudie, A.M.I.N.A., drew the cutaway drawings of a Fairmile "D" and a Vosper boat.

Most of all, my thanks must go to my wife: at the time this book was started she was my fiancée; and despite a courtship spent doing research at the Admiralty and typing most of the MS., she became my wife five days after the book was completed.

Yacht Concerto
Southwick
Sussex
September 1954

Officers referred to are R.N.V.R. unless otherwise stated, and times given are frequently zone times.

Chapter I

THE BACKGROUND

Circumstances have caused the Mediterranean Sea to play a greater part in the history of the world, both in a commercial and military point of view, than any sheet of water of the same size. Nation after nation has striven to control it, and the strife still goes on.

Therefore a study of the conditions upon which preponderance in its waters has rested, and now rests, and of the relative military values of different points upon its coasts, will be more informative than the same amount of effort expended in another field.

The Influence of Sea Power on History, 1660–1783

ADMIRAL A. T. MAHAN wrote those words in 1889, and fifty-one years later the bitterest round in the age-long battle for control of the million square miles of Homer's "wine-dark sea" began.

It began because one more dictator, blinded by his own spasms of megalomania, saw that control of the Mediterranean Sea meant control of Africa and the Suez Canal; and like Napoleon, he saw Suez as the gateway to the East, a gateway to a great new Roman Empire.

Just as Napoleon's dreams of conquering Egypt and cutting a canal through the isthmus were shattered, afloat by Nelson and ashore by Abercromby, so Mussolini's dreams of the Mediterranean as an Italian lake were turned into a nightmare by the three fighting Services, ending only as his body swung lifeless from a gibbet in a remote Italian village.

As, in this book, we are concerned primarily with Coastal Forces in the Mediterranean, it is essential that their role in the war, and the influence of the Mediterranean in history, shall be understood.

The Mediterranean has been called the "cradle of civilisation", and its shores, from Spain in the west to ancient Palestine in the east, are strewn with buildings and ruins revealing the lives and loves and battles of its people from many centuries before Christ until the present day.

A burning motor torpedo-boat may have sunk under the shadow of the island of Crete in the same position as a shattered rowing galley belonging to Minos, but the waves engulf it within seconds; and the fact that one vessel belonged to the first naval power to command the Mediterranean (two thousand years before Christ) and the other to the naval power commanding it nearly two thousand years after Christ makes no difference, because the sea keeps no record.

The strategic importance of the Mediterranean and its ports has always been bound up with trade: in early days whoever controlled its sea highways could successfully sail out his own trading ships and destroy those of his rivals.

The fabulous epochs of Castor and the reasoned prose of Mahan span the naval history of the great sea. Castor tells of the first naval power ever to attain command of it, Crete under Minos. From Crete control passed to the Lydians in 1179 B.C., and then successively to many Eastern Mediterranean powers, many of whose names are today but the names of small, sparsely-populated islands.

The importance of the Mediterranean was its role as the trade link between Europe on the one side and Africa and the Far East on the other. In the ancient days Egypt was the point where West met East, the aromatic clearing-house of the exotic cargoes of India and Asia leaving overland and by sea for the luxury-loving and sensation-seeking Europeans.

But the war against the holy cities of Mecca and Medina closed the canal linking the Nile with the Red Sea in A.D. 700, and traders were faced with an age-old problem which frequently—and often accidently—led to new countries being discovered: they had to find a new way through.

Gradually they started using the Levant ports at the eastern end of the Mediterranean, bringing their cargoes down to the sea lashed on the backs of camels—the "ships of the desert". So, for a while, the Levant ports flourished and Egypt, her "Moment in Annihilation's waste" past, slowly died.

Then Marco Polo, after incredible adventures, discovered the overland route from China across to Turkey, farther north, and in turn the Levant ports gradually fell into near-disuse.

But a century later a voyage started—in a ship displacing only slightly more than the modern motor torpedo-boat—which was to change the known face of the world: in 1497 Vasco da Gama rounded the Cape of Good Hope and opened the sea route to India and the

Far East. From then on the northern nations could deal direct with the East, without using the somewhat unscrupulous "middle-men" of the Mediterranean.

So the great receiving centres of the Mediterranean were slowly pushed out of business. No longer did the Eastern wares come over-land to Levant and Turkish ports, and then by sea to the rich ports of Venice and Pisa, Genoa and Marseilles.

Loss of trade is naturally damaging to a country—especially an ambitious country like France. As Marseilles, once one of the most important and flourishing ports of the Mediterranean, fell into disuse and decay, so one French king after another played with the idea of Egypt . . . an occupied Egypt with their engineers cutting a canal joining the Mediterranean to the Red Sea, amputating the arm of the continent of Africa which barred the seaway to the East.

To trade direct with India and Asia, northern seamen following Vasco da Gama accepted the long sea route (11,000 miles from Britain to Calcutta, for instance), but a canal linking the Mediterranean with the Red Sea would cut that voyage to 6,250 miles.

The distance from Europe to the East almost halved—but it took a Napoleon Bonaparte to act, and he wrote to Talleyrand: "The time is not far off when to destroy England we shall be forced to occupy Egypt."

Talleyrand told the Directoire and they ordered (in April 1798) the ambitious Bonaparte to sail and occupy Egypt, and "cut a canal through the Isthmus of Suez and assure the exclusive use of the Red Sea to the French Republic".

Napoleon made one big blunder, to be followed by Hitler and, to a certain extent, Mussolini: he underestimated the value and the use of sea-power. Although there were long periods during the Napoleonic war when the Royal Navy was out of the Mediterranean, Nelson was there when Napoleon sailed from Toulon, and it was Nelson who smashed his fleet at Aboukir Bay in the great Battle of the Nile.

Years later de Lesseps—without any financial backing from the British, who had not woken up to the importance of Egypt to Britain —built the Suez Canal, which was opened in 1869. But more British ships used it than any other country, and Disraeli's dramatic purchase of the Khedive of Egypt's shares soon put us in a strong position. Britain, at last, was awake, and she soon took steps to protect the Canal and modernise Egypt.

But the years passed, and while Europe, like Rip Van Winkle, slept soundly, Mussolini's ersatz star was rising: like Napoleon, he dreamed of Suez in his hands. Once he had entered the war, he visualised that with the Canal in his hands, and with Hitler's help, the Axis would strike north-east into Palestine, Syria and Iran, and advance north to outflank the Russians. The Middle East oilfields would be in Axis hands. And the sea route to their other treacherous ally, Japan, would be open. The British blockade of Germany would have failed: the Nazis and Fascists would have all the oil and rubber they needed for their ambitious, carefully-laid plans. India would be open to the Axis hordes—from the Germans and Italians in the west and the already-near Japanese to the south-east.

Yet in fact at no time did the Axis have complete control of all the strategic areas of the Mediterranean. The British Army fought in the desert on sands stained by the blood of Romans when they fought Carthage; the Royal Navy fought over the seas known to the Minoans, Greeks and Trojans, over the tideless waters which were impartial graveyard of trireme and galley, submarine and battleship.

Despite the fact that the complete northern coastline—from France in the west to Yugoslavia, Albania and Greece in the east—was enemy-held, and with the Axis dominating the Narrows between Sicily and Tunisia, the Navy fought back.

It used in the early days a few outdated battleships, a handful of cruisers and destroyers, and various small craft ranging from river gunboats to a few old MTBs.

Since this story really opens after France fell and Italy came into the war, let us look at the position then. Mussolini had built up a new fleet of fast, well-built ships. Not a big fleet, but a well-balanced one with battleships, plenty of heavy cruisers, fast destroyers, submarines and patrol craft.

By controlling the Sicilian Narrows he planned to cut the Mediterranean in half; but in fact he was not always able to do this completely. So with the fall of France, only Egypt and Palestine, the two islands of Malta and Cyprus, and Gibraltar were in British hands. The rest of the Mediterranean was in Axis or neutral hands. Our only naval bases were at Alexandria in the east, Gibraltar in the west, and Malta in the middle. Tiny, gallant Malta which Mussolini had boasted his warships and aircraft would capture in two days. . . .

Soon Axis hordes spread their particular brand of hatefulness over Yugoslavia, Albania, Greece and Crete. It was not long before the whole coastline from France to the Black Sea, and from Algeria to the Egyptian border, was Axis-held. This, theoretically, gave the Axis complete control of the Mediterranean both at sea and in the air. But only theoretically.

It was not long before vessels of the Royal Navy, ranging from battleships (ancient as they were) to motor torpedo-boats (few as they were), were fighting back desperately along the vast African coasts. It was many weary and bitter months before the MTBs, MGBs and MLs were roaming off Sicily and Sardinia, and, on the other side of Italy, ranging far up into the Adriatic among the German-held Dalmatian Islands, hiding under some cliff of an enemy-held island by day, savagely attacking his convoys by night; many gruelling months before they were fighting the enemy among the myth-ridden islands of the Aegean.

.   .   .   .   .

The Germans were under no illusions about the strategic importance of the Mediterranean right from the beginning of the war; and Grand Admiral Raeder presented a survey[1] of political developments to the senior officers on his staff which made his views quite clear, but the Germans soon found Hitler had little idea of the use and importance of sea-power at the beginning of the war and none at all towards the end. On 6th September 1940 the Commander-in-Chief, Raeder, reported[2] to Hitler:

> *Gibraltar and the Suez Canal have decisive strategic significance for German-Italian warfare in the Mediterranean area. Britain should be excluded from the Mediterranean. Control of the Mediterranean area is of vital importance to the position of the Central Powers in South-eastern Europe, Asia Minor, Arabia, Egypt and the African area.*
>
> *Unlimited sources for raw materials would be guaranteed. New and strategically favourable bases for further operations against the British Empire would be won. The loss of Gibraltar would mean crucial difficulties for the British import traffic from the South Atlantic. Preparations for this operation must be begun at once so that they are completed before the U.S.A. steps in.*
>
> *The Fuehrer gives orders to this effect.*

Three weeks later Raeder was again reporting[3] to the Fuehrer in an attempt to hammer home his ideas about the Mediterranean:

[1] *Minutes of the Fuehrer's Naval Conferences*, 1939.
[2] Ibid., 1940.
[3] Ibid., 1940.

The British Navy have always considered the Mediterranean the pivot of their world empire. Even now eight of their thirteen battleships are there; strong positions are held in the Eastern Mediterranean; troop transports from Australia were sent to Egypt and East Africa. . . .

By the time Italy came into the war Britain had managed to strengthen her position in the Mediterranean despite the desperate threat of invasion at home. It was becoming clear that, as in Napoleonic times, the Mediterranean was to be one of the decisive theatres of the war. But only Raeder and the General Staff, possibly because they alone realised the full meaning of sea-power, appreciated the danger.

Hitler had paid lip-service to their schemes, but he was a land animal, and his mind was concentrating on a land battle—the invasion of Russia. On 28th October 1940, however, a somewhat inconsiderate Mussolini invaded Greece and upset his plans.

Our last look at the strategic situation is through the eyes of a German, Vice-Admiral Weichold. In *The War at Sea*[1] he gives these views:

The entry of Italy into the war put an entirely new complexion on the military situation in the Anglo-German war. After the successful countering of the German air attack against the British Isles and when the German High Command had renounced its plan for invasion,[2] recognising the sea as the only place where British power could be brought into battle, another very vulnerable point of the British Empire was now laid open to the Axis in the Mediterranean.

The reason for the vulnerability lay in the dependency, even of a sea power, on the geographical situation. This was especially true of the Mediterranean as British sea-power relied only on a few bases.

With the fall of these, the whole edifice of British power in the Mediterranean, above all in the Middle East, must needs crumble. England's Mediterranean possessions were, however, mostly of commercial value which had increased considerably since the First World War.

Through her obligations to territories in the Eastern Mediterranean, England had now become vulnerable on land. A threat or struggle in these territories allowed the British Empire to be brought to battle on the land which had hitherto only been possible on the sea.[3]

[1] With other German admirals captured at the end of the war, Weichold was requested to write a report on the war at sea.
[2] Operation "Sea-lion".
[3] Here Weichold has, in this and the succeeding paragraph, summed up the whole question.

The practical considerations governing the exclusion of Britain's sea-power from the Mediterranean and the destruction of her imperial lifeline were the seizure of Malta, the blocking of the Sicilian Channel and the conducting of operations from Libya against Egypt. Italy's situation in the Central Mediterranean and her possession of Tripolitania secured French North Africa as a base for future land and air operations against the British on a large scale.

. . . The only presupposition for the execution of Axis Mediterranean operations was the recognition that in that sea and bordering British territories lay the possibilities of concerted action with the Italian ally.

. . . . .

World War II in Europe falls conveniently into four parts:

(1) After the fall of Dunkirk the Battle of Britain gave us breathing space to really get Britain's war production going.

(2) Victory in the Battle of the Atlantic allowed the British Isles to be built up as the arsenal and castle from which, on D-Day, Hitler's fortress could be attacked.

(3) The Battle of the Mediterranean, which finally stopped the Axis advance and then drove them back, made a German victory impossible and gave the Allies time—time to learn, time to get their strength, and time to plan the final assault on Europe.

(4) The Second Front, which gave the final crushing blow.

The fifty-four-month Battle of the Mediterranean can also be divided into four parts:

(1) The capture of all the northern coastline by the Axis.

(2) The isolation of Malta and the capture of much of the coastline on either side of the Mediterranean, a period when Admiral Cunningham seldom let the superior enemy forces take the initiative.

(3) The defeat of the Germans and Italians in Libya and, after the North Africa landings, the complete destruction of the Axis forces in Africa.

(4) The invasion of Sicily and Italy, the liberation of Greece, Albania and Yugoslavia, and the invasion of Southern France.

CHAPTER II

A STATE OF WAR . . .

N OW for the introduction to Coastal Forces, the smallest ships of the Royal Navy to sail the seas as fighting units. So small, in fact, that (with half a dozen exceptions) all the boats had numbers instead of names.

They were craft in which individual—and individualist—leadership was essential. During the war they were manned almost exclusively by the Royal Naval Volunteer Reserve—men who, in peacetime, followed many and varied professions and trades, and a proportion of whom were yachtsmen.

The boats themselves were built of wood for two main reasons: to obtain light displacement, and to allow them to be built in the many yacht yards round our coasts, thus not interfering with the building of steel warships.

Later in the war mass-production or prefabrication was used extensively—especially with the very successful Fairmile designs. But in September 1939 we had only the 60-foot and 70-foot MTBs, pioneered by the B.P.B. Co. and Vosper Ltd. respectively, together with a number of craft building for foreign governments; a modest and late start, for it was upon the experience gained in building and operating these few boats that the vast armada of Coastal Forces—mass-produced, prefabricated, and assembled in the four corners of the world—was to be founded.

The German surface fleet favoured MTBs. They were not subject to naval treaty obligations and mass-production could be achieved by building them as coastguard cutters. By 1938 Lurssen, Vegesach, were building diesel-engined E-boats[1] capable of more than 36 knots and were actually advertising them in England. They continued with the same design for E-boats right through the war.

The Germans thus started with two advantages: a high-powered diesel engine already being mass-produced, and a hull well tested and tried on coastguard duties. We were not so fortunate and far-sighted. MTBs were very very minor war vessels of the British Fleet, and the

---

[1] "E-boats" refers to the description "Enemy War Motor-boats".

pre-war design and manufacture of a diesel engine for so few craft would have been a very expensive venture.

It was thought that the needs of MTBs could be met by marine conversions of various aircraft engines, which, although they were petrol engines and would introduce a considerable fire risk in a wooden craft, were of lightweight construction, thoroughly tested and tried (in aircraft) and also "on the shelf".

Additionally Vospers purchased the manufacturing rights of a high-power marine petrol engine of Italian design. In the event, however, the R.A.F. wanted all—and more—of the manufacturing capacity of the aero-engine firms and work on building the Italian engine in this country had not started when hostilities commenced. Eventually America came to our aid with two very fine types of marine petrol engine, the Hall Scott for the "A", "B" and "C" Fairmiles and the Packard for the "D" Fairmiles and the 70-foot MTBs and MGBs.

There were four main types of Coastal Forces craft which fell into two groups—offensive and defensive. The offensive boats—similar in role to the fast fighter-bombers of the R.A.F.—were the Motor Torpedo-boats (MTBs) and Motor Gunboats (MGBs). The defensive boats (although many of them became very offensive in the Mediterranean) were the Motor Launches (MLs) and Harbour-defence Motor Launches (HDMLs).

The disadvantages of all the craft were their limited range, small fire-power, vulnerability to air attack and their inability to take much punishment from the enemy[1] or high winds and heavy seas. But their tactical advantages, although the Admiralty were slow to realise them, and even slower to utilise them, completely outweighed the drawbacks.

The MTBs and MGBs were extremely fast and highly manœuvrable. Their silhouette was low. Thus they were ideal for night fighting, where surprise, not the weight of fire-power, was often the decisive factor. They, and they alone of our surface craft, could operate close to the enemy's coast (usually about a hundred yards off, in the Adriatic and Aegean!); penetrate known minefields and harbours protected by boom defences; attack in shoal-waters; and, sailing by night and hiding in creeks and inlets of enemy-held islands during daytime, fight where destroyers, unable to get clear by dawn, would have to risk often devastating air attacks. They, and they alone, continually took the war

[1] Primarily because they were lightly constructed (for speed); unarmoured except for thin plating round the bridge; and carried several thousands of gallons of petrol, which made them highly inflammable.

into the enemy's coastal waters; to his quayside, in fact. From the
end of 1940 to 1943 they were, in fact, almost the only surface craft
continually able to seek out and fight the enemy.

It was in 1935 that the Admiralty ordered twelve 60-foot motor
torpedo-boats from the British Power Boat Company. The first six
boats were delivered in March 1937 and became the 1st MTB Flotilla.
They were based on Malta and made the passage to the Mediterranean
under their own power. The second six boats, the 2nd MTB Flotilla,
were shipped to Hong Kong. They served there until the island
fortress fell to the Japanese.

Six more boats of the same type, the 3rd MTB Flotilla, were allocated
to Singapore. They arrived in the Mediterranean in the summer of
1939, on their way to the Far East. The Admiralty then ordered them
to join the 1st MTB Flotilla at Malta, bringing the island's strength up
to twelve boats.

At home the 4th MTB Flotilla, of more advanced craft, was forming
at Portsmouth and was to have comprised of six 70-foot boats designed
by Vosper's. But during the summer of 1939, a few weeks before the
war began, three of them were sold to Rumania.

So that fateful Sunday morning in September, when a quiet voice
told us on the wireless that a state of war existed between us and
Germany, the Royal Navy at home had three boats in the 4th MTB
Flotilla, plus one experimental boat; the 1st and 3rd MTB Flotillas in
Malta; and the 2nd MTB Flotilla at Hong Kong.

There was no recognised Coastal Forces base in Britain, nor any
special training facilities. At the Admiralty itself there was no department specifically responsible for Coastal Forces; indeed the name
"Coastal Forces" was not coined. In addition the World War I
prejudice against these types of craft still existed in many minds.

The *Coastal Forces Periodical Review*, in an historical survey at the
end of the war in 1945, comments:

*We started the war with almost complete lack of experienced MTB officers
and there were no senior officers who could train the young ones; there was
no considered amalgam of doctrine and experience. The Navy generally
knew nothing about the boats. From the material aspect, while the wooden
hulls could be built quickly, there was no suitable British engine available.*

Before the war, it was assumed—quite reasonably—that U-boats
would operate in the North Sea and Channel, and we developed a

small, fast anti-submarine boat known as a Motor Anti-Submarine Boat (Masby). Soon after the war began it became obvious that the U-boats were unable to operate there, so there were no targets for the Masbys. However, when France fell the E-boats swarmed into the North Sea and Channel thick and fast, and the Masbys were converted into motor gunboats.

This was not as easy as it sounds: the right type of guns were not available at the beginning; and people like Robert Hichens, later to become one of the greatest motor gunboat leaders in Home Waters, had to beg, borrow and steal machine-guns from nearby R.A.F. aerodromes.

The success of the Masby-turned-MGB was soon obvious; they could—reducing it to its lowest terms—attack the escorts while the MTBs attacked the convoy. But there were never any set rules for the game . . . there seldom is.

Now for the boats themselves, starting with MTBs. These waspish craft are divided into two basic types—short boats under 100 feet and long boats over 100 feet. It was only the 60-foot boats of the British Power Boat Co. that had the sting in their tail, provided by two 18-inch torpedoes with stern launching gear. The later short boats of 70 feet and 73 feet which were mainly developed by Vosper's had bow-firing 21-inch torpedoes in tubes. It was a requirement that all these short boats must be capable of being carried overseas on the decks of merchant ships. In the Mediterranean other types of short boats were also used—the American-designed and built Elcos and Higgins.

Speeds and armaments of the short boats varied, depending on the particular role they were playing at the time and the stage of development reached. Generally speaking, they carried two torpedoes, several light guns (of which the 20-mm. Oerlikon was the most popular) and depth-charges. They had three engines.

The short boats—although the fastest ever to operate—suffered from the fact that they were not particularly good sea-boats and they could not keep at sea in much over Force 5.[1] It became necessary to have a larger MTB designed to keep the sea in worse weather than the short boats. Their function would be the same, although there would be an added emphasis on gun-power.

So the long boats came into being. The first were completed early in 1942. The majority of them were the Fairmile "D" class, referred to hereafter as "D" (or "Dog") boats. They proved themselves to be

[1] Mean wind speed of 18 knots.

a very fine all-round offensive boat in spite of their comparatively low speed.

Their speed was (as in the short boats) limited by the engines available; and it was also affected by the increase in weight caused—apart from increased scantlings—by the extra guns (and men to fight them), ammunition, engines and fuel.

The "Dogs" were 115 feet long and displaced about 120 tons. Compared with the short boats, their above-water shape was less pleasing to the eye (apart from being much larger), and the extra beam made them look less sleek, although somewhat more menacing.

Driven by four 1,500 horse-power Packard engines, all supercharged, the "Dog" boat's maximum speed was around 28 knots, with a range of 450 miles at 20 knots. If upper-deck fuel tanks were fitted (as they were when the boats went from the United Kingdom to the Mediterranean under their own power) the endurance was increased to 2,000 miles at 10 knots.

As with the short boats, the armament of "Dog" torpedo-boats varied. The early ones usually carried two torpedoes, a 2-pounder pom-pom, twin 20-mm. Oerlikons, four ·5-inch and four ·303-inch machine-guns. Later many additions were made. These included new 6-pounders fitted to MGBs instead of the pom-pom. A change which was not welcomed by all Coastal Forces officers in the Mediterranean.

Petrol, about 5,000 gallons of 100-octane, was carried in ten fuel tanks, divided into two compartments forward and abaft the engine-room. The boats drew less than 5 feet forward and under 6 feet aft (although again this varied, depending on the weight of the armament and fuel carried).

They were usually manned by three officers—commanding officer, first lieutenant (usually referred to as "Number One") and navigating officer (the "pilot")—and about thirty men, the senior rating being a petty officer coxswain. A leading seaman helped him with an upper-deck crew of about twenty.

In the engine-room there was usually two motor mechanics and four stokers (a misnomer: the majority of them only saw steam when it came out of a kettle. Most of them were "Hostilities Only" ratings who in peacetime worked in garages. With the motor mechanics they became past-masters in dealing with the highly-temperamental petrol engines).

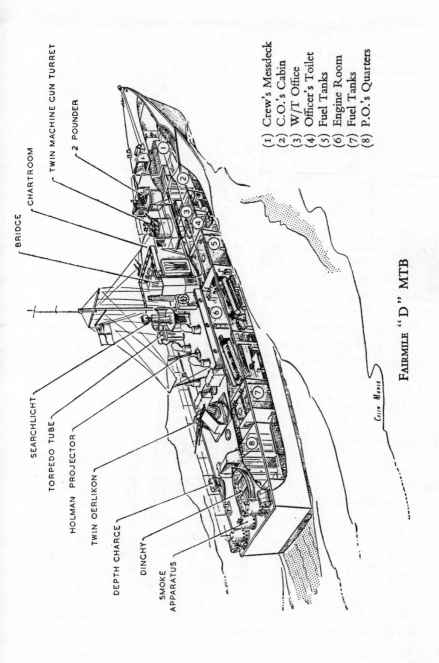

BRIDGE

CHARTROOM

TWIN MACHINE GUN TURRET

2 POUNDER

SEARCHLIGHT

TORPEDO TUBE

HOLMAN PROJECTOR

TWIN OERLIKON

DEPTH CHARGE

DINGHY

SMOKE APPARATUS

(1) Crew's Messdeck
(2) C.O.'s Cabin
(3) W/T Office
(4) Officer's Toilet
(5) Fuel Tanks
(6) Engine Room
(7) Fuel Tanks
(8) P.O.'s Quarters

COLIN MUDIE

FAIRMILE "D" MTB

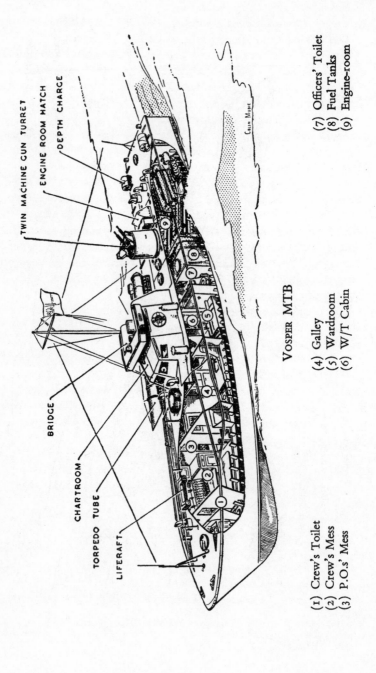

TWIN MACHINE GUN TURRET

ENGINE ROOM HATCH

DEPTH CHARGE

BRIDGE

CHARTROOM

TORPEDO TUBE

LIFERAFT

COLIN MUDIE

VOSPER MTB

(1) Crew's Toilet
(2) Crew's Mess
(3) P.O.s' Mess

(4) Galley
(5) Wardroom
(6) W/T Cabin

(7) Officers' Toilet
(8) Fuel Tanks
(9) Engine-room

The other half of the *offensive* arm of Coastal Forces is the motor gunboat. The short MGBs were generally the same craft as the short MTBs, but with the torpedo tubes replaced by extra guns.

The long MGBs were, in the first instance, a development of the Fairmile "A" design; but later some "Ds" were turned into MGBs and fitted with a heavier gun armament including a pom-pom and an ancient 6-pounder (the "goose gun").

The gun is a simpler and older weapon than the torpedo; and basic gunboat tactics have not altered much since Nelson's time. Coastal Force guns were small and were not fitted with accurate sights; all firing was by gunlayer (individual) control.

In a night action, with the boat bumping about if there was anything but a calm sea, gunners could not be expected to obtain hits at much more than "whites-of-their-eyes" range. Even in a flat calm it was difficult to hit anything much over 500 yards when using open sights.

Many action reports by MGBs contain the sentence "Fire was opened at 400 yards and the range shortly afterwards closed". This was no exaggeration; it was the only way of successfully fighting with the boats and weapon available.

The original function of the MGBs—engaging the escorts while the MTBs attacked the convoy—was officially changed in 1943 when MTBs were given a greater gun armament and took over both roles. In some theatres, especially the Mediterranean, the necessary conversions could not be carried out, and MGBs continued in existence. Apart from beating up truculent escorts, the Mediterranean MGBs were able to do a fine job sinking targets which could be dealt with by gunfire, instead of using a costly torpedo, or which (because of shallow draught) were difficult to hit with a torpedo.

So, in the Mediterranean especially, there was always a use for both MTBs and MGBs. Usually both types went on an operation, the S.O.[1] only deciding whether it was to be a gun or torpedo (or both) attack when the target was picked up.

The defensive boats of Coastal Forces were the motor launches (MLs) and harbour-defence motor launches (HDMLs). In the Mediterranean, however, they were frequently doing offensive operations, especially among the islands of the Adriatic and Aegean.

Originally designed as an anti-submarine boat, the ML became a tough maid-of-all-work: it did such jobs as minelaying, minesweeping,

---

[1] Senior Officer—usually a lieutenant-commander. He was embarked in one of the boats to command the flotilla or unit as a whole.

anti-submarine escort, anti-E-boat escort, gunboat, headquarters ship, navigational leader and rescue-ship, quite apart from being used to pick up or land agents behind the enemy lines.

MLs were mass-produced from the Fairmile "B" design. They had a nice sweeping sheer, were 112 feet long, displaced 75 tons, and were pushed along at 18 knots by two Hall Scott petrol engines.

The average armament of an ML was one 3-pounder (frequently a vintage piece), one twin and one single 20-mm. Oerlikon, and two twin machine-guns. Those equipped for anti-submarine (hereafter referred to as A/S) duty were fitted with Asdic, a submarine-detecting device transmitting waves below water which echo back (or "ping") when they hit a submerged U-boat, and a Y-gun[1] with twenty depth-charges.

The HDMLs were, as their name implies, originally designed purely for harbour defence; but they proved such fine, reliable sea-boats that they were more often used for combined operations and A/S escort.

They were much smaller than the MLs—only 72 feet long and displacing 54 tons. They were fitted with two Diesel engines which gave a greater cruising range and required far less maintenance than petrol engines. Although slower than MLs, they did a magnificent job, working with an armament[2] which usually consisted of Asdic, eight depth-charges, a 2- or 3-pounder, one 20-mm. Oerlikon, and two twin machine-guns.

[1] A depth-charge projector which lobs a charge clear of the boat and which, using one on either side, allows a "pattern" of charges to be dropped.
[2] As with the other boats, the armament varied from time to time.

Chapter III

TACTICS FOR ATTACK

HAVING described the boats, we now have to consider the tactics used by Coastal Forces in the Mediterranean. In writing about tactics, one sails in dangerous waters: each S.O., C.O., Number One and pilot has his own ideas. These will differ in varying degrees with opinions held at every executive level upwards —and every non-executive level downwards, too.

So I must emphasise that I am writing in general terms about the Mediterranean in particular. . . .

The main task for MTBs and MGBs throughout the war was, as I have said before, attacking enemy coastal shipping in areas where no other warships could operate—because of minefields, shoal waters, radar-controlled shore batteries, or (especially in the Adriatic and Aegean) the inability to get clear or hide before daylight brought swarms of enemy planes in to attack.

Usually, therefore, the boats patrolled channels which were known to be used by enemy shipping and which were usually flanked by minefields, rocks or islands—frequently all three.

Our own radar sets were good at picking up aircraft but very weak in finding surface craft. When near land they were useless because the preponderant back-echo submerged the first quarter of the scan. It was not until American PT-boats (like our short MTBs) arrived in the Mediterranean with radar sets equipped with screens (showing ships or land as distinct blobs or lines, from which courses and ranges could be accurately determined) that the problem was overcome. From then on a PT-boat operated with a British force when possible. The Germans could also detect our own radar more easily, so to use it often gave away the fact that MTBs were nearby.

In the Mediterranean the Germans made extensive use of F-lighters —cargo carriers with very shallow draught but which carried a large number of guns. They were, in effect, both convoy and escort. Thus Coastal Forces had frequently to attack ships which were almost impossible to torpedo yet which heavily outgunned our own craft.

Therefore the main weapon of Coastal Forces was surprise. There were few, if any, *successful* actions fought in the Mediterranean in which tactical surprise was not achieved. Where surprise was lost an attack frequently reduced itself to a "battle of broadsides", and the lightly-built, comparatively unarmoured MTBs and MGBs, with thousands of gallons of highly-inflammable petrol aboard, extremely vulnerable engine-rooms and great deal of complicated hydraulic and electrical systems, almost inevitably came off worst.

If it seemed that tactical surprise was impossible to achieve by normal methods, then it had to be created. There were various methods. The classic case was for MGBs to attack from one direction while MTBs came in from another. Sometimes the enemy challenge or reply was known or guessed and boats could use this ruse to get in close before the enemy opened fire. The limit of the scope for creating surprise was the limit of the S.O.'s imagination. You will read about that later. . . .

It was Nelson who perfected the system of meeting his commanding officers before an action—usually, in those more leisurely days, at dinner the day before—and discussing every aspect of it. The reason for this was simple: it was nearly certain that every possible move by the enemy would be discussed. Nelson would give his ideas and orders to meet any eventuality.

The result was that when he moved his fleet into action every commanding officer knew what Nelson would do or want the individual to do in a particular situation. Signalling, a laborious business in those days, was cut down to a minimum; and the less signalling, the less chance there was of confusion. Nelson often only signalled "Engage the enemy".

On every operation by any warships in the last war this briefing, when possible, was naturally held; but the parallel between Coastal Forces actions and Nelson's actions is even closer. Until March 1944, when bridge-to-bridge R/T[1] was fitted, signalling from boat to boat was nearly as laborious as in Nelson's day; and even after the sets were fitted the enemy and the elements conspired to put them out of action.

Thus the S.O. would, as it were, do as much of the fighting as possible in the operations-room. Because they were small boats which

---

[1] Radio-telephone, which allowed speech from boat to boat.

always worked together, the S.O. usually knew fairly exactly how any individual C.O. would react in given circumstances. Almost more important, the C.O.s knew how the S.O. would react.

Because it was necessary to attack at close range, Coastal Forces craft had a hard time keeping out of sight of the enemy lookouts but, at the same time, being able to see the enemy ships. MTBs and MGBs had a small, low silhouette (though not as low as E-boats) and usually had to shadow before an attack. It was seldom that an attack could be made "on sight".

Towards the end of the war, when the PPI (screen) radar was in general use, it was naturally possible to plot the course and speed of the enemy very accurately; and some flotillas perfected methods of approaching, aiming, firing and retiring without seeing the enemy— except as "blips" on the radar screen. And they achieved extremely accurate results, the record in the Mediterranean being five ships hit with six torpedoes. In 1945 forty torpedo hits were made out of sixty-one torpedoes fired at over 2,000 yards.

There were five main types of torpedo attacks which concern the reader:

The concentrated attack: all boats approached in formation, fired individually at separate targets, and disengaged independently. This was the most successful type of attack, but it required complete surprise and was impossible under certain conditions (extreme visibility, or an exceptionally wide-awake escort force, for instance).

The divided attack: individual boats or sub-divisions attacked from opposite directions or in succession from the same direction. This type of attack had the advantage that, since the boats were dispersed, there was less chance that they would be spotted; and avoiding action was more difficult for the enemy. On the other hand, the enemy was often able to bring more guns to bear on individual MTBs, and our own boats had identification problems.

The diversion attack: this was made when it was certain that tactical surprise could not be achieved, and has been described earlier. Towards the end of the war this type of attack, in one form or another, had to be made almost every occasion when MTBs and MGBs met the enemy because the enemy had such powerful and numerous escorts.

The zone attack: this was used against strongly escorted convoys when it was impossible to get inside the defensive screen. It is rather too complicated to explain in detail, but, as its name implies, torpedoes were fired in a "fan" or "zone", the actual timing being taken from the centre boat.

The radar attack: until the new radar sets arrived in the Mediterranean this type of attack was, of course, impossible; and as it forms an interesting stage in the development of tactics in the Mediterranean it will be dealt with later.

CHAPTER IV

BEG WHILE THE IRON IS HOT

THE story of Coastal Forces in the Mediterranean during World War II is an extremely complicated one dealing with, after the fall of North Africa, three separate theatres of operations.

To give some shape to the narrative, it is proposed to divide the story into sections: the Libyan coast actions which ended with the surrender of all Axis forces in North Africa; the invasion of Sicily and Italy, followed by Coastal Forces actions along the west coast of Italy; the switching of some flotillas to fight in the Adriatic; and the movement of flotillas to attack in the Aegean.

From the autumn of 1943 onwards Coastal Forces were fighting hard in three main areas—the Tyrrhenian Sea, off the west coast of Italy; the Adriatic; and the Aegean. So, instead of switching from one to the other every week or so, I shall follow one area for six months or so before moving on to the next: thus it will be easier to follow the work of individual flotillas and officers and see how new tactics develop.

The main story starts in 1942; but as there were some Coastal Forces activities in 1941 I shall briefly describe the events in that year.

· · · · · ·

For Britain 1941 was the most desperate year of the war: at home war production was barely under way, the Luftwaffe was battering our cities, and the U-boat campaign in the Atlantic making itself felt. The outlook was dark and dawn seemed a thousand years away. The much-vaunted Wehrmacht was but a score of miles from the Kentish coast.

The 1st MTB Flotilla was back in England, having been recalled from Malta before France fell. It made its way through the French canals and after a refit was based at Felixstowe.

The 1939 building programme for MTBs had been increased by a War Emergency Programme. Two boats constructed for Finland had been taken over; a few Masbys were completed and orders were given for MLs and HDMLs.

Throughout 1940 the build-up of coastal craft was painfully slow. We tried to get MTBs from America. The exchange of old American destroyers for British bases had been arranged, and by September Mr. Churchill was already giving one of his famous prods:[1]

Action this day.   *5.ix.40.*
P.M. to Foreign Secretary.

. . . *What is being done about getting our 20 motor torpedo-boats, the 5 PBY (flying-boats), the 150 to 200 aircraft and the 250,000 rifles, also anything else that is going? I consider we were promised all the above, and more too. Not an hour should be lost in raising these questions. "Beg while the iron is hot."*

In the Mediterranean, New Year's Day 1941 opened the toughest phase of the whole war. The Germans, alarmed by the lack of success by the Italians, brought in the Luftwaffe. Within a fortnight Nazi bombers were attacking Egypt.

The German naval view is given by Admiral Weichold:[2]

As opposed to the far-reaching defensive policy of the Italian direction of sea warfare, British eagerness for action showed itself in strategy and tactics. In spite of the great dangers to the mother country in the shape of threatening German invasion, which urged a concentration of forces in the North, the British leaders had the courage to allot as many forces to the Mediterranean as could carry on active operations. Doubtless the reason lay in the British habit of viewing things from a maritime point of view. Great Britain realised that in this phase of war the Mediterranean would become a deciding factor and acted accordingly. The strategic skill of the British admirals was equal to their tactical ability. But more than anything else the excellent co-operation between the three Services should be stressed. The great successes arising therefrom saved the British Empire and proved to the world that British power was unbroken.[3]

But the successes Weichold refers to were only at sea: on land during 1941 we reeled from one heavy punch after another. Italy had attacked

---

[1] *The Second World War*, Vol. II, p. 590.
[2] *The War at Sea*—see footnote 1, p. 22.
[3] Compare with the bickering between the German Army, Navy and Air Force over the Adriatic (p. 208).

Greece in October 1940 and the war had dragged through the winter with the gallant Greeks fighting back hard.

Then in April 1941 the Germans struck a double blow: a heavy assault on Cyrenaica coincided with an attack on Greece and Yugoslavia by motorised divisions and the Luftwaffe. Especially the Luftwaffe. In three days they spread enough high-explosive brand of German *kultur* to kill 30,000 people in Belgrade alone.

Greece fell in a dozen days, although the Royal Navy managed to get a high proportion of Allied troops away in time. Then, literally out of the skies, the attack on Crete started. Apart from heavy losses in bigger warships, most of the MTBs in the Mediterranean—five old 55-foot Thorneycroft boats—were lost with two HDMLs.

The fall of Crete, a few weeks after the capture of Greece, put the Axis in a very strong position—as Weichold points out:[1]

> *The Axis war leaders had now only to continue to exploit their advantage in the war against Great Britain in the Mediterranean. It was at this point that German leadership committed the greatest error of the whole war. It turned its attention from England, already sorely pressed, to attack a new and powerful adversary. Moreover, strong German air squadrons were transferred from the Mediterranean for their Russian campaign. . . .*

In March Admiral Cunningham had a great success: for months he had been trailing his coat across the Mediterranean to try to entice the Italian battle-fleet into action. In March he had been successful. The Battle of Matapan resulted in the loss of three Italian heavy cruisers and two heavy destroyers. More important, though, was the effect on Italian morale.

Hitler's attack on Russia started in June. Within a couple of months Britain had occupied Syria, and Britain and Russia had smashed an attempted revolt in Iran which was headed by an Axis puppet. But in Libya the Germans were building up supplies. The Royal Navy attacked when it could; for practical purposes, however, the Axis held sway over the Central Mediterranean.

∙   ∙   ∙   ∙   ∙

In the United Kingdom during the first three months of 1941 only three MTBs were completed, but thirty-seven Masbys were converted

---

[1] *The War at Sea*—see footnote 1, p. 22.

into MGBs to deal with E-boats which were attacking our East Coast convoys. Between March and June, however, six MTBs, twelve MGBs, seventeen HDMLs and more than fifty MLs were completed. The first "C"-class MGB was commissioned and an ML flotilla arrived in Gibraltar, where a base was formed.

But the Royal Navy was still desperately short of MTBs, especially in the Mediterranean. At the end of June the Admiralty signalled to the Chief of Naval Staff in Ottawa that there was an urgent need for MTBs in the Eastern Mediterranean. Efficient boats, the Admiralty said, had many opportunities there for achieving considerable success. But the only available British MTBs were operating in the Channel. . . . It was understood that a flotilla of 70-foot patrol-boats was form-ing at Halifax. Would the Canadian Government consider lending them—with or without crews?

Ottawa's reply came back promptly: five Scott Paine 70-foot boats would be available at the end of July without armament, or at the end of August with armament. Three more, with armament, would be ready in mid-September. Four others would be completed by the spring of next year. Trained crews were not, however, available.[1]

That was a help, and during the last six months of 1941 our own production was speeding up: the Admiralty's careful planning was becoming apparent, and between 1st June and 31st December 1941 twenty MTBs, eight short and twenty-three long MGBs, forty-four HDMLs, fourteen Masbys and more than a hundred MLs were completed.

What was more important, there were many young officers serving in MTBs, MGBs and MLs in the Channel and gaining valuable experience to help them fight later in the Mediterranean, where several flotillas of MTBs were being formed. Most of these would use American-built boats.

In August, Admiralty records report that "The C.-in-C. [Mediter-ranean] explained to the Admiralty the future position concerning MTBs. Sixty were being sent to the Mediterranean. Although most desirable to have a flotilla of fifteen at Malta, it might not be practical to get them there. Accordingly arrangements were in hand for the main base to be at Alexandria, and for a secondary base at Haifa. Advanced operational bases might be developed at Tobruk and Famagusta (Cyprus)."

---

[1] As will be seen later, there were many Canadian officers already serving with Coastal Forces.

So the build-up of Coastal Forces started. Their tiny force had suffered a crushing blow at Crete, and the remaining boats, old Thorneycrofts of the 10th Flotilla, were based on Egypt.

But in the boatyards of America the gaunt frames of new boats were being planked up. Late in 1941 some experienced Coastal Forces officers arrived in New York to co-operate with Elco, the firm building the boats.

Twenty boats were being completed to form two flotillas of ten boats each. In the light of experience gained while fighting E-boats in the Channel the Coastal Forces officers (Lt.-Cdr. Noakes, R.N.; Lt. A. Lennox-Boyd, R.N.V.R.; Lt. Robert Allan, R.N.V.R.; and Lt. Dennis Jermain, R.N.[1]) and two engineers, Lt. Henzell and Lt. Purser, asked for certain modifications to be made—mainly in the gun armament.

Noakes and Allan left with their ten boats before Christmas. They had to be freighted round the Cape of Good Hope and up the Red Sea to Suez. These boats, to become the re-formed 10th Flotilla, were 70-foot Elcos and were numbered from 259 to 268.

They did not prove quite so reliable as the later boats (77 feet long) which formed Jermain's 15th Flotilla. Although these had the same engines, they had better installations.

[1] Now respectively Capt. C. S. D. Noakes, O.B.E., R.N.; The Rt. Hon. A. Lennox-Boyd, P.C., M.P.; Cdr. R. Allan, D.S.O., O.B.E., M.P.; and Cdr. D. Jermain, D.S.C., R.N.

CHAPTER V

INTO BATTLE

The main tasks of the Mediterranean Fleet in early 1942 were to keep up attacks on enemy supply routes to Rommel's armies in North Africa; supply beleaguered Malta—with each convoy a major Fleet operation; and support the 8th Army in the desert. Von Richtofen's Stukas had made their debut in the Mediterranean and were stepping up their dive-bombing attacks on Malta, where an invasion seemed likely. Axis planes held sway over the vital Sicilian Narrows. . . .

TO recapitulate: at the beginning of the year Coastal Forces in the Mediterranean consisted of the remnants of the original 10th Flotilla's old Thorneycrofts, eight HDMLs of the 102nd ML Flotilla, and six more of the 101st Flotilla. These, with some MLs at Gibraltar, did not make a very imposing force.

Within a few weeks the twenty new Elcos, shipped over two by two from New York in merchant ships, were being met at Suez by a small band of engineers, who quickly got them ready to be sailed north through the Suez Canal to Alexandria. There a fairly substantial base was being set up at Mahroussa Jetty, the then King of Egypt's old yacht base. Soon this was to become H.M.S. *Mosquito*, the Coastal Forces' main base.

Jermain had had several unpleasant moments because of acoustic mines while serving in the Channel; and when leaving Port Said for Alexandria in MTB 309, the first of his flotilla to arrive, he remarked to the coxswain that at least they would not be troubled with acoustic mines in these waters. Within a few seconds two of them blew up fifty yards ahead—some of the first the Germans laid in the Mediterranean.

By the beginning of May he had collected half a dozen of his new boats (numbered from 307 to 316) and with four of them moved up to Tobruk, where Noakes had set up a skeleton base at a former Italian boom defence depot near the harbour mouth.

Jermain took over from him, installed his own flotilla staff under John Purser and started into the primitive makeshift life which they were going to get used to during the next few years. They made the somewhat wry comparison (which many new officers joining from England were going to echo over the next three years) between Channel and Mediterranean operations.

In the Channel boats operated from well-established bases—Felix-stowe, where the headquarters were in an hotel; Dover, where another hotel served as the base; and such ports as Yarmouth and Ramsgate. When they brought their boats in, a base staff took over refuelling, with the fuel coming through specially-fitted pipelines with several filters and bonding arrangements to prevent sparks, re-ammunitioning and generally getting the boats ready for sea again.

In Tobruk, however, refuelling was done from forty-four-gallon drums or petrol lorries, which, despite all precautions, often carried dirty petrol which contained water. If this was passed into the boats' tanks it would cause the engines to stop dead, so every drop of petrol had to be filtered through chamois leathers, as these, when wet with petrol, hold water.

That in itself was trouble enough; but although chamois leathers were established naval stores for MTBs, each was punched in the centre with a broad arrow picked out in holes big enough to let the water through. This thoughtful act was supposed to prevent them being sold to local inhabitants.

While the new MTBs came round the Cape, other reinforcements, this time MLs, were trying to get right through the Mediterranean from Gibraltar under their own power.

On 14th January orders were received at Gibraltar to pass the 3rd ML Flotilla through, and after some delay ML 126 and ML 130 left Gibraltar at 2130[1] on 12th March. It would have been suicide to sail blindly through, so the two boats were ordered to make the passage inside French territorial waters after passing Cape de Fer (i.e. within three miles of the Algerian coast) and fly the green, white and red Italian ensign.

The MLs arrived at Malta in time for breakfast on the 17th. The news of their safe arrival was signalled to Gibraltar, and that night two more MLs, 129 and 132, sailed eastwards from the Rock. They failed to arrive in Malta, and after being four days overdue they were given up as lost.

[1] The 24-hour clock is used throughout. To obtain p.m. times 12 must be subtracted from all times over 1200.

Later it was discovered that they had covered nearly a thousand miles before being attacked by Italian bombers off Cape Bon. ML 129 was badly shot up and sank. ML 132, which was badly damaged, picked up the survivors. Seven men had been killed or died of wounds, and the C.O. of 132 decided to enter Bone (which was in Vichy French hands) and ask—as any warship is allowed by international law to request of a neutral country—to be allowed to stay twenty-four hours to effect repairs. But the French refused, and the men were interned.

The loss of the two MLs made the Admiralty decide that the rest of the 3rd Flotilla and the whole of the 27th Flotilla would have to go round the Cape. In May, however, the 27th was allocated to West Africa and the rest of the 3rd Flotilla were ordered to stay in Gibraltar to wait for a chance to get through.[1]

That was a bad start for the MLs; but earlier the Admiralty had ordered some of these craft from Empire and Middle East countries.[2]

·   ·   ·   ·   ·

So the MTBs helped supply Tobruk, joining in the odd assortment of craft carrying troops, food, arms and ammunition up from Egypt.

Frequently one or two MTBs would go off on clandestine operations (more usually known as a "false-nose job"). Most of the time the destination was the former kingdom of Minos, German-held Crete, where agents were landed and other personnel and refugees were taken off.

Because of the great and ever-present danger of attack by heavily-gunned enemy fighters and bombers (an almost daily occurrence on the Egypt-to-Tobruk run) MTBs doing a "false-nose job" usually left Mersa Matruh during the night for a point well to the west, behind the German front line, which gave them the shortest possible "hop" north to the island. The boats would hide up in some creek or inlet, hidden by camouflage nets, and wait for the signal to leave for Crete.

One of the early tasks of the boats of the 10th Flotilla was Operation "Leader", when MTBs 259 and 264 sailed from Bardia at 1830 on 15th April to land four men on Crete. They arrived off the island running on silent engines at 0015/16th[3] and established communication

---

[1] See p. 178.
[2] The first pair, 348 and 349, were launched by a Cairo firm in February.
[3] i.e. fifteen minutes past midnight on the day of April 16th. Where the actual month is obvious from the context, this convention combining time and day will be used. Thus noon on Christmas Day would be "1200/25th".

with the shore. The four men were landed on the beach from a rubber dinghy and eight more were brought on board. The MTBs then crept away and soon were heading back at full speed, arriving at Mersa Matruh before daylight.

* * * * * *

By 26th May it was obvious that the Luftwaffe was hotting up its offensive over Tobruk. The already-heavy bombing was increased and Tobruk Harbour became an even more unhealthy spot for the small craft. It seemed probable that Rommel was planning an all-out attack.

MTBs were patrolling off the enemy coast looking for any German or Italian craft that might be moving supplies into the Bomba area, although they did not have much luck. However, MTBs 309 and 312 sailed from Tobruk and landed agents on 22nd/23rd May[1] and repeated the operation the next night. Then, on 26th/27th May, the same two boats went on patrol in the Bomba area. Lt. Jermain was embarked in MTB 309 as S.O. and Lt. Ian Quarrie was C.O. of 312.

It was a very dark night and suddenly, at 0300, an F-lighter was sighted. Jermain writes: "We fired torpedoes at it, but at least two of them ran under because of the vessel's very shallow draught. Then I had another go with depth-charges[2] and managed to explode one right underneath the craft. We were unable to find any trace of it afterwards, except for a lot of bubbles, but could not definitely say it was sunk because while disengaging from the F-lighter's heavy guns we had momentarily lost sight of it."

F-lighters were the German version of a large landing-craft crossed with a cargo lighter. Of a peculiarly humped-back shape, they could be used as cargo- and troop-carriers or as "flak" (anti-aircraft) ships. As the MTBs, and later MGBs, increased their attacks on these craft the Germans increased their fire-power until they were carrying a gun

[1] When an operation takes place during the night this convention is used throughout this book.

[2] In October 1940 Jermain was in one of two Vosper MTBs in the Channel which were patrolling off Flushing Harbour. Later they were running on noisy main engines when they found a convoy anchored off the Scheldt. The other MTB was badly damaged and Jermain's boat had trouble with the torpedo-firing gear. With no torpedoes but with plenty of sitting targets, Jermain picked the largest ship and made two depth-charge attacks, his gunners firing upwards at any German unwise enough to look over the target's gunwale. When making his second run Jermain passed so close to the target that the flare of the MTB's bow touched. The depth-charge exploded amidships, provoking the target into sending an S O S in plain language, identifying her as a 6,000-tonner.

armament of upwards of two high-velocity 88-mm. (3.5-inch), four
40-mm. (1.5-inch) and four 20-mm. (0.8-inch), and various smaller-
calibre machine-guns—far more than any MTB or MGB.

They frequently carried range-finders and predictors. They had a
very shallow draught, as little as 3 feet at times. We had great difficulty in getting our torpedoes to run shallow enough to hit them.
The subsequent shallow-draught attack technique will be described
later.

 .   .   .   .   .

The Afrika Korps was poised for the attack on Egypt. Rommel had
managed to build up some of his supplies in Libya and was putting the
finishing touches to the plan for an attack which he thought would
take him to the Suez Canal. His major problem was getting enough
petrol and oil, a problem which eventually affected all the German
forces everywhere.

But in the meantime Malta, under merciless air attack, was desperately short of supplies—especially ammunition for anti-aircraft
guns and food. During April it was estimated that at least 6,700
tons of bombs had been dropped on the island—3,156 tons of
them on the dockyard. It was considered the island might fall if
supply-ships did not get through, so it was planned to sail two convoys to the island at the same time—one leaving from Gibraltar,
at the western end of the Mediterranean, and the other from
Alexandria, in the east.

The Alexandria convoy, MW 11, consisted of ten merchant ships
and H.M.S. *Centurion* (a merchant ship rather cunningly disguised as
a battleship. She carried 1,000 tons of stores and her "main armament"
consisted of thirteen 20-mm. Oerlikon guns). The convoy escort
included seven cruisers, one anti-aircraft ship, twenty-six destroyers,
four corvettes, two minesweepers and four MTBs (261, 264, 262, 259),
the theory being that if the convoy was attacked by surface ships the
boats slipped to attack.

The MTBs, which were also loaded with stores, were to be towed
behind the merchant ships. Towing warps were fitted right round
each boat—down one side, across the transom, and up the other side,
the two ends being joined with a bridle at the bow. This was a very
clumsy affair, which in theory meant that in order to slip the cable had
to be hauled in on to the fo'c'sle of the MTB. In fact it meant cutting
with a hacksaw. The standard towing fittings were not used because
it was thought the towing speeds might be too great.

Bobby Allan was S.O. of the MTBs (which were to be based on Malta), while the whole operation, known by the code-name "Vigorous", was under the control of Rear-Admiral Sir Philip Vian, in the cruiser *Cleopatra*. The convoy sailed in sections from Port Said, Haifa and Alexandria. *Cleopatra* left Alexandria on 11th June for the rendezvous. There the convoy assembled and headed for Malta at 14 knots, with the wind freshening.

The convoy had to make 14 knots in order to reach a position off Malta on the last evening which would enable them, by steaming at full speed, to get into harbour by dawn.

Before sailing the MTB officers had been lined up for a talk by an admiral, who started off his address with the remark "I don't suppose any of you have been in action before. . . ." Several chests, adorned with ribbons of the D.S.C., swelled visibly. He concluded by saying that in the event of meeting the enemy the MTBs' job was not completed when they had fired their torpedoes: they were to continue making feint attacks, forcing the enemy to take avoiding action, until the MTBs were sunk. . . .

Soon after the convoy sailed there were white horses on the waves and the MTBs ran into trouble: the heavy wire ropes used for towing quickly tautened as the merchant ships took the strain, making the MTBs suddenly surge forward faster than 14 knots and overtake the tows, which then slackened and the MTBs slowed down until the merchant ships took the strain again. The jerky progress soon damaged the lightly-built MTBs.

Gradually leaks started. The wind was blowing Force 4 to 5,[1] increasing all the time. In MTB 259, the boat in which Allan was embarked, the leaks worsened as the towing warp round the boat squeezed and strained the frames and the thin planking. The transom was slowly being pressed in and the engine-room started flooding.

The other three boats were also being badly strained. Allan, describing the operation, said: "My boat was becoming completely water-logged. At last light I decided we would not get through the night and asked permission for the MTBs to leave the convoy and make for shelter.

"We were keeping wireless silence of course, and it took a long time to pass signals by lamp; but eventually permission came through and I ordered all the boats to slip the tows and gave them a rendezvous.

[1] 12–18 knots.

"By this time it was dark and there was quite a sea running. My boat was obviously sinking, so I sent two of the boats on to Tobruk and told Jermain, in the third, to stand by me.

"Within a matter of minutes 259's engines stopped and it was not long before the whole engine-room was flooded. We waited for Jermain to find us. He had a difficult job on a pitch-dark night like this and with the nasty short sea.

"We felt very alone. Soon our upper deck was almost awash and it was obvious she was going to sink any minute, so I ordered 'Abandon ship' and we launched our two dinghies, climbed in, and drifted around. We started firing rockets to help guide Jermain, and after about an hour he managed to find us."

All of 259's crew were picked up, and the MTBs' part in Operation "Vigorous" was over. Although it does not concern us here, the convoy did not get through: an Italian force of two battleships, four cruisers and eight destroyers sailed and placed itself between the convoy and Malta. The convoy was delayed so much that lack of fuel forced it to return to Alexandria. The other convoy from Gibraltar was relatively more successful.

· · · · ·

Then Rommel's hammer-blow fell on Tobruk. British troops started withdrawing from the main Gazala Line on 14th June, but it was decided to retain Tobruk again to continue as a fortress behind the enemy lines. Experience in 1941 had shown that with the harbour in our hands the Navy was able to supply the garrison entrenched behind the wide perimeter defences.

But Rommel thought otherwise. At 0700 on 20th June his attack started. Guns of all calibres started a big barrage, dive-bombers swept in, and then under cover of smoke his troops attacked the south-east perimeter defences.

The Senior Naval Officer, Tobruk, Capt. F. M. Smith, D.S.O., R.D., R.N.R., and the S.O., Inshore Squadron, Capt. P. N. Walter, D.S.O., R.N., took precautionary measures: demolition charges were laid, craft in the harbour were dispersed, and demolition parties stood by.

Jermain and some of his boats had just arrived back in the harbour after a night's patrol when German bombers started a heavy attack on the town and the port, while other planes started to blast a path through the British minefield for Rommel's tanks.

Jermain's boat and one other, commanded by Lt. Martin Solomon, were moored up alongside the damaged Italian warship *San Giorgio*. Several bombs hit her without damaging the two boats.

The British A.A. gunners were using a new form of barrage which involved firing shells filled with parachutes joined by wires. The idea was, apparently, that the enemy aircraft flew into them and dropped to earth wrapped in silk and wire. When the bombing attacks started the sky was suddenly spotted with parachutes, and with one voice the ships said "Paratroops!" and loosed off volumes of small-arms fire.

Ashore the situation was becoming chaotic: the Army's Divisional H.Q. said the outer perimeter had been penetrated and enemy tanks were at large inside. Capt. Smith, the S.N.O., was told that it was expected the situation "would be restored" by a counter-attack.

In the harbour shells were bursting all over the place. The base staff worked like slaves to get the MTBs ready for sea again. The small petrol-tanker lorry made trip after trip to the boats, usually chased by bursting shells and generally with an air raid going on, and by mid-afternoon all the MTBs were refuelled.

A propeller had to be changed on Lt. Charles Coles' boat, but the shelling became so bad that the professional divers refused to go under, and Coles put on a shallow-diving helmet and went down to change it himself.

Ashore the bursting bombs and shell-fire were steadily destroying the already-battered town: smoke and dust drifted over the streets and across the sands. Crumbling buildings blocked the streets.

By 1500 the situation was becoming desperate. The first sign of trouble in the military sphere came when a sergeant swam off to one of the boats lying in the eastern side of the harbour and reported that his unit had been wiped out and that the enemy was through. Jermain relayed this information to the Garrison H.Q. through the Naval H.Q. and was told not to spread alarmist rumours.

Coles had been ordered to take his boat alongside and report by telephone that soldiers who had swum off from the south shore said their force had been overrun and tanks were approaching the edge of the escarpment overlooking the south shore. He passed this news to Sub-area H.Q., where, says the official report, "apparently it was regarded as being of an exaggerated nature".

Jermain soon saw tanks and troops coming over the hills and reported them, with the same result. His next report, via Coles, was of tanks on the main road into Tobruk. This was at first treated with the same

D

disbelief. Coles invited them to look out of their windows, and a gasp at the other end of the telephone line proved that they too had just seen a German tank under their window. That was a measure of speed at which things were moving and the general confusion existing.

The official report says that by 1630 it was confirmed at Sub-area H.Q. that forty Mark IV German tanks, with guns and infantry, were approaching and it was advisable that all craft left the harbour "until the situation was restored". No demolitions were to be carried out.

By the time the Army had woken up to the situation German tanks had closed round most of the harbour and were firing on the MTBs and other craft from all directions and at close range.

All records were put aboard MTB 309. By 1830 tanks were on top of the escarpment and other tanks were coming down the Bardia road. Half an hour later the S.N.O. (previously told not to carry them out yet) asked for instructions about demolitions, "but no executive order[1] came".

The order was eventually given; but by then more tanks and heavier guns had arrived and joined firing at the jetties, quays and ships in the harbour. Capt. Smith told Capt. Walter that all craft in the harbour were to leave for Alexandria, except HDML 1069, which was to stay and pick up demolition parties.

Meanwhile the MTBs were leaving their moorings. "We found ourselves in a stream of craft evacuating the port," says Jermain, "and realised we would not be back for some time. We felt very badly about leaving the soldiers, but there was nothing else we could do."

Earlier in the day Martin Solomon had a visit from the C.O. of an ML, who had told him he had a presentiment that he would be killed within a few hours. Solomon tried to cheer him up, and offered to lay a smoke-screen to help cover the ML—and the other craft—when the time came to leave. By the time Solomon was ordered to sail with the rest of the boats shells were falling thick and fast. German soldiers were firing mortars from the shore.

Solomon, on his way out, had picked up ninety-seven soldiers aboard the schooner *Kheyr-el-Din*, commanded by Lt. Robert Chesney, which was ablaze at the harbour entrance. He then turned (having failed to persuade Chesney to leave the schooner) and made a run along the full length of the harbour, laying smoke. His boat became the No. 1 target for most the enemy guns, and he was forced to

[1] i.e. order to carry them out. Usually a preparative signal is followed by the executive signal.

stop. Ashore he could see German mortar crews shaking their fists at him.

His smoke floats must have given the impression that his boat was ablaze, because the mortar-fire stopped. He started off again at high speed. He had a difficult time dodging wrecks, on one occasion passing between the funnels and mast of one sunken ship. Still under heavy fire, he made two more runs, enabling many craft to get out under the smoke-screen.

(Solomon was awarded the D.S.C. for his day's work, and the man responsible for refuelling the MTBs from the petrol lorry received the D.S.M.)

Ashore German tanks were everywhere. Admiralty House was almost surrounded before Capt. Smith left for the harbour. With the First Lieutenant of the base, Lt.-Cdr. W. E. Harris, R.N.R., he started many demolitions himself. By the time his party reached the harbour the only serviceable craft left was a motor lighter.

The Germans were in almost complete control of the land round the harbour by the time Capt. Smith and Capt. Walter put off with their party in the lighter. Long before they reached the boom they were under heavy fire from tanks and artillery. Shells put the engines out of action and the bridge was completely smashed.

The lighter, choked with dead and wounded, drifted ashore. Capt. Walter, severely wounded, was taken prisoner. Capt. Smith, the white-haired veteran of Tobruk, died of wounds during the night.

The following ships escaped: two South African minesweepers; MTBs 309, 311, 61, 260, 262, and 267; HDMLs 1046, 1048, and ML 355; three tugs, one LCA, and one LCP. Our losses included: the South African minesweeper *Parktown*, HDMLs 1039 and 1069, three tugs, a salvage schooner, two schooners, an LCA, five LCMs, one LCP,[1] and seven other landing-craft.

To return to the MTBs. Jermain writes: "Outside the harbour I tried to re-form my boats to give protection to the escaping ships that night, but we had become badly scattered on various rescue duties and the Staff Officer (Operations) to the S.O. Inshore Squadron, whom I had collected from an ML, was anxious to get to Mersa Matruh to pass on the news of the fall of Tobruk. Unhappily E-boats did attack, and *Eskimo Nell*, a very famous harbour craft, was among those sunk.

"In the morning, at first light, when just short of Mersa Matruh,

---

[1] LCA—Landing Craft, Assault; LCP—Landing Craft, Personnel; LCM—Landing Craft, Medium.

I saw a U-boat on the surface. It dived immediately. Some landing-craft sailing eastward were heading for the diving position, and on being warned, turned inshore to get cover in a fog-bank. Unfortunately the fog-bank was perched on the water's edge and these unlucky craft ran themselves straight ashore."

From Mersa Matruh the MTBs went back to Alexandria.

Chapter VI

THE STAR OVER SUEZ

By July 1942 the grisly spectre of defeat on land had got past knocking on our door in the Mediterranean; overcome with impatience it had sidled in and now sat staring at us. Yet nine months later the only Germans left in Africa were dead or our prisoners. . . .

But on 1st July Rommel had halted at the El Alamein line: two days' march to the eastward was Alexandria and the Nile valley. In his hands were Tobruk, Sollum and Sidi Omar, shattered pawns in a seemingly endless game of desert chess. One more attack by Rommel and the Suez Canal was his.

We were about to be defeated just at the point when America—rightly called the arsenal of democracy—was at last beginning to throw her weight into the war: we were about to die of thirst in the "wine-dark sea".

But Rommel for the moment was stopped: he had reached high for his star over Suez; he ruptured himself on the 8th Army.

THE withdrawal of the Army and R.A.F. brought Rommel's Afrika Korps perilously near the main Fleet base at Alexandria. If the Germans broke through to cut the Canal the Mediterranean Fleet would be trapped, with no escape or supply route to the south and with the Luftwaffe, who controlled the Central Mediterranean, waiting at the Sicilian Narrows to the west. So it was decided that the larger ships of the Fleet had to move south of the Canal. "The Flap", as it was called, had started. As the old and damaged *Queen Elizabeth* and the other big ships passed through, the Royal Navy's striking force left in the Eastern Mediterranean consisted of four cruisers, nine destroyers, some submarines which, apart from attacking enemy supply lines to Africa, were running vital supplies to Malta, and the MTBs.[1] Some of the MTBs went up to Beirut and Cyprus on A/S work.

[1] The 7th Flotilla (Vospers): MTBs 57, 58, 59, 60, 61, 62, 63, 64, (65 still in U.K.).
10th Flotilla (Elcos): MTBs 215, 259, 260, 262, 263, 264, 265, 267, 268.
8th Flotilla (Vospers): MTB 73 (75, 76 on passage to Med.; 77, 78, 79, 80, 81, 82 still in U.K.).
15th Flotilla (Elcos): MTBs 307, 308, 309, 310, 311, 312, 313, 314, 315, 316.

MTB operations from Alexandria were not very productive: the base was too far from the enemy's sea-lanes; weather conditions—and certain types of boats—were unreliable; W/T communications were unsatisfactory; and the experiment of carrying fuel on the upper decks, to give increased range, exposed the boats to grave risks from air attacks and was only suitable when the extra fuel was used up during the hours of darkness.

Several patrols were made off Mersa Matruh, but the MTBs could not find a target. Occasionally they landed Army patrols behind the German lines.

It was some time before the MTBs were given a chance to see some action. Towards the end of August British Intelligence discovered that Rommel, starved of the petrol needed to make his final armoured thrust into Egypt, was expecting a vital convoy from Crete which would bring him much-needed supplies. MTBs 315, 312 and 311 were given the job of attacking the convoy, even though its route from Crete would be well out of their normal range. The boats sailed for Crete on 31st August, and Jermain, describing the trip, says:

"This operation illustrated the improvisations we had to make in the Mediterranean in those days. In order to reach Crete we each needed an extra 3,000 gallons of petrol. There was no chance of getting special alloy tanks or fittings that the boats in England would have been given for such an operation.

"Instead we had to embark, in each of the boats due to make the patrol, a deckload of 1,500 gallons of petrol in leaky, four-gallon tins. Other boats came part of the way with us, also carrying 1,500 gallons in tins on deck. They were to be our 'tankers'.

"After we had used 1,500 gallons from our main tanks we refilled them with petrol from our deckload and then stopped. The 'tankers' came up astern in the darkness and passed their painters, which we secured.

"With an unpleasant swell running, which was tossing the boats about a bit, the tins were passed from the bows of the 'tankers' to our sterns, being thrown from hand to hand. The total weight was about 2½ tons.

"Our one concession to safety[1] when dealing with this highly-inflammable fuel concerned the axes used to punch holes in the tins—they were made of phosphor-bronze, which did not cause sparks!

---

[1] Normally when fuelling MTBs the routine was: (a) cut engines; (b) disconnect the batteries; (c) shut down the life of the ship; and (d) generally hold one's breath.

"It was bitterly disappointing, around noon next day, to be sighted by enemy reconnaissance aircraft. We had to turn and run and suffered about five bombing attacks—from about ten aircraft at a time—before darkness. Fortunately our Oerlikons kept the planes high and we were able to dodge the falling bombs.

"However, the report of our presence caused the enemy convoy to be turned from its course and gave the R.A.F. another day in which to attack. They wiped it out, so our effort had not been entirely in vain."

CHAPTER VII

WINNER TAKE NOTHING

ON September 13th/14th came Operation "Agreement"—simultaneous raids on Tobruk and Benghazi. The object, defined in a telegram from the Commander-in-Chief, Mediterranean to the Chiefs of Staff in London, was to hold the ports for twelve hours, destroy shipping, harbour installations, petrol and supplies.

The Army had managed to hold Rommel at the Alamein line, and the planners considered that successful raids on enemy communications were most important and worth the risks.

In fact, "Both operations failed to achieve their purpose and heavy losses were sustained for few compensating gains", according to the official report. Immediately after the Tobruk raid there was a good deal of speculation as to whether or not the Germans managed to get a copy or details of the plan of the attack.

Lt. Ramseyer, one of the destroyer *Sikh's* landing party who was captured by the Germans, reported later that after being taken to the enemy's headquarters "The German general informed me that they were ready for the attack, because of the heaviness of the air raid and consequently all guns were closed up.[1] He stated that the Germans had a copy of our order, but failed to produce it when demanded. From the nature of the questions and the general atmosphere, I gathered that a landing in Tobruk was expected, but not with any degree of certainty as to the exact day or time."

The Benghazi operation was an Army-R.A.F. affair, so does not concern us here. The Tobruk plan was briefly this:

One hundred men from the Long Range Desert Group would have come overland from Kufra, and at a certain time would penetrate the Tobruk perimeter. They would then seize and hold Mersa Sciausc inlet, a creek east of the harbour, and capture the anti-aircraft batteries.

[1] Loaded and ready to fire.

They were called Force B, and as soon as they had seized the inlet they were to flash a signal to an aircraft overhead which, in turn, would pass the code-word "Nigger" to the S.O. of the MTBs (whose code name was "Staple"). "Nigger" would mean that the enemy guns at Mersa Sciausc had been captured and MTBs could enter.

Force C consisted of 200 men of the Northumberland Fusiliers, embarked in seventeen MTBs. Three MLs would go with Force C— two to carry demolition parties, and the third to take the troops off any MTB which might break down.

Force C, when they received the code-word "Nigger", would enter the creek and anchor in pairs. The troops were then to disembark and the S.O., MTBs, would set up a command post with the Long Range Desert Group men of Force B. Together they would cause as much damage as possible, and then withdraw.

A vital part of the operation was that L.R.D.G. men should set up leading lights at the entrance of the creek, which was not very easy to find even by day, to guide the MTBs in. The importance of this will be seen later.

Force A consisted of 350 Royal Marines in the destroyers *Sikh* and *Zulu*, who were to land at Mersa Mreira and seize the coastal defence and anti-aircraft guns. The submarine *Taku* would land beach guides for the destroyers.

As the Vospers of the 7th and 8th MTB Flotillas were, despite much hard work by base staffs and crews, still too unreliable to face a 700-mile journey (nor were any of the MTBs designed to operate at such ranges) it was decided to use the boats of the 10th and 15th Flotillas to form Force C. The S.O. was to be an R.N. captain who, as far as is known, had not previously handled a unit of MTBs.

The MLs were 352, 353 and 349, and they embarked the demolition parties under Cdr. Nicholls.

The MTBs and MLs sailed from Alexandria at 1800 on 12th September with the S.O. in MTB 309. Once past the Outer Channel Buoy the boats formed into two columns. Jermain, with the S.O. aboard, led one, and Allan led the other. The force moved westwards at 8 knots.

At 0300 the next day, 13th September, MTB 268 signalled that she had an engine defect. ML 353 came alongside and took off her troops. For the rest of the day the MTBs' luck held: they did not sight any enemy aircraft or surface craft. All the time they forged their way westwards on the first leg of their 700-mile round trip—which had to be made without refuelling.

Ashore the men of the Long Range Desert Group made their way across the sands towards Tobruk. Their one great danger was that they would be sighted; but they were veterans of the stealthy type of warfare needed for this operation. Further back behind our own lines mechanics loaded bombs and belts of ammunition into the R.A.F. planes due to start their attack at 2130. Pilots and crews had their last-minute briefing.

Force A, the destroyers, were already at sea: the Marines had their orders; assault craft hung from the davits; and many miles ahead the submarine *Taku* was doing her silent task.

Soon darkness fell, and the S.O. of the MTBs writes in his report: "At 2030 on 13th September speed was increased to 25 knots; and at 0030 on 14th September speed was decreased to 8 knots and the flotilla proceeded on silent engines, course of 270 degrees was shaped. At that time I observed that out of sixteen MTBs who formed the flotilla at 2030, only six were in company."

When the S.O.'s column suddenly increased speed to 25 knots two of the boats, and Allan's column, completely lost sight of it. Such a large force of MTBs had never operated together before, nor since, as a single tactical unit.

Unless every boat picks up the signal for "Increase speed"—at night a series of "I's" in Morse—from the one immediately ahead, the result is almost certain to be chaos; and even if the signal is picked up, it is hard, in the darkness, to judge just how much the leader is increasing. If a boat suddenly increases speed by, say, 15 knots, and flashes "I's" at the same time, it may be hundreds of yards ahead before the following boat can increase and catch up, and since MTBs do not run on rails it is often more a matter of luck than good station-keeping whether or not the first boat is found again.

Old MTB hands like Jermain and Allan had procedure understood for increasing speed, and before taking a unit to sea would have said: "Look, chaps. We go at 8 knots until half after midnight. We then increase speed to 16 knots and five minutes later to 25 knots. Synchronise watches. I will give 'I's' to the leader of the other column and we will both pass 'I's' down the line. You will proceed to increase speed when I make a long 'T'. First time 16—second 25. At half after five we reduce to 8."

So the S.O.'s boats headed for Tobruk. Allan kept his boats together and, although he could not find the S.O., kept on a similar course.

From 2300 onwards the MTBs could see the rapid summer-lightning flickering of the anti-aircraft guns in action in Tobruk, interspersed with the more deliberate flash-and-glow of exploding bombs.

Ashore Lt.-Col. Haselden, in command of the Long Range Desert Group force, was setting his men into position during the last few hours before he was killed. The soldiers had decided the only way of getting through the perimeter of Tobruk was in three three-ton trucks disguised as British prisoners of war, with some of the men dressed as German guards.

On this piece of bluff rested the fate of the whole operation. If they failed and were caught the Germans would have realised something was happening and the two destroyers, sixteen MTBs and three MLs would have sailed into a death-trap.

By 0145 Tobruk Point bore 270 degrees, two miles from the S.O.'s six MTBs. At 0200 an MTB closed MTB 309 and said it had received the signal "Nigger" (meaning that Mersa Sciausc was captured and the MTBs could enter) from the possessor of the call sign "T.O.R.".

The S.O. took the boats in towards the southern shore to look for the red leading lights. He writes in his report "Neither I nor my officers were able to sight the red light which should have been exhibited at the entrance".

He decided to do the next best thing—search Tobruk Harbour to see if there were any enemy ships to attack. With the other five MTBs, he searched from 0315 but found nothing. But at 0440 he received a wireless message from the L.R.D.G. saying two MTBs had entered Mersa Sciausc. He returned to the inlet and MTB 309, with 262 and 266, entered. Immediately the Germans opened up heavy cross-fire on the three boats: light artillery and small arms fired from both sides of the inlet, and heavy artillery and small arms from the north shore of the harbour.

The S.O. said in his report: "It was obvious to me, in view of the heavy opposition, that Mersa Sciausc had not been captured by British troops, or, if it had been, those troops had been driven out."

Ashore the soldiers had been having trouble. Lt. T. B. Langton, an S.A.S. officer, wrote[1] that the Aldis lamp to be used to signal the way in to the MTBs was not available, so he had to use a torch to flash the three "Ts" every two minutes in red. He says: "After a short while I saw two MTBs come in. After that, however, no more appeared. My problem now was whether to stay signalling or to go and meet the landing troops and conduct them to H.Q. as I was

[1] In a report to the Commanding Officer of the Special Air Service Regiment.

supposed to do. I decided to try a compromise by wedging my torch in a rock and leaving it alight."

Langton went down to the landing point and found the two MTBs —314 and 260—unloading. He then went back to the torch. He continues: "I resumed signalling. Heavy fire was coming from the opposite shore of the harbour out to sea. One of the MTBs got caught in the searchlights and I could see the wake, and tracer bouncing off one of them. . . ."

Allan's column of MTBs had arrived off Tobruk shortly after the S.O.'s six boats. Enemy tracer was criss-crossing the water like red lines on a fantastic graph, and searchlights swept across the sea, groping to find a target for the enemy guns. Allan could not find the break in the boom defences, so three of his boats fired torpedoes at the boom to try to blast a way in. But they were unlucky. Every time they had a look at the harbour tracer streamed out towards them.

Ashore Langton was back at the eastern signalling point. He concludes: "One of the two MTBs[1] slipped out past me during a slight lull, and appeared to get away safely. At first light I decided to abandon signalling and I returned to the landing point. . . . I saw one MTB aground."

The S.O. after attempting to enter the inlet following the Long Range Desert Group's radio message, had retired eastwards under considerable shell and small-arms fire. The MTBs became scattered. He collected three MTBs at 0545 and made a further attempt to enter Metsa Sciausc, but once again he ran into heavy fire. He withdrew again, planning to try again at dawn. Shortly after dawn the Luftwaffe joined in and attacked the MTBs, so he ordered the four MTBs, and two MLs which had joined him, to return to Alexandria.

Large-scale air attacks started. Ju. 88 fighter-bombers—a minimum of eight at a time—made heavy attacks at 0950, 1206, 1430, and 1820. The MTBs fought back vigorously and managed to dodge the bombs, although a near-miss caused some casualties in MTB 266 in the third raid.

Allan's MTBs did not leave Tobruk until the last possible minute, and all of them were running dangerously short of petrol. His boats stayed around the harbour area until daybreak, after the others had detached. The surviving boats had so little fuel left that they could only return at very slow speed. They took fourteen hours to get back.

The Coastal Forces casualties for the raid were four MTBs—308,

---

[1] This was MTB 260.

310, 312, 314—lost through air attacks, and two MLs and one MTB lost in Mersa Sciausc.

The S.O. concluded his report: "Commanding officers of all sixteen MTBs who were in company at 2030 on 13th September reported their eventual arrival off Tobruk, though I and my officers saw only seven boats from 2030, 13th September,[1] until arrival back in Alexandria. There is no doubt that C.O.s are not certain of the individual performances of their boats at high speeds, and I am of the opinion that an improvement in the station-keeping of MTBs should and can be obtained with more experience.

"In my opinion those two facts were responsible for the failure to arrive off Tobruk as a complete striking force."

Admiral Harwood, in a report to the Admiralty on Operation "Agreement", wrote: "The young officers in the MTBs were a little too untrained and inexperienced to take full advantage of the unexpected opportunities. In the light of all that happened, they had a difficult task, but there is no doubt that chances were missed."

Some, at least, of the MTB officers concerned felt that the difficulties of handling MTBs at night had not been fully appreciated when "Agreement" was planned. Sixteen boats had never operated together before as a unit—four was a more usual number; and the problem of station-keeping with such a big force was, they felt, one which should have been given more attention.

Some of the C.O.s were very experienced and veterans of the MTB versus E-boat war in the Channel, and as one of them writes: "It was hard for the planners to realise that MTBs were not equipped—nor did they have enough officers—to be handled like destroyers; and in relation to their length kept much closer to each other than destroyers would have done in similar circumstances."

[1] When he increased to 25 knots.

CHAPTER VIII

"RUMBLE BUMBLE"

Within two months of the abortive Operation "Agreement" the Mediterranean war had entered a new phase: the United Nations in November had passed to the offensive. British and American troops landed in North Africa; Rommel's army in the Western Desert was defeated and driven out of Egypt and Cyrenaica; and the Russians, after Stalingrad, began to advance.

A promising start was thus made in closing the ring round Hitler's Fortress Europe. Sea-power had helped to make this possible: now we could see the value of the desperate struggle by the Royal Navy and Merchant Navy to keep open sea communications during the previous three years—moving troops, planes, tanks and guns to the Middle East by the laborious route round the Cape; supplying, at great risk and a terrible cost in lives, munitions to Russia; and in keeping open the Atlantic trade route despite Doenitz's U-boat warfare.

IN September Coastal Forces in Alexandria were reorganised under Capt. G. V. Hubback, R.N.; but despite renewed enthusiasm, energetic training in signals, tactics, etc., and the advance of the 8th Army a few weeks later, there were no direct successes for Coastal Forces in 1942.

At home production of the new Fairmile "D"-class MTBs, destined to do fine work in the Mediterranean, was speeding up: in the last six months of 1942 forty were completed. During the same period twelve short MTBs and twelve short MGBs, nearly a hundred MLs and about forty HDMLs were completed.

After the heavy MTB losses in the Tobruk raid the Elco boats of the 10th and 15th Flotillas were formed into a single flotilla (the 10th) and Jermain was given command of it.

. . . . .

On 23rd October the third and last battle of El Alamein began at 2200 with the now-famous artillery barrage. The battle lasted until

2nd November. The Germans were forced to retreat and eight days later were driven out of Egypt. On 8th November the Allies landed in North Africa.

There was a great deal of concern in Alexandria just before the landings because it was not known how the French Fleet lying there would react. It was thought possible that they would react violently.[1]

The warships were therefore covered by anti-aircraft guns in sand-bagged positions, destroyers, and MTBs. These boats were all keeping a W/T watch and were ready to fire torpedoes—should the situation arise—at five minutes' notice. And without five minutes' notice, on one occasion.

In one of the MTBs the torpedoman woke up one morning and absentmindedly went through his daily check routine, forgetting the firing mechanism was held only by pieces of split yarn. He pulled a firing lever—and off went a torpedo, heading straight for a warship in which the British Admiral was flying his flag, at more than 40 knots.

As the horrified torpedoman watched, the torpedo hit the wire of a mooring buoy and was deflected into another part of the harbour where, unfortunately, it killed some members of the civilian crew of a small craft.

"As the reconstituted Flotilla," Jermain writes, "our first job was to prepare for our part in the Battle of Alamein, and we worked up a scheme for misleading the enemy into thinking that landings were being made in force behind his lines. We had used the technique on several occasions before with considerable success, and this particular operation was given the title of 'Rumble Bumble'."

Briefly the plan was that the feint sea-borne landing would be staged off Ras-el-Kanais, about sixty miles west of Alamein, on the night of the big attack. A force of twelve LCTs,[2] escorted by two MLs, eight MTBs and three Hunt-class destroyers, *Exmouth*, *Hurworth* and *Belvoir*, was sailed westbound in daylight from Alexandria, and a convoy of four merchant ships from Port Said continued westward after passing Alexandria astern of this force.

Shortly after darkness fell all the ships, except for the MTBs, returned to harbour. The MTBs carried on to Ras-el-Kanais, where, at 0045/24th, they closed the shore and simulated landings by sending up showers of tracer, dropping smoke-floats, and generally discomforting the enemy. This sudden dig in Rommel's ribs was a complete success.

[1] In actual fact they did not.   [2] Landing Craft, Tank.

From then on the Elco MTBs acted as sea-outriders to the 8th Army, staging fake landings, shooting up lorries on coast roads, and generally helping to make the enemy jittery.

The Vospers were still wrestling with a series of defects that maddened the base staff and depressed the crews. The defects were mostly due to the boats having to be sent to the Middle East without proper trials and with only four items of spare gear. This was not Vosper's fault; nor was it their fault that there was no properly-equipped base for dealing with big repairs.

MTB 61 (Tim Bligh) had been selected as the guinea-pig of the 7th Flotilla to try out a number of modifications, including a stern exhaust with underwater discharge for the centre engine. In order to test the changes MTB 61 was sent on a round trip from Alexandria to Beirut, thence to Haifa and back to Alexandria—some 850 miles—as a reliability test.

Halfway round, the hydraulic steering sprang a leak which could not be remedied for lack of spares. This meant a continual revolving of the wheel to keep the ship on a straight course. From Haifa to Alexandria the steering-wheel was turned 28,000 times. Otherwise the test was all right. MTB 61's steering was to break down in sterner circumstances, as will be seen later in this book. A new type of steering gear had in fact been designed and was being fitted to all new boats.

By 1st November the enemy ashore was really on the run; and on the nights of 4th November and 5th November MTBs were dispersed along the coast westward from the front line to make sure the Germans did not try to scuttle out by sea. But they found nothing.

Although the MTBs took part in many fake landings behind the enemy lines, there is one case recorded where an MTB made a real landing behind our own lines, although this happened a good deal earlier.

Lt. Ian Quarrie was on passage one night from Mersa Matruh to Tobruk in his 70-foot Elco, MTB 263. There was a considerable southerly current along the coast which was difficult to estimate, and the charts in those days showed the coastline too far to the south.

He was going along at 25 knots when, like the jumping boats at Miami, 263 hit the shelving beach at a slight angle, shot up in the air and landed many yards inland. Out of the darkness came a sentry's quavering voice: "Halt! Who goes there?"

Ian Quarrie, in a resonant deep voice, replied: "MTB Two Six Three!"

He had landed, ironically enough, outside an Army rest camp.

The boat was eventually salvaged and ended up on the dock at Alexandria, a warning, like the dead jays that gamekeepers hang up in woods, to all newcomers.

．　　　．　　　．　　　．　　　．

While the MTBs hunted along the Cyrenaica coast, the North Africa assault was going on well. Having landed in three sectors round Algiers, four near Oran and one west of Bougie, the Allies pressed on eastwards as fast as possible to get to Tunis. (The landings, since they involved only a very few Coastal Forces craft, have not been described in detail.)

For the Allies to be able to assault Sicily and Italy it was vital that they captured the great naval base at Bizerta and the secondary base at Tunis. But if Rommel was to get the reinforcements he needed to throw the Allies out of North Africa he had to hold these ports. Relentlessly he was driven back westward across the desert towards Tunis by Montgomery's 8th Army. MTBs moved in to operate up to Benghazi, and a mobile base for them was later established at Ras-el-Hilal.

Benghazi, very badly damaged and with eighty-six wrecks in the harbour, was open to Allied shipping on 26th November and an advanced base for MTBs was established there on 9th December. About this time Jermain took his 10th Flotilla over to Malta to wait for a chance to move to Tunisia to attack the German supply-lines. The Axis, determined to hold Tunisia, were moving every available man, gun, plane and tank from Sicily to Tunisia.

E

CHAPTER IX

WATCHING BRIEF

SO 1942 ended and 1943 arrived, the year in which Coastal Forces were due to make a more valuable contribution to the war at sea. The Allies' immediate problem was to stop the Germans getting supplies through to Tunisia. On 6th January General Eisenhower, the Supreme Commander, told the Chiefs of Staff: "Unless this can be materially and immediately reduced, the situation, both here and in the 8th Army area, will deteriorate without doubt."

Marshal Kesselring's Luftwaffe was firmly established in Sicily and, by controlling the air over the Sicilian Narrows, had a strong measure of control over the sea as well.

MTBs operating from Malta made several sweeps off Syracuse, Augusta and Pantelleria during January, but could not find any targets. It was decided to send some of the Malta MTBs to operate from Bone and the C.-in-C. wrote: ". . . before long we were able to send a reinforcement of British MTBs and a few of their American counterparts, the PT-boats, though the former, particularly the 'D' type, were lamentably slow and so full of gadgets and unnecessary amenities that they could hardly fulfil their functions. . . ."[1]

Jermain's 10th Flotilla was ordered to Bone from Malta. At first he did not expect to be there for more than a few weeks, so the flotilla took the minimum base staff and crammed the boats full of Commandos, who also had to be shipped round.

The flotilla organised a small base at Bone and did some patrols, but by now the enemy was being increasingly harassed at night by cruisers as well as MTBs, so he did not use these waters more than necessary in darkness. So, although the MTBs sat almost literally "moaning at the bar" of enemy-held ports, they saw nothing.

However, MTBs operating farther to the east, off Tripoli, had some success: 264 (Lt. H. W. Sheldrick), 260 (Lt. H. W. Wadds) and 313

---

[1] *A Sailor's Odyssey*, by Admiral of the Fleet Viscount Cunningham, p. 521. Although it is not understood what he refers to regarding "amenities", the gadgets were presumably radar and gunnery equipment.

(Lt. A. D. Foster), with Lt. Peter Evenson embarked in 264 as S.O., sailed on the night of 19th January and at 2225 sighted a hospital-ship off Tripoli. At 2330 they found three tugs towing a U-boat just north of Tripoli and promptly attacked with torpedoes.

The tugs abandoned their tow and made for the safety of the harbour; but they were repeatedly hit and one of them was set on fire. The U-boat was hit, reportedly by a torpedo from 260, and when Tripoli fell on 23rd January the submarine *Santorre Santorosa* was found on shoals a mile off the mole with torpedo damage aft.

.   .   .   .   .

The *Mediterranean War Diary* for 3rd February under the heading *"Malta"* says: *"MTB 309 arrived from Benghazi several hours overdue. . . ."*

Those "several hours" were quite crowded. The C.O., a Canadian, had to bring his boat from Benghazi to Malta. This island is hard to find from Benghazi for several reasons, not the least of which is that it is a long way, the island is low-lying, there are sets in the Mediterranean which vary and are difficult to estimate, and MTBs had to carry stores to Malta which altered their displacement and therefore their speed at given revolutions.

The C.O.'s task was made more difficult by the fact that a new type of propeller had been fitted to his boat, and he had not had a chance to test his new speeds over a measured mile. He did not know that he was making an extra knot or two.

When dawn came and Malta should have been in sight, nothing could be seen. The C.O. thought his new propellers had slowed him, so instead of casting east and north he decided, rather unwisely, to push on. He sighted land ahead about two and a half hours after he should have made his landfall.

He still went on, perhaps not realising that the land he had sighted was still many miles ahead of him. As they approached, the C.O. said that the island looked smaller than it should; but, as someone remarked, it had been bombed a lot. . . . And as someone else said that it was nice to see dear old Sliema again, looking just the same, the C.O.'s doubts were somewhat allayed.

Eventually the entrance of a port was distinguished and a schooner was seen just outside flying an unfamiliar flag. One of the crew was sure it was the Maltese flag, but the C.O. told his first lieutenant to check it up in the *Seamanship Manual*. He also told his signalman to make a note that the shore signal station was flashing some very unintelligible Morse.

Just as the MTB was about to enter the harbour the First Lieutenant shouted up that the "Maltese" flag was in fact the Italian merchant ensign. . . .

Very cautiously, with the feeling that every gun in the area must be pointing straight at them, the MTB was turned round and made an unhurried exit in order not to arouse suspicion.

But even then the C.O.'s troubles were not over. Halfway between Pantelleria (for that was the island, held by the Axis) and Malta the MTB ran out of fuel. Aircraft had to search for it and fuel was sent out.

At his interview with the Admiral the cost (several thousands of pounds) of the various measures which had been put into effect as a result of his mistake was pointed out to him, and what had he got to say?

The C.O. did not hesitate: "Stop it out of my pay." The Admiral, not to be outdone, replied: "As you are a Canadian, that would be possible."

·   ·   ·   ·   ·

As soon as it became clear that the MTBs would be staying in Bone far longer than was originally expected, Allan and a fairly large staff and a collection of stores were sent round to Bone in a fast minelayer. Allan then set up a permanent base in Bone.

From the operational point of view, Bone was a very long way from Bizerta and Tunis, where the targets were supposed to be. The boats had to cover something like a hundred miles before reaching the first of the enemy sea-lanes.

Nevertheless the MTBs made occasional sweeps through the Roads of Bizerta and Tunis. Lancaster, while carrying Commodore G. N. Oliver (the Flag Officer, Inshore Squadron, who liked to escape from his desk whenever possible and get to sea), made a very neat attack and sank a merchant ship near the Cani Rocks without the escorting E-boat seeing him.

The story goes that Lancaster had given the warning "Merchant ship in sight" earlier in the night, but the Commodore had pointed out just in time that Lancaster was looking at the Cani Rocks.

Later it was the Commodore who gave the warning "Merchant ship in sight", and Lancaster made the same reply. However, it was a merchant ship this time and Lancaster neatly torpedoed it. The Commodore was particularly pleased because earlier he had been captain of the cruiser *Hermione* which had been sunk in the

Mediterranean by a torpedo from a submarine, U. 205. Lancaster was awarded a D.S.C. for this action and for all the other hard work he had put in.

.   .   .   .   .

By the end of January the build-up of Coastal Forces in the Mediterranean was going ahead fast, and this is an appropriate point to give the actual and paper strength on 1st February 1943:[1]

In the Mediterranean: MTBs: 7th Flotilla (amalgamated 7th/9th) with eleven boats; 10th Flotilla (amalgamated 10th/15th) with fifteen boats. MLs: 3rd Flotilla (seven boats), 9th (six), 25th (eight), 28th (four), 29th (five), 42nd (seven), 43rd (four). HDMLs: 11th Flotilla (four boats), 101st (six), 102nd (eight), 103rd (five), 114th (eight), 115th (eight), 117th (six), 134th (eight).

Due later: 19th MGB Flotilla, to comprise eight boats; 20th MGB Flotilla (five); 32nd MTB Flotilla (eight).

These three flotillas were the new "D"-class Fairmiles.

[1] These details are taken from official records which were frequently out of date and inaccurate.

CHAPTER X

COCOA AND A CONVOY

A CLOSE watch was being kept on Tripoli as the 8th Army pushed the Wehrmacht westwards, and on the night of 19th January a considerable amount of German shipping was reported moving westwards from the harbour. The destroyers attacked it, and the next night it was the turn of the Coastal Forces: three MTBs, 264, 260 and 313, sailed from Malta to "beat up" the harbour mole and add to the general agitation of the Germans.

A postscript to the month of January is provided by Jermain: "Returning from one patrol in the last of the darkness we had an amusing encounter when, in my favourite arrow-head formation, we did a grid-iron[1] with some E-boats in the same formation—to the intense surprise of both sides."

·   ·   ·   ·   ·

Vospers of the 7th Flotilla had been operating from Malta for about three weeks, patrolling off ports on the east coast of Sicily and off Pantelleria. On 16th February three boats, 61 (Bligh), 77 (Sturgeon) and 82 (Taylor), took on board 1,000 extra gallons of petrol in four-gallon tins and left Malta at three o'clock in the afternoon to patrol to the southwards of Marittimo, a small island on the western tip of Sicily.

The Senior Officer, Lt. Hennessy, was in 77. 61 had no torpedoes, but was armed with three captured Breda 20-mm. cannon—one on the fo'c'sle and one on each beam resting on the torpedo-tube bearers—in addition to her twin 0.5-inch. Two Elco boats which had undocked only that afternoon, 307 and 315, left Malta about an hour after the Vospers to catch up en route or to rendezvous fifteen miles south of Marittimo.

An enemy report was received by W/T at 2145 of a merchant ship escorted by two destroyers approaching Marittimo from the north-

---

[1] i.e. passed through them—rather like the Horse Artillery manoeuvre at the pre-war Aldershot Tattoos!

east. It was expected that this would be the unit's target, and Hennessy considered that the rendezvous with the Elcos (which would have been before the enemy merchantman would have arrived) would provide a good interception point. So the Vospers thundered on at 20 knots. And they thundered as only Vospers could.

The boats were fuelling as they went along in order to get their dangerous deck cargo into the tanks as soon as possible.

At 2315, 61, whose hydraulic steering had broken down some hours previously, and who had to spend the rest of the night being steered by a tiller fitted direct on to the rudder bar over the stern (not the most up-to-date method of controlling a boat from a forward bridge in a fast night action), had to stop engines because of a defective dynamo and the whole unit cut engines and stopped for cocoa and a chat.

The motor mechanic, Petty Officer Matthews, thought that it would not be possible to start any of the engines for half an hour, and having delivered this salvo disappeared into the heat below to wrestle with the trouble.

It was fairly calm, but there was a slight haze which reduced visibility and added a touch of friendliness to the moon.

Shortly afterwards an enemy sighting report from an aircraft was received by W/T: four merchantmen and a number of destroyers. Hennessy went down to plot the position on the chart. At the same time Bligh spun the useless steering-wheel and looked to the north-wards at a patch of darkness. It was smoke. And suddenly there was the convoy about a mile and a half away, steering straight for the three boats lying stopped (one helpless).

The MTBs started up their one relatively silent engine, and by some stroke of luck 61 was also able to get under way. Hennessy decided to attack at once with torpedoes and sent Bligh down the port side of the convoy to be ready to stage a diversion as necessary in the rear, in accordance with prearranged tactics.

The enemy was readily identified as a convoy with four large merchant ships in a rough square, with a number of escorting vessels ahead and abeam. 77 (Sturgeon) shaped to attack the starboard column but soon had to start up her noisy engines in order to pass clear ahead of the port column. She was still unobserved and got into an ideal firing position some 400 yards on the target's bow.

Sturgeon fired one torpedo and then swung to the right to fire his second one at the rear ship of the port column. At this point the enemy woke up and everything started firing; machine-guns, 20-mm.,

40-mm., 88-mm., and some heavier guns mostly firing shrapnel to burst about fifty feet in the air.

MTB 77 nevertheless continued as planned and fired her second torpedo at the chosen ship. But, alas, it did not leave the tube, and in all the turmoil and fever of the barrage this was not noticed at the time. Sturgeon now wanted to get out of the middle of the convoy as soon as possible, and elected to do this by passing close ahead of the leading ship of the port column, dropping a depth-charge as he shaved the stem. But luck was again absent, as a burst of shrapnel killed the First Lieutenant as his hand was on the release lever. So 77 disengaged to the south-east under very heavy fire, unable to make smoke because the burst which killed the First Lieutenant also damaged the smoke apparatus.

It is difficult to see how 77 could have been better manoeuvred. She got into the middle of the convoy unseen, was able to choose three targets with precision, and had caused the enemy to hit themselves with their own gunfire as they shot at her between their ranks. But she came out of that action without having scored a definite success.

Both Hennessy and Sturgeon thought that the torpedo had hit the first ship, but in the circumstances it was difficult to be sure. (In fact she was not hit, as is shown by the German report given later.)

MTB 82 fired one torpedo at the same ship as 77 and then disengaged ahead of the convoy under heavy fire from leading enemy escorts. 77 and 82 joined up to the south-eastwards and waited for 61 without much hope, as they thought that she could not have escaped, since their last news of the breakdown was that only one engine could be used.

61 had, meanwhile, passed through unimaginable frustrations. She had gone down the port beam on her completely silenced centre engine and had started firing at the enemy and dropping flares as soon as they woke up. It was one of the techniques of diversions that one had to judge whether it was better to do nothing rather than something (as it so turned out on this occasion)—i.e. to wait until the enemy knew that something was afoot.

The enemy obliged by firing back, rather high. When the MTBs were seen disengaging Bligh stopped, about 600 yards off the port bow of the rear destroyer escort. No torpedoes could have missed that amiable vessel as she went slowly past on a steady course and speed, no doubt glancing benevolently at the E-boat on the port side; but 20-mm. were useless against her.

A real E-boat could be seen on the other side of the rear destroyer, so Bligh passed round the stern and dropped flares on the port quarter, hoping that the E-boat would come over to pick up survivors from the burning British boat. But the bait was not taken.

The same trick was tried on the enemy's starboard beam, but although the enemy got off an enormous number of rounds none of the small craft escorts detached themselves (quite rightly, of course; it would have been wrong for them to have done so). After teasing the convoy in this manner for an hour and a half without any visible result beyond a heavy expenditure of their ammunition (none of which hit 61) Bligh assumed that the MTBs were waiting at the rendezvous and would not be attacking again that night, so after rattling the bars once more along the port side of the convoy he disengaged at 0210 and went to the rendezvous. The unit was reunited towards 0230 and got back to Malta some six hours later.

The Elco boats had also had their frustrations. They had not met the Vospers at the agreed rendezvous to the south of Marittimo, but they had managed to find a target for themselves, the single merchant ship and escort which had been the subject of the enemy report received at 2145. But, as they were preparing to attack, the merchantman was sunk by a Wellington torpedo-bomber and the escort was too fast to offer a torpedo target.

The German report of the action says that the convoy was an all-Italian one of four ships—the *Prosinone*, *Alcamo*, *Chieti* and *Labor*. It was escorted by a destroyer, three torpedo-boats, and the corvette *Antiope*, and was bound for Bizerta from Palermo.

The report says none of the ships was hit by torpedoes, but "two of the MTBs made several attempts from the rear but were driven off by the escorts. Several hits were observed on one of the MTBs". This bit of hopefulness refers to Bligh's come-hither efforts: one can only presume (a) the Germans suffered from double vision, (b) Bligh had a split personality.

. . . . .

In February the MTBs were getting rather exasperated because of the lack of targets, and the 10th Flotilla turned its attention to mine-laying. Some American mines were sent up—there were 450 of them at Bone waiting for customers—and the Coastal Forces shipwrights quickly got to work fitting temporary chutes. The 77-foot Elcos were altered to carry six mines and the 70-foot boats four.

At first the MTB men were rather disheartened by the change in their role; but when the reports of enemy sinkings started coming in they were converted.

On one occasion some MTBs of the 10th Flotilla were on a normal patrol when they sighted a merchant ship on fire in the middle of a ring of blazing fuel. They closed to investigate. As they got to within a short distance of her they realised she was sinking in the middle of a minefield they had laid a few nights earlier. Since mines are no respecters of nationality, they cautiously withdrew with all available fingers crossed.

Up to the end of March MTBs laid 108 mines off Plane Island, Cape Zebib, Zambra and Bizerta, and the full extent of their successes will never be known.[1] It is interesting to compare the MTBs' total of 108 for five weeks with the R.A.F.'s total for five months, when aircraft laid only 180 mines off Tunisia, Greece, Crete, Sicily and Italy.

.   .   .   .   .   .

By the middle of March the MTBs were trying to work out a technique for attacking the Siebel ferries and F-lighters which the Germans were using more and more frequently along the coast. Under normal conditions, torpedoes would be set to run at more than 5 feet, preferably more than 7 feet, to make sure that they travelled on a steady course, unaffected by the surface waves.

But the Siebel ferries and F-lighters had a very shallow draught, and, as mentioned earlier, torpedoes ran underneath them without hitting.

At home the "boffins" were perfecting a type of pistol—the mechanism which explodes the torpedo—which fired without actually hitting the target, although it was not used in the Mediterranean until much later.

The Siebel ferry was a characteristically German contribution to naval design. There were several variations, but basically it consisted of two powered barges, about 80 feet long, with a bridge or deck which joined them together—rather like a catamaran. The space between the barges, or pontoons, was quite considerable, and the whole had a beam of 50 feet.

They were built in Holland and Belgium in water-tight sections. This, apart from making them less vulnerable if hit by gunfire, meant they could be transported in sections by rail and assembled wherever

[1] Many years later Jermain, paying a visit to Italy, was talking to an Italian woman who said, proudly: "My son sank the *Manchester*." Later in the conversation she said he was also a survivor of a ship mined off Cape Bon, to which Jermain was able to say: "Madame, I mined your son."

the Germans needed them. One assembly point, for instance, was at Naples.

The Siebel ferry was driven along at 8–10 knots by lorry engines fitted in deck compartments and driving underwater screws, one engine to each pontoon.

The ferry had two functions: with three 88-mm. guns, two 37-mm. guns, a range-finder and predictor, it could be used as a mobile "flak" (anti-aircraft) ship, river gunboat or as mobile coast-defence artillery. Without heavy armament, it could be used as a lighter carrying cargoes or as a ferry carrying troops and vehicles. They had been seen carrying 150 men without undue crowding.

.   .   .   .   .

An attack on Siebel ferries was made on 22nd/23rd March, when MTBs 311 (Lancaster, who was also the S.O.) and 265 (Oxley) left Bone for an offensive sweep off Plane Island. The two boats had been patrolling for some time when, at 0150, look-outs spotted four ships moving along in an irregular formation.

Lancaster immediately stopped the two boats to plot the enemy's course and speed. Straining his eyes in the darkness, he saw the craft were twin-hulled Siebel ferries. Rapid plotting showed they were moving at about 7 knots.

Deciding they did not warrant the possible waste of four torpedoes, Lancaster told Oxley in 265 to stand by and use gunfire to support while he took 311 in close.

After hurried shouts from the bridge, the depth-setting of 311's port torpedo was altered from 10 feet to 2 feet. Thirty minutes after sighting the enemy Lancaster took 311 in on silent engines for the attack.

He chose the third Siebel in the enemy line. Slowly the range closed —1,000 yards, 900 yards, 850 yards . . . had they been spotted? A hand closed over the port and starboard firing levers . . . 800 yards, 750 yards, 700 yards—"Fire". The hand pulled the levers, firing-pins hit the impulse charges, and two torpedoes hissed out of the tubes into the water. Within a matter of seconds the gyroscopes had taken control, bringing them back on to the direction they were heading when they were fired.

Immediately the torpedoes left the tubes the enemy reacted violently: long streaking lines of tracer from 20-mm. and 40-mm. guns curved low over 311, while more cut through the darkness close astern.

Lancaster took the MTB hard a'starboard to disengage, passing near to the fourth Siebel in the line. 311's gunners fired bursts into it while aft the C.S.A. apparatus started belching smoke to cover their retreat.

The showers of blinding tracer prevented anyone in 311 seeing whether their torpedoes had hit; but Oxley in 265 later reported he had seen an orange glow which grew in size and suddenly vanished to be replaced by dark smoke.

While the two boats were heading back to base at 35 knots, after the attack, a mine blew up in 311's wake, fortunately without damage to the boat.

.   .   .   .   .

The last action in March was one of the most successful fought in the Mediterranean up to then and was a perfect example of a surprise attack.

The weather that night—31st March—was bad. An 18–24-knot wind knocked up a nasty short sea on top of a north-westerly swell, and apart from being a very dark night, there was a good deal of haze. Altogether, it was a completely unsuitable night for the boats to operate.

But an enemy convoy was reported off Cape Zebib bound for Bizerta and four MTBs from Bone were ordered to sea to intercept it. The unit, MTBs 316 (with the S.O., Lt. Jermain, embarked), 265, 266 (Lt. R. R. Smith), and 315 (Lt. L. E. Newall), left Bone at 1700 and ploughed its way towards the enemy convoy. Sea swept the foredeck and spray whipped across the bridge, at times almost blinding the officers and look-outs huddled behind what little shelter there was.

At 2050, when they were off Cape Serrat, MTB 265 reported a man overboard. He had last been seen on board fifteen minutes earlier. The S.O. told the C.O. of 265 to search for him and not rejoin.

An hour later 316, Jermain's boat, developed engine trouble and could not go on. There was too much of a sea running for him to transfer to another boat, so he told Smith in 266 to carry on as S.O. with 315, while 316 returned to Bone.

The force was halved. Smith and Newall battered their way towards Cape Zebib until, at 2310, they were a mile north of it. Both boats cut engines to wait for the convoy.

The noise of the wind whistling through the rigging and radio aerials was emphasised by the sudden quiet after the engines were stopped. The swell threw the boats about in a bruising, senseless way and made it difficult to keep a sharp look-out.

But exactly forty minutes later ships were sighted approaching from eastwards. Bearings were plotted and it became apparent the enemy were steering 250 degrees to pass between Cape Zebib and the Cani Rocks.

Both MTBs started up and began closing at slow speed, trying to make out through the spray and haze just how many ships there were and of what type. Finally it was estimated that there were three merchant ships following an escort of two destroyers and several E-boats. Smith put the MTBs between the convoy and the land and planned to go in at 10 knots.

He waited for the destroyers and E-boats to pass and then closed to attack with torpedoes. He lined up 266's sights on the second merchant ship and fired both torpedoes, while Newall fired both his at the third ship in the line.

Smith turned at high speed, seeing one of his torpedoes hit between the funnel and the bridge as he ran across the bows of 315's target, and the ship must have sunk like a stone because Newall passed through survivors in the water two minutes later.

Both of Newall's torpedoes hit the third ship, and when the flash of the explosion had died down it had vanished.

While that was going on Smith had spotted a destroyer on the starboard quarter of the convoy and, having no torpedoes left, decided to attempt a depth-charge attack. The destroyer retaliated with heavy fire, and 266 had to run for it.

As soon as his torpedoes were fired Newall disengaged. He came out close under the bows of the same destroyer, which promptly shifted its fire to him. Both the MTBs managed to escape, and, having scored three—possibly four—hits with four torpedoes, sinking two out of three merchant ships, Smith and Newall set course for base.

But the wind increased to a full gale, with an even heavier sea. The boats were pounding so badly that Smith reduced speed to 13 knots. Before long, however, the shuddering thump of the boats crashing down on the waves threatened serious damage to frames and planking so he had to reduce to 8 knots.

But in Smith's the damage was already done: she was making water in the engine-room and after compartments. The ends of the boat were sagging six inches every time she got on the crest of a wave and she had apparently broken her back in the swell.

It took them many hours to get back in the gale, and they did not arrive at Tabarka until 1100 next day, with officers and men soaking wet, hungry and worn out—but pleased with their night's work.

CHAPTER XI

THE "DOGS" BITE

The months of April and May 1943 will probably be chosen by historians as the period when the pendulum swung, and the offensive at sea finally passed into the hands of the allies. . . .
ADMIRAL OF THE FLEET VISCOUNT CUNNINGHAM[1]

THE pendulum was also swinging for Coastal Forces: within a few months they were to get within reasonable striking distance of targets, and more boats were being allocated. Up to now it had not been possible to use the fast boats in the right way; in fact it was not until the beginning of 1944 that this was possible.

Nevertheless their star started rising in April 1943, as these extracts from the Mediterranean War Diary show:

April 8th: The Admiralty was requested to send out two flotillas of MTBs as soon as possible.

April 9th: Five ML flotillas to be formed to operate A/S (anti-submarine) striking force on the North African convoy routes. These are:

22nd Flotilla: MLs 449, 468, 494, 460, 258. Codeword "Knout".
25th Flotilla: MLs 238, 236, 273, 280, 283. Codeword "Paddington".
28th Flotilla: MLs 443, 493, 341, 307, 295. Codeword "Groat".
29th Flotilla: MLs 471, 469, 463, 480, 458. Codeword "Flail".
31st Flotilla: MLs 555, 556, 560, 561, 564. Codeword "Rackham".

The 22nd and 28th Flotillas to be based at and operate from Algiers; the 25th, based on Algiers, to operate from Bougie; the 29th and 31st to be based on and operate from Oran.

April 10th: One MTB flotilla requested by the C.-in-C. is being supplied from the United Kingdom and the Admiralty have asked Washington to arrange to supply the other.

[1] *A Sailor's Odyssey*, p. 534.

April 12th: 20th MTB Flotilla (MTBs 291–298) allocated to the Mediterranean from U.S.A. construction. Four boats are now ready for shipment and four will be completed on May 15th. This was later changed, and MTBs 287–294 are being allocated, half for the 18th and half for the 20th Flotillas. This was done because the latter four boats of the 20th will not be completed as early as expected.

April 19th: 168th MTB Flotilla allocated to the Mediterranean— MTBs 81, 85, 86, 89, 97, 226, 242, 243. (This flotilla became the 24th.)

. . . . .

It would not be fair to give those entries and omit two others referring to Coastal Forces. The first, for 14th April, reported that five out of six MGBs at Bone were unable to operate because of the lack of spares. The second on 16th April, provoked, no doubt, by the first, reported that the C.-in-C., Mediterranean (Admiral Cunningham) had pointed out to the Admiralty that the failure of supplies of spares for MGBs and MTBs was resulting in a large number of these boats being made unfit for operations.

It took a long time to sort out this problem. The arrival of the American PT-boats in the Mediterranean helped to a certain extent because the British were able to get spare parts—including engines— from them, usually on the "old boy" basis rather than through any official arrangement.

A small example of the shortages the MTBs faced was in the supply of fluid for the hydraulic gun turrets. The engineer of the 32nd Flotilla (which arrived in the Mediterranean later), Lt. Dennis Taylor, R.N., was forced to make up some of his own. The ingredients were lubricating oil and paraffin. The first time it was used it burnt out after a few minutes; but it kept the guns going long enough to justify his unofficial alchemy.

. . . . .

In April the first "Dogs"[1] began to bark: the 32nd MTB Flotilla, (MTBs 633–640), the 33rd MTB Flotilla (MTBs 651 and 656—the other six boats were still being built in the U.K.) and the 19th MGB Flotilla (MGBs 641–647) were starting operations, and more flotillas were due later.

These "D" boats were in fact a complete success. Such "amenities" as these boats had allowed them to be lived aboard for long periods

[1] Fairmile "D"-class MTBs—see p. 28.

when the boats started operating among the islands of the Adriatic and Aegean.

The "amenities" were, in fact, comparative. The Vospers were designed to operate from bases where the men would live ashore, and had picnic accommodation. The "Dogs", being bigger boats, had more space for living quarters (as will be seen from Colin Mudie's cut-away drawings). But corvettes, the "next size up" in warships, had the *comparative* comfort of the *Queen Mary*.

What the "Dogs" lacked in speed they made up for by the way in which they were handled; and in the first few weeks they made a name for themselves in the Mediterranean, mainly due to the work of the 32nd Flotilla under Gould[1]—who was to be killed a few weeks after arriving while fighting one of the bravest actions of the war.

Steward Gould was a born Coastal Forces leader and had been fighting in MTBs for three years before he brought the 32nd Flotilla to the Mediterranean. He had seen the beginning of MTB-MGB operations in the Channel, and was commanding a Vosper which made a brave but fruitless attack on the two German battle-cruisers, *Scharnhorst* and *Gneisenau*, and the heavy cruiser *Prinz Eugen*, when they made their dramatic dash up-Channel on 12th February 1942, catching the R.A.F. and the Navy unawares.

.   .   .   .   .

The first noisy action by the Mediterranean "Dogs" was on 14th/15th April, off the Tunisian coast where Rommel and his Afrika Korps were still fighting hard to prevent the "Big Squeeze" by the Allies from east and west driving him out of Africa.

Two boats of Gould's flotilla, MTBs 634 (Lt. A. S. Eason, with Gould embarked) 638 (Lt. E. Rose), and MGB 643 (Lt. G. Hobday) of the 19th MGB Flotilla, left Bone after dark with instructions to destroy two enemy vessels stranded near Cape Zebib and then bombard the beach east of Ras-el-Dukara.

The three boats arrived off the reported positions of the ships in darkness and soon spotted them. Gould stopped the unit at 0025 and had a good look. One of the ships, the larger, was of 4,000–5,000 tons and appeared to be afloat, half-laden. Gould decided it was the best target.

The three boats lay with their engines stopped, keeping a watch on the ships and also the approaches to nearby Bizerta, in case any more likely targets came in sight.

[1] The late Lt. P. F. S. Gould, D.S.C., R.N.

As they watched, the larger ship started signalling by lamp to a coastguard station 500 yards along the beach to the westward. Still the MTBs waited. Then, at 0055, several four-star red flares were seen in the sky in the direction of Bizerta.

Gould decided to attack the ship and then go off to investigate the flares. He took 634 in to 700 yards range and told Eason to fire one torpedo with a depth-setting of 5 feet. As soon as the sights were on the port torpedo was launched, but instead of running straight for the target at 40 knots it slewed round to starboard and exploded on the beach. After ordering a second torpedo to be fired, Gould told all boats to close and shoot up the ship and the coastguard station. The second torpedo ran true, much to Eason's relief, and hit the ship amidships, apparently breaking her back.

The three boats then closed, firing all guns that would bear for about four minutes. Gould then ordered them seawards to check up on the flares. Two searchlights along the coast came on and started groping their narrow white beams across the sea, trying to find the MTBs.

Suddenly two large U-boats were sighted on the surface a mile to seaward and on an easterly course. Rapidly Gould ordered Rose in 638 to attack with torpedoes while he and Hobday, in MGB 643, followed up with gunfire and depth-charges.

Rose fired both torpedoes at one of the U-boats from its beam, but unfortunately they passed close ahead. Immediately Gould took 643 in at high speed for a depth-charge attack, but the startled U-boats had crash-dived and escaped. Half a mile beyond, however, Gould saw single-funnelled destroyers or large torpedo-boats.

As 634 had previously fired both her torpedoes at the merchant ship, Gould ordered her to attack with depth-charges, and she ran in at full revolutions. But the enemy ships retired at high speed—at least 30 knots. Gould immediately followed them and opened fire. The rear enemy ship replied with 3-inch or 4-inch and 20-mm., but her fire was inaccurate. 634's motor mechanics strained to get every ounce of power out of the four Packards, but within ten minutes the enemy was out of range.

The three boats then went on to Ras-el-Dukara to carry out the bombardment as ordered. They arrived back at Bone at 0845 with no casualties or damage to report.

F

"ONE WAS SET ON FIRE"

The African stage was set for the final act of the drama. Rommel, fighting a rearguard action, was hemmed in round Bizerta and Tunis. He was still fighting strongly, backed up by dive-bombers which Hitler had recalled from the Russian front to help him. General von Arnim had made two attempts to break out; but both failed.

Montgomery's decisive tactical victory at the Mareth Line on 29th March was followed by Rommel's recall to Berlin, and von Arnim took over. Gabes fell the same day, and Sfax on 10th April.

AT sea the MTBs and MGBs began to make up for the frustrating and weary months which had gone before. They were operating in force almost every night from Bone and Malta. Sousse was captured on 12th April, and by the 17th enough petrol had arrived to let them use it as an advanced base.

Four nights after the attack on the U-boat two MGBs of the 19th Flotilla, 640 and 644, left Bone for the Cape Guardia area, north of Bizerta. They found three E-boats and attacked, hitting one badly. It retired on fire under a smoke-screen. The other two E-boats, also hit by the MGBs' fire, covered its escape. German night-fighters attacked the MTBs without success, although they appeared to have some success against their own E-boats.

On 16th/17th April, MTB 634 (Lt. Eason) of the 32nd Flotilla, and MTB 656 (Lt. D. G. Tate), one of the early boats from the 33rd Flotilla, were on a sweep from Bone when they found a convoy of four destroyers and two merchant ships between Zembra and Zembretta. Torpedoes from 634 hit a 4,000-ton merchant ship, which burst into flames. The boats were engaged by the destroyers, but luckily escaped with little damage.

・　　・　　・　　・　　・

About this time it was decided to try a new way of attacking the enemy sea-lanes with the MTBs and MGBs. Despite the efforts of the

Royal Navy during darkness, the enemy were still managing to get their ships across to Sicily and Pantelleria. This was, for the most part, because Kesselring's Luftwaffe squadrons still controlled the Narrows during daylight and made it impossible for us to operate destroyers until after dark.

However, as an experiment, it was decided to see if MTBs could successfully operate in daylight. The plan was for MTBs to leave Sousse in the evening in order to be in position ready to operate at first light.

Stewart Gould, who had his 32nd Flotilla at Bone, was picked for the operation, which was to take place on 27th/28th April. He was told that "no undue risks were to be taken" and ordered to return to Sousse "if air opposition was too heavy".[1]

Before the operation Gould, who was in Bone, took two of his boats up to Sousse on 25th/26th April to join MTBs 633 and 637, discuss the plan and get last-minute instructions for what was to prove his last action.

The two boats, MTB 639, commanded by Lt. G. L. Russell, with Gould on board, and MTB 635, commanded by Lt. R. Perks, D.S.C., left Bone for what should have been a quiet passage. But, as Lt. Eric Hewitt wrote nearly eighteen months later,[2] the two boats were crossing Bizerta Bay at about 2300 in line ahead in a slight mist (no radar watch being kept) when—

Suddenly two F-lighters loomed up at very close range, fine on the port bow, crossing left to right. MTB 639 (Gould's boat) stopped suddenly and fired both torpedoes, MTB 635 going hard-a-starboard to avoid collision. . . .

No explosions were heard. MTB 635 engaged the leading ship with gunfire and MTB 639 engaged the second lighter. Both quickly caught fire and the crews abandoned ship. MTB 635 stood off to seaward as guard and MTB 639 picked up survivors (believed to be 11).

Both boats stood by for about half an hour after the action and the two F-lighters burned furiously, with sundry explosions, and finally sank. . . . Prisoners stated that they thought the MTBs were an E-boat escort for entering Bizerta.

[1] The lesson of Tobruk was still fresh in many minds.

[2] The original action report was lost—probably because of Gould's death two days later. When Capt. Stevens, Captain, Coastal Forces, heard of the action in December 1944 (it took place before he assumed command) he told Lt. Hewitt, then a sub-lieutenant and First Lieutenant of 635, to write a report, which was forwarded to Admiralty.

The two boats then went on to Sousse, where Gould talked over the plan for the next day's operation with Commodore G. N. Oliver, R.N., the Senior Officer, Inshore Squadron, under whom the MTBs were, at that time, operating.

Gould finally took three boats on the operation—MTBs 639 (Lt. G. L. Russell), 633 (Lt. H. E. Butler, D.S.C.) and 637 (Lt. E. F. Smyth). They sailed from Sousse at 0130/28th and headed in the darkness for Ras Mahmur. Arriving there at 0500, Gould took the three boats along the coast. It was daylight by then, and Gould, who wanted to see what was going on ashore, kept only a mile off the beach.

They cruised along quite slowly for two hours. Through binoculars they could see German and Italian working parties on the beach; but no one fired at them; nor did they sight any enemy ships.

At 0730 the boats rounded Kelibia Point—later to lend its name to the Royal Navy operation against German vessels trying to evacuate Tunis, which was dubbed the "Kelibia Regatta".

As gun emplacements and shore defences were sighted, the MTBs took cross-bearings and plotted the positions on their charts—it was the sort of information which always came in useful; in fact, during later operations against Sicily, MTBs had the job of going through the Messina Straits at night and deliberately provoking batteries into firing, in order that they could plot their positions.

Still Gould took his boats northwards. Many pairs of binoculars swept along the shore and to seaward—there was a wrecked Italian destroyer on Ras-el-Mirh Point; nearby were some enemy fighters on the beach—apparently in good condition; four miles further on a wrecked Siebel ferry was perched grotesquely close inshore.

They rounded Cape Bon at 0850: the visibility was perfect and still the enemy kept quiet. There was Ras-el-Amar, and a mile and a half before they reached it they sighted a wrecked destroyer lying on its beam ends. The time was 0920.

A few minutes later they sighted two Italian motor minesweepers. Increasing speed, they closed to within point-blank range of the two ships—which were of about 300 tons—and opened fire. The enemy did not reply and both ships were rapidly destroyed.

Five minutes after first opening fire on the Italians the three boats were attacking a German R-boat (similar to an ML). This was left burning from stem to stern, the crew starting a long and lonely swim to the shore.

After that several three-engined Ju. 52 transport planes—used by German airlines before the war and the backbone of the airborne attack on Crete—were sighted on the beach. Gould signalled the boats to close the shore, and the planes were raked with pom-poms.

At 1000 an unsuspecting Feiseler Storch plane was seen to be preparing to land on the beach at Ras-el-Amar. Within a very short time it was lined up in sights of the 20-mm. Oerlikons and badly hit before it had time to land of its own accord. It was claimed as a "probable".

While the gunners were busy shooting at the plane a large ship was sighted hull-down on the horizon in the Bay of Tunis. It had apparently been attacked by the R.A.F. because dense smoke was coming from it.

Gould then decided to carry out a sweep farther offshore, and the boats moved out to a position of twelve miles north-east of Cape Bon. Sighting nothing there, the boats moved even farther out.

At noon they saw a large enemy ship and went up to investigate. It turned out to be a German hospital ship and Gould turned the unit back towards Kelibia Point.

About this time look-outs reported aircraft. They turned out to be enemy fighters, which were patrolling in small numbers. At 1240 the MTBs found out what they were doing—they were part of a large air umbrella protecting a convoy consisting of a merchant ship and two destroyers. (The British report says there were two destroyers, but according to the Italians there was only one, the *Sagittario*. They say the merchant ship was the *Teramo*, formerly the French *Marie Therese le Borgne*.)

The MTBs moved in to attack. Gould's boat, 639, had used up both her torpedoes in the earlier encounters, and he decided to attack the leading escort, thus giving the other two boats a better chance to fire their torpedoes. The following passages in italic type are taken from Italian naval records:

Near Ras Idda the convoy was attacked by three MTBs which were repulsed by the escort's gunfire and by the fighter escort. One of the MTBs was set on fire and a second damaged. . . .

There were more than thirty German fighters overhead, and ashore coastal guns were getting the range, awaiting the order to fire. Aboard the *Sagittario* gunlayers watched to see what the MTBs were going to do next.

Gould closed the *Sagittario* and his tiny 20-mm. Oerlikons opened up. Immediately the shore batteries and the *Sagittario* started shooting. Groups of two and four fighters swung down in shallow dives to rake the boats with cannon and machine-gun fire.

Gould's boat continued shooting while the other two MTBs headed for the *Teramo*. At 1252 MTB 633 (Butler) fired both her torpedoes at 2,000 yards and 637 (Smyth) fired two shortly afterwards.

Commodore Oliver, the S.O., Inshore Squadron, in his report on the action wrote: "Several observers claim to have seen explosions, but the result was not seen by commanding officers owing to smoke-screen, gunfire, and general activity."

More and more fighters concentrated on attacking Gould's boat and finally cannon shells set it ablaze. At 1310 the other two MTBs saw that they were abandoning ship.

The burning MTB stopped in a position ten miles south-east of Cape Bon. . . .

On board Gould's boat the C.O., Lt. Russell, and three ratings had been killed. Gould, the first lieutenant (Lt. A. Heyburne), the navigator (Midshipman A. Youatt) and two ratings had been badly wounded. Smyth brought 637 alongside the blazing wreck and took off the wounded and the few men left aboard. Butler, in 633, picked up survivors in the water.

Enemy fighters were still attacking. There was no chance of saving 639, even though the coxswain, P.O. Patrick Crossey, rigged towing gear despite a leg wound; so she was riddled with pom-pom shells until her tanks caught fire and she sank.

As soon as the sixteen survivors were on board and MTB 639 had sunk, the two boats disengaged southwards at high speed, still being attacked by the fighters and shore batteries.

These attacks were kept up for nearly half an hour, with the boats weaving at high speeds. This made the gunners' job difficult, but 633 managed to hit one fighter with Oerlikon fire and brought it down. At 1400 Gould died of his wounds aboard Smyth's boat.

At 1525 the convoy was the target of a second violent air attack during which the Teramo *was hit and set on fire. The* Sagittario *took the killed and wounded on board and steered for Tunis. At 1630 she was again attacked by a Liberator squadron without result; some aircraft were shot down and three aviators rescued. . . .*

Admiral Cunningham, describing the action as "a praiseworthy exploit", had the day before signalled: "I am following the work of Coastal Forces with intense interest. Please assure them that they are contributing greatly to the discomfort of the enemy. . . . Keep going full out."

The gallant Gould, holder of the D.S.C. and Bar, was buried next day at Sousse.

CHAPTER XIII

"SINK, BURN AND DESTROY . . ."

The beginning of the end for the Axis in Africa came with General
Alexander's plan for a general offensive. This started on 22nd April.
On 13th May the Germans surrendered. . . .

NEVERTHELESS at the beginning of May German resistance
in Tunisia stiffened; but it was von Arnim's last fling. Destroyers of Force Q were making nightly sweeps south of
Marittimo and those of Force K in the Sicilian Channel. Every available MTB, MGB, ML and HDML was put to sea, operating from Bone
and Sousse.

The Prime Minister was at this time again becoming concerned
about the MTBs. One of his minutes[1] said:

P.M. to First Lord, First Sea Lord and General Ismay. 2 May 1943.
The activities of the motor torpedo-boats from Malta and Sousse are
becoming extremely important. Can we not strengthen them? What is
there at Malta? What is there at Alexandria? Are there any more suitable
vessels which can be sent to Malta, Tripoli and Sousse? I presume all this
can be settled by Cunningham without further reference here. Let me know
what he is doing.
I should be willing to send a message to the MTBs, who seem to be
putting up an extremely sporting fight.
There is a question whether all these fast small craft should not have a
name. I have thought of them as the "Mosquito Fleet", but would it not
be more dignified to call them the "Hornet Fleet"? Or, again, perhaps the
"Shark Fleet"—"Sharks" for short.[2]

The month started off with the loss of an MTB. On 2nd May three
"Dogs" sailed to sweep from the Gulf of Tunis towards Marittimo,

---

[1] *The Second World War*, Volume IV, p. 853, Appendix C.
[2] The Coastal Forces base at Gosport is in fact called H.M.S. *Hornet*.

while three Elcos of Jermain's 10th Flotilla operated inshore between the Cani Rocks and Zembra Island.

But they had tempted the minefields once too often, and one of the Elcos, commanded by Lt. J. D. Lancaster, MTB 311, was badly damaged and had to be abandoned. MTB 316 picked up the survivors—three of whom were hurt—and 311 was sunk by gunfire.

About this time HDML 1154 failed to return from a patrol off Bizerta and was believed to have hit a mine. The HDMLs were working hard—one of them spent seventeen consecutive nights on patrol.

Ashore, on 7th May, the Americans reported they had captured Bizerta and the naval base at Ferryville. Next day the S.O., Inshore Squadron sailed for Bizerta in MTB 637 (Smyth) with another MTB in company. He reported: "At 0300 (exactly six months and one hour after the assault on North Africa had begun) I hoisted my broad pendant in MTB 637. . . . We entered the avant port, whereupon fire was opened."

Although Bizerta had been declared captured, the Germans were still in possession of some parts of the town. Machine-guns and cannons opened up on the two boats at close range.

Almost immediately Smyth and his first lieutenant were severely wounded and a motor mechanic was mortally wounded. S/Lt. Arundale,[1] took over the boat and brought it out of the harbour, still under heavy fire.

He brought MTB 637 back to Bone on one engine. Commodore Oliver successfully arrived in Bizerta overland the next day, and the day after hoisted his broad pendant, at Fort Koudriat, where headquarters was established.

On 7th May sixteen destroyers were patrolling the coast of Tunis, searching for any Germans escaping by sea. All available Coastal Forces craft from Bone and Sousse established night patrols farther inshore, between Bizerta and Kelibia. There was a lot of activity on the enemy beaches, but no craft were seen to leave.

Admiral Cunningham had his forces all ready. The next day (8th May), when he had brought all his available destroyers in for a close day-and-night patrol off the Cape Bon peninsula, his orders to them were brief: "Sink, burn and destroy. Let nothing pass."[2] Operation "Retribution" had begun.

---

[1] This was Arundale's first experience of handling an MTB. He was in fact the navigator of MGB 645 (Lt. Basil Bourne) and had been lent to 637 for the Bizerta trip.
[2] *A Sailor's Odyssey.*

The MTBs and MGBs continued their patrols. On 9/10th May MTBs 316, 265 and 313, operating off Sidi Daud, intercepted an enemy craft and captured thirty-six German soldiers and airmen. The next night MTBs off Tunis picked up six Austrian transport drivers who were trying to cross to Sicily in a rubber dinghy. MTBs 75, 76 and 78, inshore off Kelibia on the same night, picked up thirteen Germans in a fishing-boat.

On 11th/12th May boats of Jermain's 10th Flotilla reaped a very large harvest. MTBs 316, 309 and 265 were off Cape Bone when they picked up 117 prisoners between them.

Jermain, describing that night, writes: "Our bag included some German paratroopers. The boat I was in did not have enough weapons to arm every member of the crew, so we had to give some of them the tommy-guns we had taken off the paratroopers.

"Soon after that there was a burst of sub-machine-gun fire from just behind me. I looked round in alarm to see one of the paratroopers standing there with a smoking tommy-gun in his hand. The stoker who was the guard for that particular part of the boat said: 'It's all right, sir; he's only showing me how it works'."

A few nights earlier Jermain had been out with some of his boats hunting for enemy shipping operating from Cape Bon. Some American PT-boats were also out in the same area, under Lt.-Cdr. Barnes, U.S.N.

"We met," says Jermain, "while each was stalking the same object which looked like a merchant ship. 'It's your retribution,' Barnes called; but, sad to relate, it proved to be a rock, and Barnes while moving off found a genuine merchant ship to torpedo."

.   .   .   .   .

A couple of nights before Jermain's bag of 117 prisoners, the C.O. of MTB 61 was engaged on an operation which earned him the unwanted and embarrassing description, in a Sunday newspaper, of being "The Man Who Laughed at Death".

One unit of MTBs of the 7th Flotilla, which was then operating from Sousse, had passed fairly close to Kelibia on its way to a more northerly patrol area and had thought it saw a number of low-lying, barge-like craft lying close to the shore in the northernmost part of the harbour. This was a likely sort of report, although it was not known whether it was confirmed by aerial reconnaissance.

On the evening of 8th May Lt. Hennessy, R.N., in MTB 77, with

61 (Lt. T. J. Bligh) and the American PT-boat 209, was patrolling in the area immediately to the north of Kelibia. Hennessy had discussed with the boat captains the report about these barges; and as all was very quiet and 61 was fitted with captured Breda 20-mm. guns in the place of torpedoes, Bligh requested permission to enter Kelibia, seek out the enemy and attack with gunfire. This was granted.

Kelibia Harbour is shaped like a sickle, with the handle going north and south along the coastline and the cutting edge facing to the east. There had been reports of a battery on the raised ground right on the tip of the sickle, so 61 kept very close to the shore, intending to steer up the handle and round the blade and then to attack from the west the barges lying at the top of the harbour. This seemed to offer the best chance of minimising interference from the battery.

The chart showed 10 feet of water. 61 drew 5 feet. It looked all right. But it wasn't. Whilst going ahead on the silenced centre engine 61 struck the bottom and went firm aground with the bows down.

The usual drill was put into operation. All the crew went aft, jumped up and down with the engine going full astern. This had no effect. Then the depth-charges were disarmed and dropped over the side, most of the ammunition was jettisoned and any other weighty objects were thrown overboard (including the captain's library). All this was done with as little noise as possible and all orders were given at the whisper.

The next move was to put the Carley float into the water, tow it to the bows and lower on to it the main anchor which was attached to all the lines of 61 joined together. The float was then paddled away to the starboard quarter as far as the lines would reach. The anchor was tipped off the float and soon held firm on the bottom. The four officers (there were two spare ones on board that night) went over the side and stood by the bows in something under five feet of water. The coxswain was put in charge and whilst the engine went full astern the crew all pulled on the anchor line and the officers pushed on the hull. But she did not move one inch.

Bligh made a survey, mostly on foot, of the sea-bed all round the boat and reached the dismal conclusion that 61 was not likely ever to float again. Up to that point the whole business had, strange as it may seem, been conducted without any overt hostility from the land.

They may have been hoping for boats to come, and might just, perhaps, have been surprised that the visitor should spend so long in the business of berthing. But it was extremely likely that if 61 had started up her unsilenced wing engines, which made a characteristic noise quite unlike anything German or Italian, her true sympathies would have been revealed. And she was lying at such an angle down by the bows that it seemed to be a move not worth making. The main factor now, as it appeared to Bligh, was the safety of the crew.

Hennessy had been kept in touch with the developing situation by R/T, and on learning that 61 was irretrievably grounded he sent the signal "Destroy your boat". He also despatched the PT-boat to get as close to 61 as possible and pick up the crew. Lt. J. B. Sturgeon, R.N.V.R., the captain of 77, went in the PT-boat to assist with communications.

Meanwhile the enemy had decided that the visitor was behaving altogether too suspiciously and a number of men began shouting from the beach. "Qui va la?" they said, a lot of times. A 20-mm. fired a tentative burst which mostly passed overhead (they must, understandably, have overestimated the range).

There clearly was not long to go before 61 might well come under heavy fire from the shore. Bligh ordered the First Lieutenant, S/Lt. F. Johnson, to sink the confidential books and signal publications, in the weighted eyeleted canvas bag, in the deepest bit of water he had been able to find in his perambulations of the grounded boat.

He told Petty Officer Motor Mechanic Matthews to empty tins of petrol in all the spaces below decks and to pump a lot of petrol into the engine-room bilges. He then pocketed the loaded two-star cartridge pistol from the bridge rack and told the crew to prepare to abandon ship. He would give the order for this when the PT-boat came as close as she could or when the enemy, who had kept up a rather sporadic aimless firing, began to bring heavy fire on the boat. And then the little black dot to seaward was sighted and began to grow bigger. Enemy attention was riveted on 61. The PT-boat grew closer.

She stopped. She was about 200 to 300 yards away. Brian Sturgeon's voice came floating softly over the still water. "We can't come any nearer. You'll have to swim." "Bless him," thought Bligh, as he gave the order to abandon ship, "he doesn't realise we shall be able to walk most of the way."

The crew jumped over the side and started for the American. The enemy opened fire on 61 with a number of 20-mm. guns. Bligh glanced at his watch—it was two hours and ten minutes since 61 had run aground—took a deep breath and fired the signal pistol into the petrol-soaked fo'c'sle. There was a great roar of flame and the whole foredeck lifted away from the sides, like a giant crocodile snapping at a bird.

The upward and outward jerk threw Bligh over the corner of the bridge on to the after part of the torpedo-tube mounting on the starboard side. But he was only slightly hurt and was able to follow the crew, who were first walking, then swimming towards the American.

MTB 61 burnt like a huge torch, with great yellow petrol flames pouring up into the sky. And as the harbour was lit up by this sad pyre the enemy decided that all available guns should fire at the now harmless boat. And at the same time, by one of those odd triumphs of timing that so rarely occur when they are planned, a large four-engined aircraft slowly circled the harbour at about 1,000 feet.

But the captain of the PT-boat did not move and had soon picked up the men in the water. 61 lost one man—Leading Stoker F. Adshead, who, though seen in the water halfway between the boats, was never found.

Bligh was mentioned in dispatches for these events.

.   .   .   .   .

On the 13th May Colonel-General Jurgen von Arnim, Commander-in-Chief Axis Forces in Africa, surrendered to the 4th Indian Division near St. Maria du Zit, and, except for small detachments, all resistance in Africa ceased.

CHAPTER XIV

"THERE LIES A LAND CALLED . . ."

THE day before the last Axis forces surrendered in Tunisia plans[1] were made to regroup various MTB and MGB flotillas, some of which had yet to arrive. Bone was to become the main repair and training base for the Western Mediterranean, while Bizerta was to be used only by operational boats. H.M.S. *Vienna* was ordered to sail for Bizerta to act as an MTB base ship.

The 7th and 32nd MTB and the 20th MGB Flotillas were to operate from Malta, while the 18th and 23rd MTB and the 19th MGB Flotillas were to use Bone and Bizerta.

A fortnight later, 27th May, the Admiralty's offer to send seven American-built MTBs to the Mediterranean from the United Kingdom was accepted by the C.-in-C. Although the supply of spares was to be arranged locally, and crews were to be provided from MTBs undergoing large repairs, the Diary records that—

"It was pointed out to the Admiralty that despite the arrival of a small number of spare engines for MTBs and MGBs, these craft are still being made useless through engine and gunnery failures and [it was] requested that 150 per cent spare auxiliary engines and gunnery parts be sent out as soon as possible."

The C.-in-C., perturbed by the number of boats experiencing engine trouble, told the Prime Minister of the difficulties he was experiencing, and Mr. Churchill acted at once.

P.M. to First Lord.

Admiral Cunningham has expressed the opinion to me that our light naval craft could have achieved even more in the Mediterranean if the engines of the motor torpedo-boats had been more reliable. Let me have a report on this, and let me know whether this is a local problem connected with the maintenance of these craft or whether there is a basic weakness in the design.[2]

·   ·   ·   ·

[1] Mediterranean War Diary.   [2] *The Second World War*, Vol. V, p. 565.

Up to now we have been dealing mostly with MTBs and MGBs; but the MLs and HDMLs were doing hard and often monotonous work. Many of the MLs had for a long time been busy on anti-submarine patrol ahead of convoys and the extra flotillas sent to Gibraltar at the time of the North Africa campaign were steadily being reinforced.

With the gradual opening up of the Western Mediterranean, more and more merchant ships and landing-craft were coming through the Straits of Gibraltar in preparation for the evisceration of "the soft under-belly" of the Axis, the assaults on Pantelleria, Sicily, and finally Italy, thus providing the MLs with a good deal of extra patrol duties.

The work of the small HDMLs must not be forgotten. These flotillas were also being reinforced, although usually at a slower rate because they had to be shipped out.

Earlier in the year HDML 1229 made a strange voyage out to the Mediterranean. She, with two other HDMLs, was loaded on the deck of the S.S. *City of Christchurch*, which sailed for Algiers in convoy KMS 11.

On 21st March, while the convoy was off the Portuguese coast, the *City of Christchurch* was bombed and badly damaged. Her master hoped to make Lisbon and the ship left the convoy, with H.M.C.S. *Morden* escorting her.

But she was unlucky, and by 1645 on 22nd March her stern was awash. The master decided it was time to abandon ship, and after cutting the lashings holding the HDMLs the crew were taken off by *Morden*.

Morden then fired at the forward part of the ship to try to make her sink horizontally, thus giving the HDMLs a chance to float off. Three hours later she took the final plunge, and two of the HDMLs floated clear of the wreckage. One of them, however, had broken her back. The other, 1229, was intact.

The C.O. of the *Morden* then called for volunteers to get her under way. They were quickly forthcoming and soon 1229 was making 9 knots towards Gibraltar, shepherded along by *Morden*. In spite of a strong gale, she arrived in Gibraltar two days later.

Apart from A/S work, certain MLs were taking part in special operations, usually landing small parties of troops on enemy-occupied territory.

.   .   .   .   .

Out in the dark blue seas there lies a land called Crete, a rich and lovely land, washed by the waves on every side, densely peopled and boasting nine cities. . . . One of the ninety towns is called Knossos, and there, for nine years, King Minos ruled and enjoyed the friendship of almighty Zeus. . . .

So Homer makes Odysseus describe Crete. As the centuries passed, it was described in rather more mundane phrases. How the Special Service MLs regarded it is not recorded, but frequent and clandestine visitors in the spring and summer of 1943 were MLs 355 and 361.

A typical visit, on 7th May, was called Operation "Headstrong". ML 355, under the command of Lt. G. W. Searle, had the task of landing passengers on the island.

The ML sailed from Derna at 1000. The sea was smooth and at first the visibility was good, but as darkness began to fall and the ML neared Crete mist closed in like long-awaited sleep.

Soon the island's coastline was sighted and the ML approached the rendezvous. Lt. Searle writes in his report: "Several small lights were seen right ahead on the beach (these were caused by the cigarettes of the party awaiting evacuation)."

At 2220 Searle cut the engines and waited for the correct signal to be flashed from the shore. This came ten minutes later, and using her Asdic the ML closed the shore and anchored at four fathoms.

"It had been intended to make the ML's stern fast to the shore with a rope and work a rubber dinghy as a ferry by having a line on each end," Searle continues.

"The ship's dinghy, towing the rubber boat with lines, went ashore, taking Lt. Matthews, an R.N.V.R. officer on board, but they found confusion among the party on the beach. Many more than intended were struggling to get on board and force was needed to prevent them rushing the dinghy.

"In these circumstances no one helped with our ropes. The stern line came adrift and the dinghy lines became so entangled and jammed in rocks that the idea of using them was abandoned."

The passengers were taken ashore, and after the dinghy had made several trips backwards and forwards to the beach Matthews reported that "all Imperial troops and agents were aboard and no one else of the remaining people ought to be evacuated".

The ML, with sixty-eight passengers, then sailed. Searle adds: "After we left, those who stayed continued to flash lights wildly for some time, which made them conspicuous for many miles to seaward.

Also, through having to keep the engines running slowly for one and a half hours, we emitted a considerable display of sparks from the funnel during the first hour's run."

For the next few months there were several such operations—including "Chair", when ML 361 landed some passengers and embarked an Army officer and fifty-seven Cretans on 6th June, and "Emolument".

In this operation ML 361, commanded by Lt. R. M. Young, R.C.N.V.R., had to land some passengers on Crete; but, unlike previous trips, her return passage was not uneventful.

She had left Crete at 0200, shaping a course for Tobruk. At 0655 look-outs saw three aircraft coming over the horizon on a parallel course. They were identified as Arado 196s and "Action stations" was sounded.

The three aircraft altered course towards 361 and then, when they were two miles away, split up. One came in on each quarter and the third came in over the bow.

Young, in his report, writes: "At 0700 the first run was made, and the ship opened fire at 1,000 yards. This aircraft veered off and fired from the rear gun positions. From then on each aircraft attacked in turn, firing from the wings and then veering off at very close range and firing from the rear guns."

Young sent a signal giving the ML's position, course and speed, but the course was relayed incorrectly and a Beaufighter, sent out to help, could not find her—although the officers in the ML did in fact sight the aircraft.

"Early in the action," Young continues, "the after Oerlikon and port Breda 20-mm. scored hits on an aircraft coming in on the port quarter, but a moment later both guns' crews were hit.

"This aircraft immediately broke off the action and withdrew. From then on our forward Oerlikon, starboard 0.5-inch Browning and starboard Breda 20-mm. kept in action, although the gunner of the Breda was badly hit.

"Avoiding action was to go from hard-over to hard-over to try to keep them from getting a straight run over our stern, and bring as much fire-power to bear as possible.

"One able seaman [A.B. Cooney], although wounded in the stomach and ankle, the sights of his gun blown away by a bullet which struck his tin hat, continued firing with accuracy throughout the action, and immediately the action was broken off attempted to repair the

G

damaged Breda, refused to leave his action station until we reached harbour, was then discovered assisting other wounded on to stretchers, and did not get into one himself until directly ordered, when he had almost collapsed.

"Another seaman [A.B. Higginbotham], with three shrapnel wounds in the leg, was knocked to the deck and in the space of a very short time was [again] firing his gun. After the action he remained on his gun until he fainted."

Several of the guns scored hits on the aircraft. The first lieutenant, firing a stripped Lewis, was also successful and "observed the tracer in some cases ricocheting off the aircraft".

The planes made eight attacks within fifteen minutes, and then flew off to the northward, leaving seven wounded in the ML. One of them, Ordinary Seaman Derbyshire, had his foot blown off at the beginning of the attack. He managed to drag himself out of the way of the rest of the crew, and when asked what was wrong replied: "Just a hit in the foot."

Able Seaman Turner, who received through bullet-holes in his left foot and shoulder which knocked him from his gun, tried to continue firing from the deck until he found the gun had also been hit and put out of action.

Young adds: "The gunners showed exceptional coolness and intelligence in picking out their targets in such a manner that there was no useless firing and that no plane escaped engagement while attacking.

"All wounded ratings, with the exception of three seriously wounded, succeeded in getting back on their guns, although most of them were in serious pain."

.   .   .   .   .

Almost every month small convoys of Coastal Forces craft were leaving the United Kingdom, rounding Ushant and crossing the Bay of Biscay on their way to the Mediterranean. Usually they had trawlers acting as navigators and "escorts"; and although they mostly managed to get through without any severe brushes with the enemy, the weather was often far from friendly.

A typical convoy left Milford Haven in March, bound across the Bay at the time of the equinoctial gales. It comprised five "Dog" boats, five MLs and two trawlers, the *Bonito* and *Grayling*.

One of the MLs was 555, the "State Express", commanded by

Lt.-Cdr. J. Ivester Lloyd, D.S.C., R.N.V.R., Senior Officer of the 31st Flotilla. He describes[1] part of the voyage:

"The convoy formed up in two columns. Ahead of us was the trawler *Bonito*, and astern four more Fairmile 'B' MLs, each a replica of my own 555. On our starboard hand, led by the trawler *Grayling*, were five 'Dog' boats. These were longer and beamier than our own boats. . . . But while we looked like miniature destroyers, the 'Dog' boat designers seemed to have sacrificed all claim to seamanlike appearance in producing a floating war machine.

"It was an old joke in Coastal Forces that when the first 'Dog' was delivered a senior officer asked: 'Is this the ship—or the box it came in?' However, despite their appearance, the 'Dogs' did magnificent work."

The convoy made its way westwards to get clear of the west coast of France, which was liberally spattered with German air bases. Crews went into sea routine, cooked meals arrived regularly, and Lloyd, in peacetime a writer on sporting and country subjects, and more popularly known as "Farmer", settled down to read *Mr. Sponge's Sporting Tour* for the fourth time.

After the convoy turned south it came on to blow, and the bad weather continued for many bitterly cold, sleepless hours. Then an aircraft diving down on the convoy sent the crews to action stations; but it proved to be a Sunderland flying boat, which, after flashing "Good luck", climbed back effortlessly into the anonymity of the clouds.

An aircraft which appeared the next afternoon proved to be unfriendly—one of the lean and hungry-looking Focke-Wulf Condors. It circled and then, its curiosity satisfied, flew off again. The next afternoon it appeared at the same time, did its prescribed orbit, and departed.

On the third afternoon most of the crews were on deck at the appointed time to see if the Germans would live up to their reputation for being methodical. They did; only this time the Condor came in higher and dropped four bombs which burst between 555 and *Bonito*—on the spot where 555 would have been had she not lagged astern of her station.

·   ·   ·   ·   ·

The next Coastal Forces convoy to pass this way had a livelier time. It assembled at Milford Haven during the early part of April and

[1] See Preface.

consisted of eight "Dogs"—four MTBs and four MGBs of the 20th and 33rd Flotillas (later the 56th and 57th)—and seven MLs.

The "Dogs"—all of which will become familiar later in this book—were MTB 670 (with the S.O. of the 33rd Flotilla, Lt.-Cdr. Ashby, acting as S.O. of the convoy, on board), MTB 667 (Lt. C. Jerram), MTB 654 (Lt. Tom Fuller, R.C.N.V.R.), MTB 655 (Lt. Greene-Kelly), MGB 657 (Lt. Douglas Maitland, R.C.N.V.R.), MGB 658 (Lt. Cornelius Burke, R.C.N.V.R.), MGB 648 (Lt. Bailey), and MGB 663 (Lt. T. Ladner, R.C.N.V.R.).

Three of the Canadians, Maitland, Burke and Ladner, had been to school together. When war broke out the trio joined the Navy, and all three managed to get over to England in 1940 to join Coastal Forces. After two years in MTBs or MGBs they had returned to Canada on two months' leave, having first "fixed" that on their return they should be appointed to "Dogs" of a new flotilla going to the Mediterranean. So the prevalence of Canadians in this convoy was not altogether a coincidence.

The convoy sailed on 30th April in four columns—the MTBs forming the starboard, and the MGBs the port, with the MLs making up the two inner columns. Two trawlers, *Coverleigh* and *Breen*, sailed with the convoy.

Apart from patches of fresh wind and rough seas, the voyage went smoothly until 3rd May, when a four-engined Focke-Wulf came along and had a brief look at them. It reappeared later, but did not attack.

That night the convoy altered course and speed. Lt. Leonard Reynolds, R.N.V.R., then a midshipman and "pilot" of 658, writes: "Corny [Lt. Burke] and I were on watch when, at 0100, the peacefulness of the night was suddenly shattered. As from nowhere a stream of tracer came floating in from the port bow, well forward of us but hitting 657 ahead. Corny's reactions were immediate: 'Action stations —port wheel, Cox'n'. . . ."

Burke steadied up on the bearing from which the firing had come, ringing down for all engines and more speed. The tracer had lasted only a minute or two, and 657 could be seen over to starboard, with a fire raging amidships.

"From 658 nothing could be seen in the pitch blackness," writes Reynolds, "and Corny made a wide circle and struck our original course again, although no other ships were visible. . . .

"At 0220 queer things began to happen a mile or so on the starboard beam—searchlights from three craft were sweeping around, and we assumed then that these might be enemy craft. However, there was no tracer, and the risk of collision in our convoy was too great to career about."

The rest of the story is told by Lt. Jerram,[1] who was C.O. of MTB 667, in the starboard column. The attack was made by two U-boats from a pack which was on its way out into the Atlantic. They opened fire on Maitland's boat, setting some petrol ablaze. They were not sighted and later Jerram thought he smelled fuel oil.

With Fuller and Ashby he went off to search. "After a short while," he says, "we found some men in the water and lit them up with Aldis lamps. They were wearing submarine escape apparatus, and while Ashby circled round I picked up a couple of them and Fuller picked up the rest.

"They turned out to be Germans from a couple of U-boats which apparently, after attacking the convoy with gunfire, had gone round to make a torpedo attack and collided with each other."[2]

The two survivors aboard Jerram's boat proved to be an engineer and a rating. Both of them, apart from suffering with shock, were terrified. S/Lt. Dean, 667's navigator, went below to offer each of them a nip of brandy, but they were suspicious and refused to drink it. Dean, after failing to persuade them, drank it himself—to prove, he explained later, that it really was all right.

They were given clothes to wear—including white jerseys of the type worn by Coastal Forces, and they soon became friendly with the crew, who discovered that the engineer could bake excellent bread. From then on he spent a good deal of his time in the galley.

Ashby had sent a signal saying that some German prisoners were arriving with the convoy, and when 667 arrived in Gibraltar Ashby came on board to find the Germans being given farewell tots of whisky in the wardroom.

Before long a Royal Marine major arrived with two guards. He had come, he said, to collect the prisoners. Jerram invited him into the wardroom for a drink, and when that hospitality had been dispensed the major inquired after his prospective charges. Jerram pointed to the two men in white jerseys, each of whom had a glass in his hand.

---

[1] Now Lt.-Cdr. Jerram, D.S.O., D.S.C.*, R.N.V.R.
[2] The Mediterranean War Diary differs, suggesting one of the trawlers hit one U-boat and that the other had been sunk by aircraft. This idea seems hardly likely.

The major was not amused, and insisted that they were blindfolded before they were led ashore. The Germans were co-operative, and after handkerchiefs had been tied across their eyes politely told the guards "I can see a bit". When this error had been remedied they were marched ashore, with the crew calling out their farewells.

·   ·   ·   ·   ·

The convoy had arrived in Gibraltar on 7th May, six days before the Axis surrendered in Tunisia. The "Dogs", after their deck tanks had been removed, went on to Algiers and then moved up to Bone, where the Coastal Forces base under Lt.-Cdr. Allan was working smoothly and efficiently.

ML 555, which had arrived at Gibraltar in the earlier convoy, had gone up to Oran, where the other seven boats of the 31st Flotilla were operating. Ivester Lloyd, their new S.O., describes their work: "The boats of my flotilla were at sea, three at a time, for spells of seventy-two hours, patrolling the convoy routes and keeping Asdic watch for U-boats.

"If the weather blew up rough I could act on my own discretion, and so contrived to visit some amusing little ports. Once it was the old stronghold of Barbary pirates, Nemours, and several times it was Mostaghanem, where we willingly helped the Americans, who were in charge of the port, out of a difficulty.

"They had salvaged the cargo of a torpedoed British ship, and part of this was a mountain of unmarked cases. The officer in charge complained that it was 'the durndest stuff' and that his sentries 'got real crazy guarding it'. He wished, he said, that someone 'would take the goddam stuff away'. After one glance at those cases we agreed to take it all off, even if it meant loading every boat of the flotilla down to water level. For each case contained two two-gallon jars of Army rum.

"One evening, with no other excuse than the attractive appearance of the place, we dropped anchor under the lee of a big rock off El Marsa and rowed ashore in our dinghies. While the officers drank wine with a French farmer and his charming family, one watch of each crew went into the village.

"Returning to our ships at sundown, we were treated to the extraordinary spectacle of my coxswain running down the beach followed by a crowd of admiring visitors. Under his arm he carried a live goose, but his trousers were missing. 'I offered her everything I could think of for the goose, sir,' he explained, 'but she'd only have my white duck trousers.'

"As a change from patrols, an escort job sometimes came our way. Once it was a French submarine to be taken from Oran to Algiers, and I led the way in 555 while 556 came astern of the submarine. We were off Cape Tenez just before sunset and I saw two of the newly-arrived American patrol craft come roaring out of Tenez Harbour. One of them ranged alongside me, and her commanding officer, a keen-faced boy, shouted across: 'Say, are you British?'

"I looked aloft at the White Ensign and mildly replied: 'Yes.'

" 'Okay,' he shouted back. 'And that submarine—is she friendly?'

" 'I hope so,' I replied. 'She's followed me all the way from Oran.' "

CHAPTER XV

THE TWIST OF THE CORKSCREW

'Tis not so swift a business to prepare
A landing force; to moor, to take full care
The cables hold; then, anchors, too, may slip,
And time goes ere the shepherd of the ship
Can lose his fears. . . .

AESCHYLUS

ITH Tunisia in Allied hands, the spotlight of war swung eastwards towards Sicily; but for a moment it paused on three islands, Linosa, Lampedusa and Pantelleria—Pantelleria, the gaunt island, as big as the Isle of Wight, which Mussolini had fortified to be the Gibraltar of the Sicilian Narrows.

These were the three islands the Allies wanted as fighter bases to cover the assault on the Italian homeland; and they also menaced our convoys as they moved somewhat more freely through the Mediterranean.

In the United Kingdom production was beginning to keep pace with the gluttonous appetite of war. On the Coastal Forces side thirty-one "Dogs" (fifteen MTBs and sixteen MGBs), twenty-six short MTBs, about fifty MLs and sixty HDMLs were to be completed in the first six months of the year.

In Germany, however, all was not well on the production front. Doenitz met Hitler at the Berghof on 11th April to present a strong case[1] for increasing the allocation of iron to the Navy. He also told Hitler that owing to its value as an offensive weapon it was urgently necessary to increase the production of E-boats. The memorandum he left with his Fuehrer that day showed that Germany's yearly warship production was—apart from destroyers, the building of which was to stop from 1945 (extraordinary foresight on the part of the Naval Staff)—eighteen torpedo-boats (small destroyers), seventy-two E-boats,

---

[1] *Minutes of the Fuehrer's Naval Conferences, 1943.*

seventy-four R-boats, and nine hundred transport barges (many of these were F-lighters).

Operations against Pantelleria started even before von Arnim surrendered in Tunisia. On 11th/12th May a close patrol of MTBs was established off the island and bombers of the North African Air Force attacked its airfields. On the 13th the cruiser *Orion* fired twenty broadsides into the harbour from 100,000 yards while MTBs kept in close to attack any enemy ships which might try to escape the *Orion's* belting. They hopefully fired their 20-mm. Bredas into the dust and shell smoke which almost completely hid the harbour.

From the end of May the sea and air attacks on the island were intensified. It was hoped that intensive shelling and bombing would force the island to surrender; but the defenders stuck it out, so plans went ahead for seaborne landings.

Operation "Corkscrew", the Allied invasion of Pantelleria, started on 11th June. Two of the convoys carrying troops, protected by destroyers, gunboats, trawlers, minesweepers and MLs, arrived off the beaches at 0955, when the signal to lower assault craft was made.

At 1032 these craft began to approach the port, and at 1100 the cruisers *Newfoundland*, *Orion*, *Aurora* and *Penelope* began to bombard selected targets, followed by the destroyers and a gunboat, the gallant *Aphis*.

Just before noon the Allied assault troops began to land with only slight opposition, and staff officers went ashore in MTB 84 to try to find a responsible officer from whom the surrender could be accepted.

A signal was then received by Rear-Admiral McGrigor, naval commander for the assault. It had been intercepted earlier in Malta and was from Admiral Pravesi. It read: "Pantelleria begs surrender, due lack of water." Although the latter part of this somewhat dry signal later proved to be an overstatement of the case, the former was true enough.

Lt. R. Aitchison, then first lieutenant of MTB 84, writes: "Little was required of the MTBs at the actual landing until 84 was detailed to embark the G.O.C. and his staff and land them in the harbour.

"Pantelleria harbour is very tiny and was so completely devastated that we had to secure alongside an LCI to land our party. On the way in 84 passed close to a large and succulent-looking fish floating on its side in the water. It had evidently been killed by the explosions, and the crew were most incensed that there was not time to salvage it.

"We then rejoined MTB 77 and lay cut with her a short distance from H.M.S. *Largs*, the H.Q. ship. MTB 73 had been detached on Air/Sea Rescue duty.

"Most of the ships of the landing force were stationary at that time, and the sky was thick with friendly aircraft. One of the crew remarked that something had fallen out of one of them.

"And, indeed, something had. Two bombs fell close to 84 (although they had obviously been intended for *Largs*). The FW 190—for that was the aircraft—then departed without hindrance from our own aircraft. Another attempt was made to dive-bomb the H.Q. ship, but with no more success, and this time the offender was shot down.

"A little while later 84 was ordered to close a landing ship some way to seaward, and I was told that I was to be put aboard 73, as she had been attacked by aircraft and both officers had been killed.

"We found 73 alongside the landing ship, having been brought in by the coxswain. She was already disembarking casualties. She did not appear to be badly damaged at first sight, but the crew were already washing away the traces and clearing up the boat.

"It appeared that 73 had been detached to search for 'ditched' airmen some three miles from the landing force. While searching she had been attacked by an FW. 190 which made two runs on her—from ahead and from astern.

"The second burst from the fighter had made a direct hit on the bridge, and converging fire from the wing guns killed the C.O., Lt. F. L. Tomlinson, and his First Lieutenant, but left the coxswain untouched at the wheel.

"With casualties disembarked, 73 was got under way and I set a course for Malta, the other MTBs joining me. Auxiliary engines were started and pumping began as she was making water forward and also in the engine-room.

"It very soon became apparent, however, that it was petrol, not water, that was flooding the boat. It was coming from damaged tanks in the 'midships compartment.

"All engines were stopped, switches were broken, and the boat was taken in tow by 84, with 77 leading. We made every effort with the hand pump to transfer the petrol from the damaged tanks to the undamaged ones; but the pump was hopelessly inadequate and the engine-room had eighteen inches of petrol in the bilges. No one could survive in that atmosphere for more than a few minutes at a time.

"We kept on pumping for some time, but it was doubtful if anything effective was being achieved. The night passage was long and tedious, as everyone was exhausted and sleep was almost irresistible. We made Malta in the late afternoon of the following day."

.   .   .   .   .

Two days after Pantelleria was captured Lampedusa surrendered, and Linosa, the last of the trio of islands, was captured.

CHAPTER XVI

THE "HUSKY" BITES

THE assault on "Fortress Europe"—Operation "Husky", the invasion of Sicily—began on 10th July 1943. It was the greatest amphibious operation ever undertaken up to that time; and it was a complete success.

It is impossible to describe here the complete story of the work of Coastal Forces in "Husky", so it is proposed to give an outline of the operation as a whole, the disposition of certain boats, and then some of their activities.

At the outset, it is important to remember, eighty-three boats (and finally more than a hundred) were operating from Malta (thirty-nine MTBs and MGBs, twenty MLs and twenty-four HDMLs), with seventeen MTBs and MGBs from Bizerta and fourteen MLs and HDMLs from Sousse.

The craft had a variety of jobs: the MLs escorted convoys to the beaches and provided A/S protection for the vessels at anchor, apart from dozens of smaller tasks. The little HDMLs, fitted with radar, acted as escorts and navigational marks, and also helped with A/S patrols.

The plan for Operation "Husky" was that on D-Day seaborne landings would be made on the south-east coast of Sicily by British and Canadian troops with Americans on the south coast, thus forming two separate but adjoining sectors, stretching about a hundred miles between Syracuse and Licata.

· · · · ·

Between the end of the Tunisian and the beginning of the Sicilian campaigns MTB and MGB operations had eased off. Approximately 15 per cent of the boats at Malta were operating nightly, while at Bone the percentage was slightly less. This lull allowed the boats to be prepared for what was to come.

Three flotillas of Vospers (the 7th, 10th and 24th) and one of Elcos had been operating from H.M.S. *Gregale*, the Coastal Forces base at

Malta; and for the invasion they were joined by many more boats, including those from the 19th and 20th MGB and 32nd and 33rd MTB flotillas.

On D-Day 75 per cent of the boats were operational. The long lines of boats in Msida Creek at Malta on the day before the assault "Reminded one," wrote C.C.F., Captain Hubback, "of the Solent in the days of peace".

The task of the MTBs and MGBs was to cover the north flank of the assault force—the narrow stretch of sea which stops the toe of Italy kicking the rugger ball of Sicily. To achieve this, the boats were to patrol this stretch, the Straits of Messina, nightly while the other MTBs patrolled farther south, off the approaches to Syracuse and Augusta.

The 3rd, 22nd and 31st ML Flotillas were to work from Malta, escorting the convoys to the beaches and protecting them at anchor. On D-Day all thirty boats were operational, a considerable achievement by the base staff.

Although it takes us ahead of the narrative, we may as well deal with the rest of the organisational side: the seventeen MTBs and MGBs at Bizerta had little to do, and they were transferred to Malta three days after D-Day. This, with the moving of MLs and HDMLs from Sousse, meant that over a hundred craft were, at one time or another, being handled at Malta.

After the invasion an average of eight MTBs sailed daily from Malta at 1300, returning at 1330 next day. When Syracuse fell Bobby Allan's mobile MTB base moved in, and four days after D-Day the boats returned there instead of Malta. They moved up to Augusta when that port fell, and from 15th June it was the policy to have twenty-four MTBs and MGBs at Augusta, the boats spending about ten days there while others refitted at Malta and the crews rested.

The mobile base was a unique organisation commanded by Lt.-Cdr. Allan (shortly to be promoted commander at the age of twenty-nine), who had, starting with virtually no equipment at all, accumulated an organisation which included: a tractor air compressor and tractor three-ton crane, torpedo tools, a machinery lorry, a light lorry with full fuelling equipment, a stores lorry with a coppersmith's and welding trailer, a stores lorry with shipwright's machinery trailer, and three camping and general-purpose lorries.

Most of this gear had been obtained by "scrounging"—and as usual the Americans were very generous. Allan spent several days after the

German surrender in Tunisia combing the Cape Bon battlefields to see what vehicles and equipment the Germans left behind. If he found anything he wanted, it was driven or towed into Bone and added to his organisation.

. . . . .

On 6th July (D-Day minus 4) all the Coastal Forces C.O.s were called to a meeting and told that Sicily was to be invaded on the 10th. It was natural that on going ashore for the last time before the assault a bunch of Coastal Forces officers should start a party. One of the unusual features of it—held at Monico's—was the sight of a Canadian C.O. chewing his beer glass. It was a habit he had.

MTBs were sent from Malta to patrol the approaches to Messina and off Cape Punto Stilo on D-Day. The patrol areas were (a) north of 38° North and (b) south of 38° North.

Six long and two short MGBs sailed from Malta to patrol off Augusta and carry out a diversionary demonstration off the mouth of the River Simeto.

Shortly before noon on D-Day the Luftwaffe increased its activities, concentrating on dive-bombing the ships anchored off the beaches. The 20th MGB Flotilla had just gone alongside the H.Q. ship *Gloriana* when a dive-bombing attack started. The unit scattered as thirty Ju.88s made three runs. One bomb near-missed MGB 657 (Maitland) and caused four casualties. These were transferred to a hospital ship, which was bombed next day.

. . . . .

On the night of 11th July, MGBs patrolled off Augusta while MTBs operated in the Messina Straits. At 2015 MTBs 76, 62, 65 and 95 found an abandoned Italian minesweeper fifteen miles off Catania. The S.O., Lt. A. C. B. Blomfield, R.N., put a party aboard to search the vessel. They found various documents, and after these had been collected and the party taken off the ship was sunk.

An hour later MTBs 640, 651 and 670, under Lt. R. R. Smith, attacked and damaged a U-boat with gunfire and depth-charges. The U-boat returned the fire and caused seventeen casualties among the MTBs.[1]

After that MTBs and Force Q (two cruisers and two destroyers) were involved in a case of mistaken identity. Force Q was steering

---

[1] The Mediterranean War Diary and Battle Summary disagree over the boats involved. The numbers given here are taken from a Coastal Forces summary of action reports.

close to the Sicilian coast when radar detected two small targets closing rapidly from the north. They were suspected of being friendly MTBs; but as they failed to answer when challenged, the cruisers *Euryalus* and *Cleopatra* engaged with a flashless barrage on the line of approach, fired star-shell and turned ninety degrees away.

The MTBs, according to official records, were from the 7th and 32nd Flotillas, and they fired three torpedoes. There was a brisk action until the participants mutually recognised each other as brothers in arms, and no damage was done.

This may account for the story, told some time after, of the cruiser which repeatedly challenged MTBs which were approaching in bad visibility. At the last moment the MTBs answered the challenge and the cruiser signalled: "You are very lucky: I was about to blow you out of the water." The MTBs replied: "You are even luckier—we've fired four torpedoes and missed."

However, if one wants to think what might have happened, here is a passage describing a British cruiser's fire against an attacking E-boat:[1]

At 0305 the noise of an E-boat was heard by Edinburgh *on the port side, and immediately afterwards its wake was seen. It was promptly illuminated and raked with pom-pom, 0.5-inch and Oerlikon fire at 1,500 to 2,000 yards range, the target appearing to be enveloped in a hail of tracers. The E-boat stopped out of control, and at this moment the main armament fired a broadside of twelve guns at fixed sight range. When the splashes subsided nothing was seen. . . .*

[1] Operation "Substance", 21st July 1941: dispatch from Vice-Admiral Sir James F. Somerville.

CHAPTER XVII

"NUTS TO STARBOARD"

A S it was vital that we secured control of the Messina Straits, the C.-in-C. assumed control of British MTBs and MGBs at Bone on D-Day plus 2, 12th July, and the F.O.I.C. Tunisia was accordingly instructed to sail all available boats to Malta (as mentioned earlier). Twelve MTBs and five MGBs left for Malta next day.

Immediately Syracuse was in our hands Lt.-Cdr. Allan left Bone in an MGB to arrange to move in with his mobile base. The equipment followed early next day in an LST, arriving that night. Allan had the base working by the next afternoon (the 14th) and "quite extensive" repairs were being carried out on boats.

Off the south-eastern beaches of Sicily events were moving swiftly, to bring about one of the busiest nights that the MTBs and MGBs had had up to then. At 1945 MGBs 662 and 659 were detached to accompany the *Ulster Monarch* and *Tetcott* while they landed a special reconnaissance column right inside the vast harbour at Augusta.

At Malta three MTBs of the 24th Flotilla, 81 (Lt. L. V. Strong), 77 (Lt. J. B. Sturgeon) and 84 (S/Lt. G. R. Smith), sailed at 1245 for a night patrol in the Straits of Messina. The S.O., Lt. Christopher Dreyer, R.N.,[1] was embarked in 81.

Fifteen minutes later three MTBs of the 33rd Flotilla also sailed from Malta for their patrol area, which was to the south of the 24th's hunting ground. The boats were 655 (Lt. Tom Fuller), 656 (Lt. D. Tate) and 633 (Lt. A. B. Joy). The S.O. was Lt. E. T. Greene-Kelly, embarked in 655.

Two U-boats were off the north coast of Sicily at this time. They were U.561, commanded by Oberleutnant Henning, and U.375, commanded by Kapitanleutnant Konenkamp.. They had left Toulon on 10th July—D-Day for "Husky"—with orders to patrol in the areas south and east of Sicily. They had decided to go to their patrol areas through the Straits of Messina.[2]

[1] Now Cdr. Dreyer, D.S.O., D.S.C.*, R.N.
[2] This and subsequent references to the U-boats, in italic type, are taken from captured German naval documents.

Dreyer describes the 24th Flotilla's patrol as follows:

"We had planned to reach the Straits just before dusk. We had noticed previously that the period lasting about half an hour between dusk and full darkness was a very effective one in which to operate. Searchlights and star-shell were useless against us and it was difficult for us to be seen in the ordinary light, while we, being low down, could see reasonably well. This gave us the opportunity to get right up to Messina undetected.

"We arrived at the entrance to the Straits just before dusk and slowed down to about 10 knots until we got nearly as far as Reggio. Here we slowed right down to about 6 knots and went on until we were just off Messina, where we stopped engines in the middle of the Straits.

"The three boats lay close together here, with engines cut, pointing roughly towards Messina, for some time."

At 2215 a vessel was sighted on the starboard bow, 300 yards away. It was U.375 on the surface, heading for her patrol area.

"I told Laurie Strong to start up," continues Dreyer, "and shouted to the others, and we made a signal to the C.-in-C. 'Nuts to Starboard'.[1] Almost immediately we saw clearly a submarine bearing down on us and we went astern, and she passed unpleasantly close ahead.

"It was clear that we were too close to fire torpedoes and we were just going to chase her when we sighted another submarine astern of her. I told Strong to continue to go astern and fire at that one. He did this and, while going astern on all three engines, fired a torpedo at a range of about 80–100 yards. The submarine blew up and showered us with bits."

This was U.561. Henning had been following Konenkamp when U.375 passed about twenty yards ahead of Laurie Strong's boat.

"We heard someone shouting in the water (for some reason we took him to be Italian), but we hurried off to join the attack on the other submarine," continues Dreyer.

"The other two boats had managed to place themselves on each side of the first submarine, which had jinked to starboard when his partner was blown up.

[1] Enemy in sight to starboard.

"By a cruel chance Brian Sturgeon, in 77, had a double misfire of his torpedoes from an ideal firing position. Smith, in 84, fired his torpedoes just as the submarine crash-dived, with the result they missed ahead. He was quick to appreciate this and followed his torpedoes straight in to do a depth-charge attack.

"By the time we arrived on the scene there was nothing more to be done. I ordered Sturgeon and Smith to stay in the area in case he came up again, while we went to look for survivors. We were somewhat above ourselves with success, although we were also kicking ourselves for missing the second one—we certainly should have got both. However, we made a signal to amplify our enemy report 'My —— was two submarines. Regret only one sunk.'

"We searched the area where our submarine had sunk but failed to find anybody, and after a few minutes we were interrupted by sighting the enemy again."

At 2200 Konenkamp, in U.375, signalled to U-boat Command, Italy, that they had been attacked and that U.561 had been sunk. But Konenkamp did not return from this attack, so no complete account is available. Henning himself had in fact survived the explosion of the torpedo and had succeeded in swimming ashore at Messina. One rating reached the shore at Reggio.

MTB 81 had sighted one vessel moving south along the Italian shore, and it was thought to be a U-boat moving at 15 knots. A second vessel was then sighted astern, and Dreyer altered course to attain a firing position on the leading one. An enemy report was made and the port torpedo was fired from 800 yards. It missed astern by a considerable distance and it became evident that the vessels were E-boats travelling at 25 knots. Dreyer then made an amplifying report.

"We saw the E-boats to the end of our patrol area," he continues, "and then turned them over to our larger neighbours. . . . It was now about midnight and we rejoined 77 and 84. We proceeded in formation back to our original patrol area, but we were fairly soon picked up and held by the searchlights."

These searchlights had been very active on both shores, and the three boats were now held by six of them. Shore batteries opened fire with time-fused high-explosive shells, estimated to be 4-inch or 5-inch.

Dreyer had previously that night seen that the enemy recognition signal from an aircraft was a three-star red, so they decided in 81 to manufacture one for themselves to see if it would fool the enemy shore gunners, whose attentions were becoming rather oppressive.

While there were no three-star red cartridges on board, they had in fact a single red and a two-star red. Dreyer fired one and Strong the other; and despite the fact that they did not time it very well, the shore batteries stopped shooting, although the searchlights still seemed distrustful.

Dreyer's patrol was not yet over, but we can turn for a while to the three boats of the 33rd Flotilla who had picked up the two E-boats which the 24th had left on their doorstep.

Greene-Kelly, the S.O., had begun the patrol with his three "Dogs" at 2100. Nearly two hours later he received Dreyer's enemy report from farther north that he was chasing two E-boats on a course of 180 degrees at 20 knots.

In his action report Greene-Kelly, who was killed some months later in another action, wrote: "The 33rd Flotilla unit therefore set an intercepting course at 20 knots, boats in cruising line to starboard. At 2340 two E-boats were sighted half a mile to starboard and up moon, course 330 degrees, speed 6 knots, in line ahead."

The MTBs were steering due south and altered course to close. When the range was 100 yards Greene-Kelly altered course to engage on a reciprocal course, and reduced speed to 8 knots.

At 2344 the MTBs opened fire, Tom Fuller's boat engaging the rear E-boat and Tate and Joy the leading one. "The enemy was completely surprised," wrote Greene-Kelly, "and did not return fire for at least fifteen seconds, when they increased speed and turned towards the Sicilian shore, then only 300 yards distant."

The MTBs then turned to starboard on a northerly course and kept up a heavy fire, driving the two E-boats towards the shore. Soon the rear E-boat was seen to be on fire and burning fiercely from amidships aft. Her guns were silenced and she ran aground.

The other E-boat was trying to escape north, although she too was on fire, low in the water, and had only one gun firing. The three MTBs concentrated on her while moving at 8 knots, the flames providing a good aiming point, and she was last seen well down by the stern, her upperworks ablaze, and heading for the shore only fifty yards away.

Meanwhile shore batteries had opened fire on the MTBs, and searchlights were casting their lime-white glare on the scene, adding their illumination to the yellow and red flames spurting from the E-boats. Greene-Kelly, considering both E-boats destroyed, ordered the unit to resume the patrol.

When the patrol finished the unit altered course for Malta. It was just off Cape Alessio when two vessels, believed at first to be MAS-boats,[1] were sighted on the port quarter. Greene-Kelly altered course to port and increased speed to 22 knots (the boats' maximum at that time), but the chase had to be abandoned because the enemy were considerably faster and quickly drew ahead out of harm's way.

Two minutes later seven more enemy craft were sighted on the starboard bow steering north-west, in line ahead and at full speed. Greene-Kelly immediately altered course to starboard, increasing speed again to 22 knots. His own boat found itself 800 yards ahead of the other two MTBs, and fire was opened on the fifth boat in the line.

The MTBs continued altering course to starboard, and there was a running fight with the enemy, the last two boats in their line receiving the MTBs' concentrated fire. But the enemy boats were faster, and Greene-Kelly had to abandon the chase.

His boats had suffered slight superficial damage, but there were no casualties. Some idea of the rate of fire can be gained by rounds of the ammunition expended on the patrol:

	MTB 655	MTB 656	MTB 633
2-pounder	168	56	72
Oerlikon	800	180	280
0.5-inch	1800	700	1000
.303-inch	800	250	350

In the meantime Dreyer's boats had finished their patrol, and at 0445 they moved slowly south, increasing speed to 20 knots at daylight fifteen minutes later. At this time an enemy report was received from Greene-Kelly and immediately afterwards two enemy craft were sighted steering north.

Dreyer altered course to intercept, and then seven more were seen to be disengaging from the 33rd Flotilla in line ahead. He writes: "They were not a pleasant sight at this time of the morning, since they were faster and much better armed than us, and the odds were three to one and we were a long way from home.

---

[1] Motoscafi Anti-Sommergibili (Italian MTBs).

"There was no point in running away, so we passed on opposite courses at about 1,000 yards range. It was quite amazing that they let us do this, but we accepted the situation thankfully. As we passed they opened fire and we promptly replied, all the shooting being pretty ineffectual."

The boats then returned to the advanced base at Syracuse. The only casualty in Dreyer's unit was a rating in 81 who was slightly wounded. The damage, too, was slight—MTB 81 had a 20-mm. shell through a turret, 77 had a 20-mm. shell pass through the wardroom and another through the forward messdeck, with some 9-mm. bullets in the bridge and the warhead of her starboard torpedo.

CHAPTER XVIII

UP TO AUGUSTA

THE mobile base had not been at Syracuse very long before Augusta, farther to the north, was captured; and the C.-in-C. ordered that the 20th MGB and 32nd MTB Flotillas were to be based there.

A preliminary reconnaissance had already been made by Cdr. Allan. This consisted of riding a motor-cycle from Syracuse towards Augusta while the fighting for the port was still going on, and at one stage of the journey he was somewhat startled to find himself the most advanced British unit.

The first of the MTBs to arrive in Augusta had made quite an impression; but the impression was on the shore, where she had run aground. As mentioned earlier, two MGBs, 662 and 659, had been detached to cover a landing from the *Ulster Monarch*.

This landing had been strongly opposed; and while 659 was sent for more ammunition, 662 was ordered to Syracuse at midnight. She was singled out for ten dive-bombing attacks while on her way there.

Meanwhile, 659 had stuck herself aground only 600 yards from an enemy fort. Despite all the efforts of her C.O., she would not come off. Fortunately it was a dark night and the Germans in Augusta were apparently too busy fighting off land attacks to worry about a trespasser in the harbour.

The story goes that when 659 signalled her plight to a cruiser outside the harbour, the *Newfoundland*, and asked for instructions, she received the somewhat ribald reply: "Fight to the last man."

However, at first light on the 13th, the 20th MGB Flotilla were passing Augusta when the cruiser *Newfoundland* called them up. Her message was to the effect that, although Augusta was still in enemy hands, the 20th Flotilla were to render 659 all the assistance they could. Rather gingerly the MGBs entered the port, which was the most-coveted in Sicily, and gave assistance.

·   ·   ·   ·

By 14th July, the day after Dreyer's action against the U-boats, the initial activity connected with the landings was easing off, but the MTBs and MGBs were still busy keeping a watch in the Straits of Messina.

On the 14th/15th MGBs 646, 643, and 641 were on patrol south of Messina when they sighted a U-boat, which they engaged with gunfire before it submerged. Shore batteries on the mainland then opened up on the three boats and 641 was hit and sank. At first it was reported that all her crew were lost, but it later became known that many of them, including her C.O., managed to get ashore and were taken prisoner.

The next night, the 15th/16th, the short boats had their first real brush with E-boats since the assault on Sicily started. Four boats of the 7th Flotilla, 77 (under the temporary command of S/Lt. E. Lassen), 82 (Lt. C. A. Rees), which was fitted out as a gunboat, 57 (Lt. J. Aimers), also a gunboat, and 62 (Lt. C. Finch), were under the S.O., Lt. Blomfield, who was embarked in 77.

The unit was lying stopped in the Messina Straits when, at 2240, five unidentified vessels were seen steering south and hugging the Italian coast.

Blomfield ordered the four boats to crash start, sent a sighting report, and turned at high speed on to a south-easterly course with the four boats forming line abreast to starboard.

The vessels were soon identified as six E-boats travelling at 20 knots. Fifteen minutes after being sighted the E-boats swung right round and headed north again, still hugging the coast.

Blomfield altered course northwards and ordered his four boats into line ahead. Then the E-boats disappeared, lost to sight under the land. For a few anxious moments the MTBs searched for them, then sighted them again, silhouetted by flares conveniently dropped from aircraft over Reggio. The E-boats were now heading north-west at 15 to 20 knots.

Blomfield gave chase. The four MTBs became strung out as they headed north-westwards after the E-boats, and within a very short while Blomfield in 77 was well ahead of the other three.

At 2300 MTB 77 fired both torpedoes, set at 3 feet and 5 feet, the point of aim being three cables (600 yards) ahead of the leading E-boat. Blomfield then increased speed, and two minutes after firing the torpedoes he opened up on the rear E-boat with gunfire.

Immediately all six E-boats opened fire on 77, and two shore

batteries on the Sicilian coast joined in. At this moment the leading
E-boat (which was not being engaged by gunfire) blew up, having
probably been hit by 77's torpedoes.

For the next fifteen minutes the four MTBs, going full out, chased
the E-boats. 77, 82 and 62 were firing at the fourth in the line when it
suddenly burst into flames. The second in the line then hauled out and
stopped.

By this time four shore batteries on the Sicilian coast and two on
the Italian had joined in and were shooting accurately. At this point
the Straits are less than four miles wide, and 77 was repeatedly hit by
shell splinters and fire from small-calibre guns. Blomfield therefore
decided to disengage south under cover of smoke.

The shore batteries, however, kept up their fire. From 2320, when
they disengaged from the E-boats, until 0215 next day they were
accurately shelled. A near-miss on 82 severely wounded Rees, her
C.O., and killed a rating. Blomfield ordered her to return to Augusta,
which was by now operating as a base.

At 0500 he headed his unit back towards Augusta, but fifteen
minutes later five E-boats were sighted to the eastward. They were
steering north at 30 knots and being engaged by units of the 32nd
Flotilla (MTBs 634, 670, 640 and 651).

Blomfield altered a course to close and increased to full speed, and
within thirty minutes his boats were opening fire on the E-boats at
1,000 yards, closing to 500 yards. Blomfield's attack, reinforcing the
32nd Flotilla's efforts, forced the E-boats to make smoke to try to
escape.

One large-type E-boat was seen to be in trouble, and Blomfield in
77 closed for the "kill". His Breda gun chose that moment to jam, and
as the 0.5-inch turret had not had time to reload he disengaged to port.

The other two MTBs, 62 and 57, continued the chase at high speed
until the Italian coast was eight miles distant and anti-personnel fire
from batteries caused them to disengage.

All three boats had been damaged. Blomfield's boat, 77, and 82
had both been hit below the waterline, and 77 was leaking badly.
The only auxiliary engine available had been hit and was out of action,
so the crew had to bail by hand until she got back to Augusta.

·   ·   ·   ·   ·

The night after that, the 16th/17th, four more MTBs were up in the
Straits looking for E-boats and landing-craft, but they did not see any.

They found instead a large and angry-looking cruiser which came round the corner with the belligerent-turning-bewildered attitude of a bull skidding into the arena.

The boats were MTBs 315 (Lt. L. E. Newall, R.N.Z.N.V.R.), 260 (Lt. H. F. Wadds, R.A.N.V.R.), 313 (Lt. A. D. Foster) and 316 (Lt. R. B. Adams). The S.O. was Lt. Denis Jermain, embarked in 315.

Jermain writes: "I was caught completely napping. We were lying with engines stopped about two miles south of Messina, in a flat calm with a full moon to the south silhouetting us nicely.

"We had stopped engines in order to be able to listen to the engines of E-boats or landing-craft, which were the kind of target we expected to see.

"We never dreamed that a cruiser would be able to get down there unseen through all our patrols. Anyway, the first thing I knew was seeing this cruiser[1] round the bend in the Straits and come straight for us. I gave the alarm and we started up and scattered."

There was no time for signals, and 315 went east, so that the cruiser had two MTBs on each bow. Jermain's idea was that if, in attacking a warship like this, most of the boats got into a firing position quietly while another boat made a fuss, the warship might go for the noisy (i.e. most visible) one, leaving the others a clear field for their attacks.

"At any rate," Jermain continues, "here was the chance to try it out, and I told the C.O. of the boat I was in to lead the way. The enemy seemed to respond and I got the impression that my method was working. He turned towards me and followed a little way across to the eastern side of the Straits. As a result the cruiser made a good target for the two boats left to the west of him (260 and 313).

"Alec Foster (313) fired his torpedoes from a very favourable position, even though his firing levers were shot away just as he was about to pull them, and he was wounded.

"Adams (316), who had followed a little way over to the east, tried to turn and fire from the enemy's port beam, but he was too close and his boat blew up in a sheet of flame. There were no survivors."

Here is the action up to now as seen from the *Scipione Africano*:[2]

---

[1] The Italian cruiser *Scipione Africano*, mounting eight 5.3-inch, five 40-mm., and eight 20-mm. guns, and with a speed of 41 knots. She was given to France at the end of the war and renamed *Guichen*. She is now rearmed with German 105-mm. guns.

[2] The subsequent paragraphs in italic type are taken from the Italian report of the action.

The Scipione Africano, *having rounded Pezzo Point in the Straits of Messina and turned south, sighted four craft about five miles ahead. Being doubtful whether the ships sighted were Italian, she kept the formation ahead of her and increased speed from 24 to 30 knots. By 0213 there was no longer any doubt that the craft were MTBs, which at that moment began to move slowly ahead.*

The Scipione *altered course slightly to port, whilst the leader of the formation turned decisively towards the cruiser [this was Jermain in 315] This manœuvre convinced the* Scipione *that she was dealing with enemy vessels, and she therefore increased to full speed and steered directly for the gap between the second and third vessels, which by now were distant only 1,500 yards.*

The four MTBs then increased to full speed; the two to starboard [260 and 313] beginning to make the usual movements previous to attack, the two to port assuming a course directly away.

A few seconds later the MTB nearest Scipione *[313] on her starboard bow fired two torpedoes, an action which was probably followed by the farther vessel; but scarcely had the torpedoes touched the water before every gun in the* Scipione *opened accurate and violent fire.*

At the same time she was watching the two vessels on the port side which had not yet worked up to full speed. After a few seconds one of the starboard-hand MTBs, perhaps hit by a broadside of 5.5-inch, blew up and sank; the more distant one was on fire; the nearest port-hand boat exploded when not more than fifty yards away, some of her woodwork falling on board the cruiser.

One of 260's torpedoes were thought at that time to have hit the cruiser, while 313's (Foster's) starboard torpedo passed ahead. The port one misfired owing to a faulty impulse charge.

There remained afloat only one of the four vessels, and she returned to the attack at 0223 [this was 315] by firing two torpedoes from the port beam of the Scipione, *which turned at once to starboard, opening fire with her stern guns. At that time the* Scipione's *speed was about 36 knots, course 200 degrees. The fourth MTB eventually drew off. . . .*

The *Scipione* was optimistic. Three of the MTBs remained,[1] and they all saw the cruiser shelled by her own shore batteries.

[1] The Italian report quoted here said the planking picked up on board came from MTB 305—which was not in the Mediterranean.

Damage and casualties sustained by the MTBs were: MTB 316 lost with crew; 313 and 260 superficial damage. One officer was killed (apart from 316's crew) and one officer was seriously wounded.

Jermain followed the *Scipione* down the Straits and watched it turn for Taranto. He also saw it being attacked by an Italian patrol plane. This gave a slightly farcical twist to the proceedings because there were no R.A.F. planes available at Malta to act on his original enemy report.

.   .   .   .   .

By this time it was the policy to operate twenty-four MTBs and MGBs from Augusta, and the base was hard at work keeping the maximum number of boats at sea. The MLs and HDMLs were still very busy.

Nightly operations continued off the Sicilian coast. On the 18th, the night after Jermain's attack on the *Scipione Africano*, shore batteries had another success against a unit of MTBs, and MTB 75 (Lt. L. M. Bulling, R.C.N.V.R.), was badly damaged by a direct hit and had several casualties. On the next night boats of the 10th Flotilla sighted a U-boat off Reggio and attacked it with depth-charges. Shore batteries joined in, engaging the boats very heavily.

But for all the successful interceptions, many of the boats were going out on patrol night after night without sighting any enemy craft. Many of them returned in the morning to ports like Augusta, where they were heavily bombed. On the nights they were not operating they had to sleep amid the noisy aggression of anti-aircraft guns.

On the 19th, D-Day plus 9, the Inshore Squadron and Coastal Forces craft were put under the orders of the Flag Officer, Sicily, and the next day the 10th MTB Flotilla was ordered to operate from Palermo, on the north side of the island. This avoided the boats having to risk the explosive hazards of shore batteries to get to the northern end of the Straits.

Air raids on ports like Augusta continued for several days. Various ships were hit, and on the 21st July MTB 288 was sunk at 0345 by a bomb which burst close to her stern.

CHAPTER XIX

THE REEF-KNOT SLIPS

ASHORE, both on Allied and Axis field-territories, events were moving fast. Whereas the mass of the German people had plighted their troth with Hitler because they saw in him a saviour who would restore them to what they considered their rightful place in the world, Benito Mussolini was in a vastly different position.

The average Italian did not see himself as one of a master race. The dreams of a new Roman Empire were exclusive to Mussolini and his clique. Whereas Hitler built up his war machine on a solid foundation of industrial resources and was backed by men who, if they did not follow him through blind fanaticism, followed just as sure-footedly through self-interest, Mussolini's bombastic plans bore no relation to Italy's extremely limited industrial resources and the unwarlike attitude of her people.

The Italians had previously struck a medal because they were sure of capturing Egypt. Part of the design was the Italian fasces and the German swastika linked by a reef-knot which symbolised the alliance.

The reef-knot, however, can only successfully join two pieces of rope of equal thickness. The knot was beginning to slip. Hitler was getting sick and tired of his dangerously-impulsive and weak partner. Until the Germans backed them in Libya, the Italians were being chased about by smaller numbers of British and Dominion troops. In Greece Mussolini needed Hitler to extricate him.

The Allied plans for invading Italy were complete, and then, on 25th July, Rome Radio said that the King of Italy had accepted Mussolini's resignation and had taken over. Marshal Badoglio formed a cabinet which met two days later and dissolved the Fascist Party. The bearings at one end of the Rome-Berlin Axis were running hot.

· · · · ·

One of the last Coastal Forces actions of the month was against a town, for a change. After having been bombed regularly in Augusta—

where some of the boats applied to miss their stay in harbour, preferring to be out on patrol where at least some of the officers and crew
could get some sleep—boats of the 20th MGB Flotilla left Augusta
on the 26th/27th. Lt. Reynolds, who was in 658, writes:

"We received orders to bombard the railway station and sidings at
Taormina, right by the sea, and set out at 1930 with Norman Hughes,
the S.O., aboard us, and Doug Maitland in 657 and Bob Davidson in
659.

"It was obvious that the R.A.F. had been there first, as there was
already a big fire blazing in Taormina. However, we crept in to 500
yards and then straightened out parallel to the coast.

"On the signal 'Flag 5'[1] everyone opened up with all guns, and shells
simply pumped into the target. 'Y' gun, the old 6-pounder, was
handled so enthusiastically that the captain of the gun had to cease fire
to let it cool for a moment."

[It should be noted here that Lt. Reynolds is frequently quoted
because the majority of the 20th flotilla C.O.s are in Canada;
and Reynolds served with them all the time they were in the
Mediterranean.]

The next day 658 sailed for Malta. Some indication of what the
"Dog" boats were standing up to is shown by the fact that in nineteen
days 658's engines had run for nearly 300 hours—equal to twelve and a
half days' continuous running—and she was long due for both the
100- and 200-hour routines which were normally strictly carried out.

·   ·   ·   ·   ·

On 28th July Capt. J. F. Stevens, R.N.,[2] relieved Capt. Hubback,
R.N., as Captain, Coastal Forces, with his headquarters at Malta.

From the beginning of August the aim was to keep as many boats as
possible at sea in case there was a "maximum effort" call to stop the
enemy evacuating Sicily. Between the 7th and 19th August forty-
seven boats were based on Malta and available for Sicily, and during
that period thirty to thirty-two were operating—a serviceability
figure of about 65 per cent.

There were few targets for the boats, although there was still
considerable opposition from the shore batteries on both sides of the
Straits, and they continued to take their toll of men and boats.

On the 9th/10th a unit of short MTBs were attacked by shore batteries, and an Elco, MTB 265, was hit. The C.O. was wounded, and

[1]Attack with guns.   [2] Now Vice-Admiral J. F. Stevens, C.B., C.B.E., R.N.

the boat was towed back stern first by MTB 464 with most of its bows missing. (See photograph facing p. 49.)

By 13th August it was obvious that the end was near in Sicily, and monitors, destroyers and MGBs were ordered as far up the Straits as possible to stop the Germans withdrawing to Italy. But a large proportion of them managed to get across.

On the 15th/16th the second division of the 33rd Flotilla was on patrol in the Straits when, at 0124, they were caught by the groping, octopus-like arms of searchlights, and guns on both coasts opened up. The boats turned 180 degrees at high speed, making smoke.

But MTB 665, commanded by a Canadian, Lt. Peter Thompson D.S.C., received a direct hit on the engine-room, which set her on fire, and she stopped, a searing and explosive torch.

As, in the S.O.'s words, the shelling was "intense and accurate", the other two boats, 640 (Lt. C. McLachlan, R.C.N.V.R.) and 670, were unable to help and sped southwards to get clear of the hail of shells.

Once clear, the two boats stopped, and then at 0154, thirty minutes after they had been picked up by the searchlights, a boat of the 7th Flotilla signalled "Do you require assistance?" She was MTB 76, (Lt. W. Keefer, R.C.N.V.R.) and the S.O. requested her to come alongside.

Hoping to reach the burning 665 in the smaller MTB, the S.O. boarded 76 and headed north, hugging the coast until the shelling again got too bad and he was forced to turn back.

Two other MTBs, 315 and 85, both fitted with silencers, then tried to get up to 665. They managed to get fairly near, but the batteries ashore soon got their range and heavy shelling beat the two boats back.

They could see 665 drifting towards the Sicilian coast, burning fiercely and shaken by sporadic explosions. The boats searched for survivors until first light at 0445, but did not find any.

Several of the crew, including Thompson, did in fact escape from the boat and were taken prisoner. Earlier that night Thompson had embarked a Royal Canadian Navy press officer, Lt.-Cdr. E. H. Bartlett, who had expressed a wish to get some first-hand experience of MTB operations.

·   ·   ·   ·   ·

All organised resistance in Sicily stopped on the 18th. The island had been occupied in thirty-eight days and the Germans had lost

30,000 in killed, wounded and captured, while the Italians lost 300,000 or more, mainly captured.

The dry dock in Messina was found to be in good condition and the floating dock was repairable. The torpedo depot was in good order, and on 3rd September, the day we landed in Italy and exactly four years after the war started, the C.-in-C. reported that Messina Harbour was open to the Allies.

. . . . .

With the complete occupation of Sicily there was a lull, and as many boats as possible were overhauled in Malta. Some idea of the scale of the work done is shown by the fact that between 20th August and 3rd September seven MTBs and MGBs, twenty-three MLs and fourteen HDMLs were overhauled. In addition eighteen other boats were docked or slipped.

The total Coastal Forces casualties for the Sicilian campaign were ninety-six officers and ratings, killed, wounded or missing. MTBs 316, 665, 288, and MGB 641 were sunk, and MGB 657 and MTBs 265 and 75 were badly damaged.

The officially-claimed successes were one torpedo hit on a cruiser;[1] three E-boats destroyed and one possible; ten E-boats damaged; one U-boat sunk and two damaged; one minesweeper destroyed; three FW.190s, two Ju.88s, one Do.217 and one unidentified aircraft destroyed; and one FW.190 possible.

With plans in hand for the invasion of Italy and the occupation of several islands off the Italian coast, a big effort was made to get every craft into first-class condition.

The MLs had been working hard, doing unspectacular jobs for the most part, but logging a vast amount of sea time. They escorted many convoys and the 3rd, 31st and 33rd Flotillas and the 140th HDML Flotilla were recalled for a "brush up" for the main assault.

. . . . .

On 2nd September the battleships *Valiant* and *Warspite* bombarded targets south of Reggio: the invasion of Italy had begun. Next day every available Allied gun opened fire across the Straits of Messina to give covering fire for Operation "Baytown", the landing in Italy, which began at 0430. It was the day the armistice was signed with

[1] This was on the *Scipione Africano*, mentioned earlier. Although the claim was made in good faith, no hit was actually registered, according to Italian naval records.

Marshal Badoglio (although it was not announced until the 8th). It was the fourth anniversary of the beginning of the war. It was truly the turn of the tide.

The landing was made on three beaches stretching between Catona in the north and Reggio in the south. There was some opposition, but the Germans were retreating from the toe of Italy.

With the Germans departing fast, it was hoped to cut some of them off. An ideal spot for a landing was at Vibo Valentia, forty miles north of the Straits of Messina, where the main road cuts into the hillside.

This landing was called Operation "Ferdy", and it was timed to take place early on 8th September. Forty-four landing craft were to put the 231st Brigade ashore and they were to be covered by the monitor *Erebus*, gunboats *Aphis* and *Scarab*, two LCGs and two LCFs, apart from some Coastal Forces craft.

The first wave of troops got ashore at 0430 but ran into unexpectedly heavy opposition. Instead of landing as planned several miles behind the enemy lines, they had run into the vanguard of the retreating German Army, whose rate of retreat had been underestimated.

The road which they hoped to cut was packed with retreating Germans, who shelled the landing-craft as they came in and then tried to pin down the troops with cross-fire as they landed. As soon as it was light, heavy dive-bombing attacks developed.

For Operation "Ferdy", MTB 77, under Brian Sturgeon's command, had been allocated to Rear-Admiral McGrigor,[1] who was Flag Officer, Sicily and was supervising landing operations.

At 0800, MTB 77, with the Admiral on board, was closing an LCI about three miles west of the small harbour when a sharp air attack developed. A bomb from an FW.190 fell two feet from MTB 77's starboard quarter, hurling the boat violently into the air and ripping off her bottom from right aft to the forward mess-deck. She sank, but all on board were taken off by HDML 1128 (Lt. Brown, R.A.N.V.R.).

Rear-Admiral McGrigor, describing the attack, said: "I was on the bridge when the bomb burst. When the splash subsided I found myself on the deck aft with a sprained leg. I just had time to pick myself up, collect my binoculars—which had started off round my neck but had been blown across the deck—and haul down my flag before the boat sank.

[1] Now Admiral of the Fleet Sir Rhoderick R. McGrigor, G.C.B., D.S.O., First Sea Lord and Chief of Naval Staff.

"My cap had been blown off, but oddly enough the badge and band stayed on my head. Fortunately there was only one casualty—a broken shoulder-blade—although we were all scratched.

"We were taken off by HDML 1128, my flag hoisted, and we carried on."

MTB 77, a Vosper, had been on thirty-three operations and several successful actions. She had received action damage on seven occasions and had never abandoned an operation because of defects.

Rear-Admiral McGrigor was soon hard at work again directing the landing (despite the leg injury which later kept him in hospital for a fortnight). There was, for instance, an LST, carrying guns and vehicles, which had to unload its cargo despite the heavy fire. She was led in to the beach by HDML 1128 and immediately became a target for all the guns. She was eventually hit more than forty times. The landing of her guns proved to be the turning point in the operation.

The situation ashore eased during the day, and eventually all troops and equipment were landed as planned.

.   .   .   .   .

On the same day as the Vibo Valentia landing, the Admiralty sent a general message to the Navy giving the news of the Italian surrender. This was followed, half an hour later, by a signal from the C.-in-C., Mediterranean, saying that all operations in progress were to proceed, but that Italian armed forces were to be treated as friendly unless they took a threatening or hostile attitude.

The Italian Fleet honoured the agreement made with the Allies by their new government and sailed to Malta, and on the morning of 11th September the C.-in-C. signalled the Admiralty: "Be pleased to inform their Lordships that the Italian battle-fleet now lies at anchor under the guns of the fortress of Malta."

On 26th July, the day Mussolini fell from power, the Combined Chiefs of Staff in London had told General Eisenhower that he should plan an operation ("Avalanche") for amphibious operations against Salerno, using forces which would be available after "Husky", the Sicily landings. The plan was to land south of Salerno and fight the twenty-five miles to Naples, past Vesuvius.

"Avalanche" started on September 9th. On the same day the island of Ventotene, thirty-seven miles west of Naples, was captured by a raiding force made up mainly of MLs. Salerno was occupied on the 10th. The island of Capri was captured by three MTBs on the 12th, and the island of Procida in the Bay of Naples fell to four MTBs and MGBs on the 15th, to be followed next day by Ischia. Sardinia, an island sixty-five times as big as the Isle of Wight, was captured by two MGBs, an American general and an Italian colonel on the 18th.

It had been hoped that Mussolini would be found on Ventotene, but when our forces arrived there they were told that he had left for Sardinia. The two MGBs arriving to capture Sardinia learned that they had missed him by a matter of hours.

It has been necessary to give this brief outline of these rather crowded days so that the reader can have a clearer picture of the situation. The narrative will now be described more fully.

CHAPTER XX

WAR BY GRAMOPHONE

WHILE the big Salerno landing was going on a Task Group under Capt. Charles L. Andrews, U.S.N.,[1] had other work to do. Rear-Admiral Andrews (as he is now) writes: "I had command of Task Group 80.4 under Admiral Hewitt, U.S.N.[2] In my force were—my flagship, the destroyer *Knight*, minesweepers, U.S. PT-boats, a force of U.S. ARBS (small PTs without torpedoes, rigged for acoustic diversions, since at night they could project the sound effect of a complete amphibious landing), two Dutch gunboats and a British force of MTBs and MLs.

"I also had a small landing force of fifty paratroopers (without parachutes!) from the 82nd Airborne Division. I also had a British captive-balloon expert.

"We were a diversion force. The main force was to land on the Salerno beaches at 0345, and we proceeded with them to the northward in convoy formation with radar reflectors hung above our small craft by means of the captive balloons.

"This gave the picture, to the German radar, of a strong amphibious force with escorts moving northwards against the beaches north of Naples.

"Having created this illusion, we concentrated on the island of Ventotene in the hopes that Mussolini was still there. I landed my force with British MLs and we captured the island; but Mussolini had been taken off by a German submarine five hours before we landed."

The actual force, apart from the *Knight*, minesweepers and Dutch gunboats, was four American sub-chasers, one PT-boat, six MLs of the 31st Flotilla, three "Dogs" and two short MTBs, and the boats flying balloons.

---

[1] Now Rear-Admiral Andrews, U.S.N. (Retd.).
[2] Vice-Admiral H. Kent Hewitt, U.S.N., was the overall Naval Commander of "Avalanche".

The 31st ML Flotilla, along with the other MLs, had been doing useful work—carrying out A/S patrols, acting as despatch boats, making smoke in air raids to hide possible targets from the Luftwaffe, and performing various escort tasks.

A fortnight after Palermo had fallen and the British were in the outskirts to Messina, "Farmer" Lloyd, the S.O., had orders to "take H.M. ships of the 31st Flotilla under your command and proceed to Malta".

There the officers and men had spells in the rest camps, and then the flotilla sailed. The first division, under a black-bearded Scot, Lt. Robertson, D.S.C., for Tripoli; and the second division, under Lloyd, to bucket through wild weather to Bizerta, "where my orders were to report to 'U.S. Naval Unit 80.4'," writes Lloyd.

This is how he describes the next few days:

"When I reported to him, Capt. Andrews grasped my hand and cried: 'Mighty glad to know you. This is no ordinary assignment we're on. No, I'll say it isn't; but I'll take you to my Chief of Staff and he'll give you the whole set-up.'

"He led me to a good-looking, rather serious young man whose face seemed vaguely familiar. 'Here he is, Lootenant Fairbanks. Duggie, this is Lootenant-Commander Lloyd. I want you two to get together.'

"I remembered Lt. Douglas Fairbanks, Jun., then, for he had been on the Dieppe raid in command of a tank landing-craft. 'It's an amusing job we have to do,' Duggie told me, 'a real game of pirates, for we are to go round capturing islands and so on. We start with Ventotene. That's Italian for hold your wind.'

" 'Where on earth is that?'

" 'Due west of Naples. As you probably know, there's to be a landing in the Gulf of Salerno. Four hours before that comes off we are to stage this little operation of our own. The object is to land a force of Rangers, sixty strong, who are to establish a fighter control station on the island. Another thing which may interest you— Mussolini is thought to be hiding there.'

"Truly the whole enterprise savoured of one of Duggie's own films, and I went back to my boats bursting with the news. . . . The chart was small-scale and there was no separate plan of the harbour of San Nicolo. We tried the pilot book of the Western Mediterranean and found only a small paragraph stating that this harbour had been hewn from solid rock by the Romans and would accommodate only small craft. . . .

"One morning in Bizerta—'Bizerty' to the Americans—I was taken to a room in the big, airy naval barracks. There, in just a pair of slacks, perspiring on a camp bed, lay a fat and jolly man. 'This,' said my guide, 'this is John Steinbeck, who wrote *She Was Poor But She Was Honest.*'

" 'Oh yeah?' I said, taking the outstretched hand as well as the invitation to help myself to a whisky. It was three days before I realised that even though this man, who had become a firm friend, did not write that famous song, he was indeed John Steinbeck. He was acting as war correspondent for a New York newspaper and had a trick of turning up wherever anything interesting was happening, complete with his dilapidated portable typewriter.

"We held our final conference in Palermo. It was an informal affair with interruptions for wine. When interest flagged, Duggie Fairbanks would try to revive it by announcing 'We will now ask Farmer Lloyd to tell us one of his stories', and I would oblige with one of the chestnuts which my own lads were weary of hearing.

"The Rangers had boarded us in Bizerta and were living on board, most of the G.I.s preferring to sleep on deck. They were a magnificent bunch who had fought their way through North Africa. Most of them came from the southern or western states, and I have always found the southerners and westerners easy to get along with. In peacetime, their C.O., Capt. Howland, farmed in Alabama.

"In the early morning we set out across a glassy sea to capture the island of Ventotene. Our flagship and navigational guide was the *Knight*. Away to starboard was the main Salerno-bound convoy. Before dusk it had become just so many columns of smoke. . . .

"An American PT-boat came roaring alongside 555. A sailor tossed over a can with a written signal inside it. Here was news indeed. The Italian Government had surrendered! I read it out loud to the crew, standing by their guns, on look-out, at the wheel. They gave a cheer. Then 'Yorky', A.B. Gell, looked thoughtful, rubbed his neck and said in a tone of disappointment: 'We shan't get a scrap after all then, sir?'

" 'I am not so sure about that,' I said, thinking of the German garrison which was said to be on the island. . . .

"The moon was floating in a clear sky when the Rangers began leisurely to climb into their equipment and look to their tommy-guns. The Alabama captain was by my side on the bridge. 'All that gear must be damned hot,' I remarked, thinking of the tin hat, shorts and life-jacket that formed my only attire. 'Aw, shucks,' said he. 'We get used to it.'

"The worry had gone now and the excitement was back as I looked across a shimmering sheet of moonlit sea at the silhouette of Ventotene Island. I tried to visualise its harbour, cut from the rocks, and to imagine how I should manoeuvre 555 in through what must be a very narrow entrance.

"We stopped and cut our engines, lying silently on the silver sea, where everything looked as peaceful as a lily-pond. I started as a voice came out of the night, speaking inhumanly loud and in a foreign tongue. Then I realised that it was from the loudspeaker of the destroyer *Knight*.

"A speech in Italian, played on a gramophone, calling on the inhabitants of Ventotene to send up three white rockets in token of surrender. After the speech the silence was uncanny as we lay there.

"The moon was dropping towards the island. Soon it would be dark and *then* how was I to find my way to San Nicole? Twice the destroyer repeated the speech. The moon dropped below the horizon and darkness was upon us. . . . Three vivid flashes from the shore, three reports, three streaks of white light as the rockets went up. The signal of surrender.

"I started up 555's engines and the Rangers stood-to. *Knight's* cutter slid alongside. 'Follow me and we'll lead you in,' called Capt. Andrews. In the darkness and in that glassy calm it was hard to tell reflection from reality, and I kept close on the stern of the cutter, ready to reverse engines if her leadsman found very shallow water.

"Two fathoms, nine feet, seven . . . only an inch or two now between our keel and the rock, and there was what looked like a solid wall in front of me. I tensed myself for the bump. I kept in my mind the vague picture of the harbour, conjured up the quite inadequate paragraph of the pilot book.

"The cutter had gone into the darkness. I heard the voice of the leadsman, 'Eight feet'. We were over the ledge. 'Look, sir, look, right alongside!' cried an agitated rating, pointing down to where our wash was breaking on the rocky shelf. I dared not look and my reply was brief and impolite.

" 'Can you see anything ahead?' I called.

" 'Solid rock,' replied Roy Brotherton, my Number One. At that moment there was a bright flash, a hissing sound as a red rocket went up, and the glare and report of an explosion.

" 'Guess that's the Jerries,' said Capt. Howland in a matter-of-fact voice. 'Looks like there's work for us to do, after all.'

"I was praying hard that there was not even one solitary machine-gun mounted on the commanding wall of cliff which the explosion had revealed. The flash had also shown me the one jetty in that tiny harbour. It lay at right angles to the entrance and there was some sort of small craft alongside. I took the way off 555 and, by reversing her port engine, began swinging her stern towards this other craft.

" 'One foot to spare ahead!' called Roy from the bow.

" 'Six inches astern!' sang out Aussie from the poop.

"More explosions ashore. The sound of crumbling buildings. A flicker in the strange little vessel as we bumped alongside her, and I saw she was on fire. My motor mechanic, Petty Officer Neville, appeared from the engine-room with an extinguisher, jumped aboard and had the blaze out in a twinkling.

"The Rangers were at the rails.

" 'Jump!' I yelled, and they went thudding on to the other's decks. Capt. Howland paused for a moment. 'Thanks for the trip, Commander,' he said. 'Gee, these lads'll have the damnedest tales to tell. But what can I bring for you?'

" 'The flag of the island,' I replied. 'Good luck!'

"Eight months later Capt. Howland sought me out to give me the huge flag of Ventotene.

"Three more white rockets went up, to be quickly followed by a defiant red one and a few more explosions. I became aware of a movement at my elbow and turned to see, by the light of the fires ashore, Aussie truculently presenting a pistol at a German sergeant as he persuaded him on to the bridge.

" 'This is the bastard who set fire to the petrol lighter.'

" 'To the *what*?' I asked, horrified.

" 'Petrol lighter. The one we're alongside.'

"Curious about what was happening ashore, I told Sharrocks, the signalman, to use the Aldis lamp as a searchlight. Its beam showed a musical-comedy scene on the jetty. The 'chorus' was a long line of Italian soldiers in their 'number one' uniforms, all smiling delightedly, their kit packed and at their feet.

"There was also an individual in striped pyjamas who was hopping gingerly over the stones on his bare feet, exclaiming 'Me no militaire!' while a gaunt Ranger corporal tried to marshal him into line with persuasive jabs in the ribs from a tommy-gun. 'Me no militaire!'

protested the barefooted one, to which the corporal replied: 'Aw, shucks. Fall in with the rest!'"

.   .   .   .   .

Leaving the MLs to consolidate the island, the three "Dog" boats under Lt. Greene-Kelly went on to a planned demonstration at the mouth of the River Volturno, which was successful.

The two short boats, under Lt. the Hon. F. A. Shore, with Lt.-Cdr. Kremer, U.S.N., embarked as S.O., had meanwhile attempted to land agents in the northern part of the Gulf of Gaeta.

They found several F-lighters, Siebel ferries and R-boats moving along the coast, so their operation was impossible to carry out. Instead they found a convoy of seven lighters, attacked with torpedoes, and MTB 298, Shore's boat, blew up one of them. It was hit with two torpedoes and was carrying ammunition.

On 12th September Greene-Kelly sailed with his three "Dogs" to capture Capri. Capt. Andrews and Lt. Fairbanks were embarked. They found the Italians only too willing to co-operate, and they undertook the continued defence of the island. Steps were taken to establish an MTB base there and install radar. An Italian motor torpedo-boat flotilla of seven boats was placed under U.S. command.

Greene-Kelly accepted the surrender of Capri, and these were the terms:

TERMINA DELLA RESA

I, the undersigned, Commanding Officer of the Axis Armed Forces on the island of Capri, do hereby surrender unconditionally all men, arms and equipment and possessions of the said island of Capri to the Allied forces, acting herein by and through Lt. E. T. Greene-Kelly, R.N.R., under the direction of Commander, Task Group 80.4, Capt. C. L. Andrews, Jr., U.S.N., and of Commander, Western Naval Task Force and Gen. D. D. Eisenhower, Commander-in-Chief of Allied Forces, North African Theatre of Operations.

Signed C. M. MICHELANOLI, G. MASSILLIO.
Signed E. T. GREENE-KELLY, D. FAIRBANKS
FREDERICK A. WARNER.

Chapter XXI

SARDINIA FALLS TO TWO MGBs

A COMBINED force of four MGBs went to capture the island of Procida on the 14/15th, and the subsequent proceedings are best described by Lt.-Cdr. J. D. Archer, R.N.V.R., who wrote: "A naval party under my command formed from volunteers of the non-duty watch of the British boats not taking part in the operation was landed. The island acclaimed our arrival and the Italian Army fled to the nether side of the island, thinking we were the Germans."

Ischia surrendered to naval forces on 16th September.

Then it was Sardinia's turn. It was an ironical twist of fate that it should be captured in this way. After the North African landings it was vitally necessary to keep the Germans guessing about where the next assault would take place.

To fool them the body of a man, dressed as a Royal Marine officer and carrying false papers, was put into the sea from a British submarine off the Spanish coast. Among the papers on the body—which was washed up on the beach, as planned—was a broad hint in an allegedly personal note to General Alexander that it would be Sardinia.[1]

In many ways Sardinia must have looked a likelier target as far as the Germans were concerned, since if it was successfully attacked by the Allies it would have provided a good jumping-off place for a large-scale landing in the Rome area.

An American brigadier, an Italian colonel and two British MGBs. Not perhaps a well-balanced force, but it was enough to capture the island of more than 9,000 square miles.

It was a warm September morning about a fortnight after the invasion of the Italian mainland. A number of "Dogs" were lying in Messina Harbour enjoying a short rest and not bothered about anything very much except engine defects and shortage of spares and the

[1] See *The Unknown Courier* by Ian Colvin (William Kimber, 15s.).

paradox of getting the boat ready in front of the other chap only in order to grumble that he never went to sea.

Not that there was anywhere to go at this particular stage of the war except for uneventful patrols in the Tyrrhenian Sea. But it was nice to be ready. Bligh (in MGB 662) and Moore (MGB 660) were, as so often, ready; and on the evening of the 15th September received orders to proceed to Bizerta and to report to the C.-in-C. in H.M.S. *Laurana.*

No indication was given about the ultimate destination, but there seemed to be a general air of relaxation about the whole thing and it was, anyhow, a relief to get away from Messina, which was a sad mess.

The boats reached *Laurana* at noon on 17th September—a Friday. 662 had two defective carburettors, but fortunately the American PT base was equal to this (and would have been able to take on a good deal more besides).

Later that evening Bligh went aboard *Laurana* and received the operation orders from C.-in-C.'s Chief of Staff. The boats were to proceed that night to Cagliari and absorb Sardinia.

Bligh asked, "What military support do we get, sir?" and answer came, "Brigadier-General Theodore Roosevelt of the United States Army and Colonel de Carli Paslo of Italy." It seemed modest enough.

"Are we expected, sir?"

"You must assume that you are not."

"Aye aye, sir."

Moore looked thoughtful when he heard the news. Not that he doubted the ability of the unit to discharge effectively the orders. It was just that he looked a little more reflective than usual.

At about ten o'clock that night the boats embarked the soldiers. Bligh took the general, his A.D.C., Capt. Cooke, the colonel and two U.S. Army interpreters, while Moore took Sqn.-Ldr. Finn, R.A.F., and four officers of the U.S. Army. The unit slipped just before 2300 and after negotiating the unspeakable mouth of the harbour steered northward into the night and a question-mark.

The weather was pleasant and the surface of the sea uniform, and beyond slight queasiness on the part of one of Bligh's entourage the force was in good heart. And it was nice to smell the cigar smoke on the bridge whenever the voice-pipes from below decks were opened to give or receive messages.

Sardinia was sighted at 0530 on Saturday morning. The landfall was identified as Cavoli Island Point and course was altered to pass close to Cape Boi. The temperature went up a little at 0620 when a vessel was sighted ahead. Bligh semaphored to Moore "Any minute now", but it is possible that Moore thought it was too early for badinage, as he only gave a protracted "R".[1]

The general, when told, indicated that Bligh should do whatever was thought appropriate. After a quarter of an hour—not exactly of suspense but of unmixed or indifferent speculation—the ship was recognised as the *Marion Banco*, a lighthouse service auxiliary. The unit maintained course and speed (about 16 knots) and waved caps at the Italian. She did not wave back but fell out her guns' crews and turned up the wake.

An hour later, with Cape St. Elia abeam, a battery of four coastal guns could be seen on the starboard bow with guns' crews fallen in in ceremonial display. They waved white handkerchiefs as the boats sailed by and the general said, "Well, Captain, a nice summer cruise." Bligh, still cautious, said, "So far, sir", and stared hard at a small armed auxiliary which was hovering ahead.

It was probably Petty Officer Briddon at the wheel of 662 who muttered, "Got to watch out for these damned dagoes." But they were, in fact, very helpful; and although Bligh indicated that he could berth without a pilot it was suggested that it might hurt the feelings of the locals if their offer was refused, and it was to meet this point that Bligh allowed the pilot on the back of the bridge. Another nail in Hitler's coffin. Bligh berthed alongside on the northern harbour wall and waved to Moore alongside two deep. Armed sentries were placed on the jetty, and shoreward guns manned against the possibility of bands of armed desperadoes (this visibly lowered the morale of the inhabitants, but only for a while).

The reception was satisfying but restrained. No bunches of flowers, no kisses, no gifts. Just a bunch of Italian and Sardinian generals and a number of citizens to watch the disembarkation of the troops. Col. Obolensky of the U.S. Army was there to meet the general, who bade Bligh an affectionate farewell and said that he had no more for the boats to do.

.   .   .   .   .

Lt. Jermain had by this time left the 10th Flotilla to go to join a frigate in the Atlantic, and the new S.O. was Lt.-Cdr. Peter Evenson,

[1] R—"Your message received and understood."

who had been the senior of the team from the 15th Flotilla when the two Elco flotillas combined after the Tobruk raid.

Six boats of his flotilla were doing Air/Sea Rescue work from 9th to 12th September, working with Force V (one aircraft-carrier and four auxiliary carriers). The boats picked up twenty-two airmen—most of them Germans or Italians.

CHAPTER XXII

WAR IN THE EAST

ASHORE, the Allies were strengthening their hold. On the Italian mainland the enemy were ejected from the area south of a line from Brindisi to Taranto by 10th September, Brindisi itself being captured next day.

Three days later the Germans attacked Rhodes, the large island off the Turkish coast, at the entrance to the Aegean. With Rhodes and Crete in their hands, the Germans should have been able to seal off the whole of the Aegean.

But small Allied parties had already been sent to take islands in the Dodecanese, and the first of them landed early on 10th September, within a few hours of the Italian armistice becoming effective. Their story will be told later.

The Germans captured Cephalonia, an island off the west coast of Greece, on 22nd September, and Corfu, barely sixty miles east of the heel of Italy, the next day. Other Ionian Sea islands fell later.

It was during the next few weeks that the affairs of Coastal Forces became more widespread and settled down into three main theatres of operations—the west coast of Italy, the Adriatic, and the Aegean. It is proposed, at this stage, to follow the operations on the west coast of Italy until the end of 1943, and then move to the Adriatic and then on to the Aegean. Mention will be made, however, of flotillas leaving the Malta area for the eastern islands.

One such flotilla was the 10th. Peter Evenson had taken it back to Messina after working with Force V, and by the time he arrived there it was obvious that the Germans were stirring in the Dodecanese. Evenson was therefore ordered to take his flotilla to the Levant, sailing on 21st September and calling at Malta, Benghazi and Tobruk. The flotilla covered the 1,000 miles to Alexandria in five days, and later moved up to the Aegean.

For operations off the west coast of Italy it was obvious that MTBs and MGBs could use the former Italian naval base of Maddalena, in

Sardinia. On 21st September, on the order of the C.-in-C., Cdr. Allan sailed for Maddalena in MGB 646.

His mobile base had earlier moved up to Messina from Augusta. Now, while he went off to have a look at Maddalena, the whole mobile base was embarked in three LCTs, ready to sail on his return. When he came back and reported favourably, the convoy sailed—the three LCTs, the tanker *Empire Damsel*, six MGBs and MTBs and two mine-sweeping MLs (the latter sweeping the last twenty miles into Madda-lena, working on charts of the minefields which Bobby Allan had obtained from the Italians at Maddalena).

The convoy, calling at Palermo on the way, ran into heavy weather. However, it reached Maddalena safely and Allan wrote: "I feel that Coastal Force history has been written by our arrival here. For Coastal Forces to bring their own base and fuel and to do their own minesweeping into a hitherto-unentered port is unique."

The MGBs began operations from Maddalena almost immediately, patrolling off the north-west coast of Italy and particularly round Elba, the island just off the mainland south of Leghorn.

On 7th October reinforcements arrived at Maddalena. They were eight boats of the 7th MTB Flotilla and three "Dogs". About this time the 20th MTB Flotilla (not to be confused with the 20th MGB Flotilla at Maddalena) and the 24th MTB Flotilla left for Taranto to operate in the Adriatic.

The Maddalena boats were very soon in action, two Vospers of the 7th Flotilla being in an inconclusive engagement with a heavily-armed trawler between Elba and the mainland on 10th/11th October.

On 14th/15th October, Lt. Greene-Kelly was killed in a very con-fused action in the Piombino Channel,[1] when Burke, in 658, sank two "flak" ships by gunfire.

·   ·   ·   ·   ·

Although the main base was at Maddalena, an "advanced-advanced base" was set up at Bastia, and boats moved up there to operate for a few days at a time. For the whole of October the boats operated along the Italian coast from the River Tiber to Spezia.

American PT-boats shared the Maddalena base from fairly early on, and when they arrived they had no base organisation. Coastal Forces helped them with supplies and maintenance, glad of getting a small chance of repaying some of the assistance the Americans had given in

[1] Between Elba and the mainland.

the earlier days. Within a very short time Coastal Forces boats and the American PTs were operating together.

The American Higgins boats were the first to be fitted with really effective radar. The British boats had a form of radar, intended for plotting aircraft, which was no good for use against surface craft.

So the British boats frequently operated with the British S.O. embarked in a PT-boat in order to use the American radar set. This form of co-operation worked very effectively.

Before the invasion of Sicily the PT-boats were seldom allowed to operate as they would have wished. They had had a bad experience on one of their earliest patrols because they had not fully appreciated the lesson that Coastal Forces had so painfully learnt—not to use radio transmitters more than absolutely necessary.

Coastal Forces used, at that time, to reckon that a fighter attack would start with twenty minutes of transmitting;[1] and, sure enough, it happened to the PTs when they began passing manoeuvring signals by radio, and they sustained many casualties.

However, they soon settled down; and although their tactics were usually to fire torpedoes at rather longer ranges than those used by the British boats, they began to score successes against the enemy.

It was in Bastia that an American PT-boat came in collision with what it took to be a "Dog" boat and got sworn at in German.

Four "Dog" boats were in Bastia and Lt. Jerram was acting temporarily as S.O. Jerram was on board one of the boats one night playing poker (and losing) when the S.O. of the PT-boats came into the wardroom.

He said that an American air ace had arrived in Bastia and wanted to go out in a PT-boat. Jerram offered to light in the PT-boat after its trip, and off the American went. Later, apparently, a divisional leader of the PT-boats noticed that the French troops manning the harbour guns looked rather businesslike. They were in constant fear of the Germans returning and tended to be rather nervous.

The American officer asked what was the matter, and one of the Frenchmen said, "Alerte." This was interpreted literally by the American, who promptly took all the PT-boats out of the harbour in darkness, manned by what crews were available. Jerram was quite unaware of all this activity, since the Americans used another part of the harbour.

---

[1] The enemy could fix their position by direction-finders.

Outside, the PT-boats cruised up and down until they saw three boats which they took to be "Dogs". They tailed on to the end of the column. Eventually one of the PTs overran and hit the transom of the "Dog" ahead and was roundly cursed in German. The "Dogs" were in fact three E-boats who had just mined the entrance to the harbour.

Next morning Jerram had to go out in a rowing-boat to investigate. He found that the mines, well placed and quite visible in the clear water, had sealed the boats into Bastia, and MLs had to be called up to sweep a way out.

. . . . .

November on the west coast opened with MTBs of the 33rd Flotilla on the 3rd/4th chasing a submarine which was escorted by E-boats, but it managed to escape into San Stefano.

The boats from Bastia and Maddalena, however, were running to their worst enemy of all—the weather. For several nights it was impossible to operate, and on others the boats went out to find that worsening weather forced them back to base. Full patrols were possible on only six nights between 4th November and 2nd December.

At the beginning of November plans were being made for the eventual capture of the island of Elba, where Napoleon lived for a year. It is a curious coincidence that boats of the 20th MGB Flotilla should have played a small part in the forming of those plans by an operation from Napoleon's birthplace, Corsica.

MGB 658 was detailed off to land French officers on the island so that they could report on the enemy garrison, its positions, and the general feeling for or against the Germans on the island.

On the morning of the 17th four French officers boarded 658, bringing a rubber dinghy, packs, a wireless set and various other pieces of equipment which was dumped in Burke's cabin.

They then pored over the chart, and the point where they were to be landed on the island was established. In the evening, at 1740, 658 sailed with an American boat, PT 201, in company. The plan was that 201, with her radar, would act as guide. When off Elba she gave 658 a fix from which to begin her dead-reckoning approach.

The MGB then launched the dinghy and towed it astern, closing the little sandy cove at Pointe Zanca on silenced engines until only a hundred yards off the shore. At 2255 the operation began. It is best described by Burke's report:

"At 2255 the dinghy was manned by the three French agents, complete with radio equipment, and by Capitaine de Corvette ——,

The sea of a million mirrors. A Vosper MTB at speed

MTB 265 being towed back stern first to Augusta after being damaged in a Messina Straits p
on 9th August, 1943

MTB 422 leaving Leghorn harbour for a patrol

LCG 19 – one of Bobby Allan's "Battle Squadron" for Operation "Newt"

An F-lighter brought back to Ancona by Tim Bligh after the German surrender

A German I-boat

Another F-lighter

MTB 376 leaving for a patrol

MTB 422 at high speed

MTB 378, loking rather naked without a mast

After the German air raid on Bari in December 1943

There was not much room between the islands.... The channel between Pag and Vir in th

MTB 81 being towed back after colliding with MTB 372 during an action

Bligh on the Bridge of MGB 662. *Left to right*: Bligh, A.B. Stone (later killed in action), P.O. Bridden, Captain Stevens (C.C.F.) Tommy Ladner and Stan Turner

One of Bligh's victims – the schooner *Tritone* –

and one of the F-lighters he destroyed in the big Vir Island action

Commander Robert Allan, D.S.O., O.B.E., M.P.

The Coastal Forces base at Bastia with two "Dogs" alongside. The nearer one is Cornelius Burke's

Castal Forces arrive at Vis
Commander Welman astride his famous white horse.   *Right* Lieut. David Scott, D.S.C. steering
a less famous one

Marshal Tito inspects the first Dalmation Brigade on Vis Island

Cornelius Burke (658) and Tommy Ladner (663)

Marshal Tito's headquarters at the Town Hall, K

Komiza harbour, with an MTB and an MGB alongside. Partisan "Tigers" are moored up on the side of the harbour

A part of the German schooner *Tritone* which arrived on board when she blew up

(Above) MTB 405, one of the Vospers. *(Below)* An MGB embarking troops after a raid on the Greek island of Kithera

Partisan "Tigers" returning from a raid

Partisans of the 4th Army set off for the attack on Fiume (Rijeka)

GB 657 unsuccessfully trying to tow two Vospers, MTBs 371 and 287, off Levera Island after they had run aground while on patrol

1 air photograph of two of the E-boats sunk by Lieut.-Commander J.A. Montgomorie during the last days of the war

The *Partenope*-class destroyer torpedoed by MTBs under Montgomorie's command

The victorious "Dogs"

The vanquished Axis: the White Ensign flies above the Italian and Nazi ensigns (and a white flag) aboard an MTB in the Adriatic

t) On board an
at after the surrender
eft: Walter
nt. Bottom left to
: Ennis, Eric Hewitt,
Tim Bligh

w) An E-boat
enders

The old and the new: an Aegean schooner, H.M.S. *Racea*, re-arms an MTB with torpedoes aft attack

French Navy, who was in charge of the party, and who was to bring the dinghy back.

"Considerable difficulty was experienced in getting the party to man the dinghy in a seamanlike manner, and the party set off. However, after travelling a distance of some few feet, three of the dinghy's occupants simultaneously decided to trim the boat by moving in a body up to the bows. This, in spite of the efforts of several officers and men to dissuade them, advice being given in rather doubtful French.

"As predicted by those in MGB 658, the dinghy at once assumed a sharp list, was seen to go down by the bows and shortly after capsized. Loud and prolonged cries for help were immediately heard from the former occupants, and prompt steps to render assistance were made by those in 658.

"A confused situation then developed owing to the apparent inability of those in the water to take advantage of the lines, life-belts, and other aids to rescue which were quickly placed within easy reach.

"However, after many brave efforts by the majority of my crew, two of the party were manhandled inboard. The pandemonium raised by the two still in the water was such as to convince without doubt any nearby inhabitant of the island that a landing in force was about to take place!

"One of these two thereupon announced that he had broken his arm, but further remarks on this subject became inaudible when he managed to place himself under the considerable discharge of water from the four exhaust pipes in the boat's side. We were relieved to discover, after finally accomplishing his rescue, that his injuries were of a minor nature.

"Our attentions then turned to the remaining member of the party, the Capitaine de Corvette, who had contrived to wedge himself out of sight under the chine near the bows. The situation was not improved by the fact that a northerly wind was bearing him and the boat towards a point on which there was reported to be a German battery.

"Efforts were therefore redoubled to persuade the seemingly unwilling unfortunate to extricate himself. After jolting by the surging of the boat he appeared and was shortly afterwards hoisted inboard.

"We returned to a position some two miles offshore in order to reorganise the French forces. Since the wireless equipment had been lost, it was decided to land one agent alone. He was therefore dried off and put into some warm clothes.

K

"At 2355, MGB 658 returned to the same position off the beach, and the agent was rowed ashore in a small rubber dinghy, accompanied by the French officer and one rating from 658."

· · · · · ·

In December the strength of Coastal Forces on the west coast fell to the lowest level there had been. This was inevitable for two reasons. Boats were being dispersed to the various other theatres of operations, and as early as mid-October the four running boats of the 19th MGB Flotilla (later renamed the 60th) had left Malta for the Aegean, where the 10th Flotilla were already operating.

These four boats, 645 (Lt. Basil Bourne), 643 (Lt. Hobday), 646 (Lt. Knight-Lacklen) and 647 (Lt. Mountstephens) had started off their voyage to the Aegean from Malta by calling at Tobruk for fuel. It was a fine sunny afternoon, and they had communicated with the shore signal lamp to arrange for berths.

The crews were lined up on the foredecks, and C.O.s were bringing their boats in when suddenly the Army ashore turned hostile and offensive. The crews stood firm while the S.O. using the signal lamp, forcibly pointed out to the shore batteries the friendly nature of the boats, and they ceased fire.

Two months later, on 19th December, four more "Dogs" were sent from the Maddalena-Bastia force to reinforce the boats operating in the Adriatic. In addition, the old Vospers of the 7th Flotilla were being paid off.

Experience had shown, the Captain, Coastal Forces reported at this time, that "There were many tactical advantages in a mixed force of MTBs and MGBs, and for some time I have been operating the 'D' type of boats in this way".[1]

Owing to the reduction in the number of "Dog" boats on the station through enemy action, it was proposed to reorganise them into four flotillas of six boats each, with all flotillas containing MTBs and MGBs. The C.-in-C. approved this change, and the 56th, 57th, 60th and 61st Flotillas were re-formed accordingly.

The Coastal Forces strength[2] a month later totalled: the 7th (seven boats), 10th (seven), 20th (four) and 24th (eight) MTB Flotillas; the 56th (six boats), 57th (seven), 60th (six) and 61st (six) MTB-MGB Flotillas.

[1] As will have been seen from the narrative.
[2] Taken from official records and possibly out of date.

The ML strength had increased considerably in recent months and consisted of the following flotillas (the details again being taken from official records, which were detailed rather than accurate): the 3rd (thirteen boats), 8th (five), 9th (nine), 22nd (six), 25th (seven), 28th (six), 29th (six), 31st (eight), 24th (eight), 42nd (eight), and 43rd (seven). MLs 576, 360, 361, 841 and 842 were on Special Service.

The HDML Flotillas were the 111th (five boats), 115th (eight), 117th (eight), 134th (eight), 139th (eight), 140th (ten), 141st (eight), 142nd (ten), 101st (nine), and the 113th (seven).

When the "Dog" flotillas were reorganised, the 3rd ML Flotilla (which was doing minesweeping) was expanded into three divisions, and a new flotilla, the 8th, was created.

In December new boats arrived for the 7th MTB Flotilla. Four of them were American-built Vospers and five were the American Higgins boats. They were at Algiers and were sailed through to Malta, by which time the old boats of the 7th[1] had either been paid off or were in the process of doing so.

The new Higgins were 420 (Lt. A. C. B. Blomfield, S.O. of the 7th), 419 (Lt. T. Finch), 421 (Lt. R. Varvill), 422 (Lt. Cochrane) and 423 (Lt. Silas Good). The American-designed and built boats had a 20-mm. Oerlikon forward, a twin .5-inch Browning on each side of the bridge, a twin Oerlikon amidships, a Bofors aft, and two 21-inch torpedo tubes.

The four Vospers were 375 (Lt. Johnson), 376 (Lt. S. Moore), 377 (Lt. R. Aitchison), and 378 (Lt. Nick Ilett). These boats had the British radar, two torpedo tubes, a 20-mm. Oerlikon forward, and a twin .5-inch turret amidships (later replaced with Oerlikons).

·   ·   ·   ·   ·

Having brought the narrative in the Western Mediterranean up to the end of 1943, with the force depleted but with a flotilla of new boats delivered, we now have to turn first to the Adriatic and then to the Aegean.

In the Adriatic the position was confused in the early days simply because we did not know exactly what was going on inside Yugoslavia. In the first instance we started dropping supplies by air to Gen. Mihailovich's Chetniks; but later, when Brig. Fitzroy Maclean[2] established contact with Tito, it was soon made clear that it was Tito's

---

[1] Vosper boats which had been in service for nearly two years.
[2] The envoy sent by Mr. Churchill.

Partisans who were doing most of the fighting against the Germans. The Chetniks had gradually ceased to fight and had in some cases started to co-operate with the Germans.

The Partisans were, of course, Communists, while the Chetniks were, for the most part, Royalists. The Allies decided to help whoever was fighting the Germans, and the choice was Tito and his Partisans.

Chapter XXIII

THE ROAD TO THE ISLES

THE MTBs and MGBs operating in the Adriatic began by attacking enemy shipping along the east coast of Italy, sailing mostly from Bari; but there were no targets to the south of Ancona, which was not within convenient operating distance. This lack of targets coincided with the need to help Tito, and the centre of operations moved to the Dalmatian coast.

In May 1943 Mr. Churchill, talking with Gen. Eisenhower at Algiers, said:[1] ". . . The occupation of the southern part of Italy, or even the whole of the toe or heel, would give us access to the Adriatic and the power to send shiploads of munitions to Adriatic ports, and also agents and possibly Commando bands. We should not have the troops to engage in any serious operations there. . . ."

A month earlier, in a message[2] to the Chiefs of Staff Committee, and referring to the question of Italy remaining in the war with a certain amount of German help, he said: ". . . It must be considered a most important part of the objective to get a footing on the Dalmatian coast, so that we can foment the insurgents of Albania and Yugoslavia by weapons, supplies, and possibly Commandos."

In a message[3] to President Roosevelt on 26th July 1943, headed "Some thoughts on the fall of Mussolini", he wrote: ". . . It will become urgent in the highest degree to get agents, Commandos, and supplies across the Adriatic into Greece, Albania and Yugoslavia. It must be remembered that there are fifteen German divisions in the Balkan peninsula, of which ten are mobile."

On 3rd September 1943 the Prime Minister received a message from Gen. Smuts giving friendly criticisms of the conduct of the war, and expressing his dislike of the plan for the Allies to fight their way northwards through Italy. His views were, he said,[4] that "We should take Sardinia and Corsica and immediately attack in North Italy without

[1] *The Second World War*, Vol. IV, p. 736.
[2] Ibid., p. 839.
[3] Ibid., Vol. V, p. 53.
[4] Ibid., pp. 113–14.

fighting our way all up the peninsula. We should immediately take Southern Italy and move on to the Adriatic, and from a suitable point there launch a real attack on the Balkans and set its resurgent forces going".

In November 1943 Mr. Churchill prepared "What was in effect an indictment of our mismanagement of operations in the Mediterranean during the two months which have passed since our victory at Salerno".[1] This he gave to the Chiefs of Staff and it said, in part:

> *We have failed to give any real measure of support to the Partisans and Patriots in Yugoslavia and Albania. These guerilla forces are containing as many [German] divisions as are the British and American armies put together. Hitherto they have been nourished only by supplies dropped from the air. It is more than two months since we have had air and naval superiority in the mouth of the Adriatic, yet no ships with supplies have entered the ports taken by the Partisans.*
>
> *On the contrary, the Germans are systematically driving them from these ports and acquiring mastery of the whole Dalmatian coast. . . .*
>
> *How has it happened? An imaginary line has been drawn down the Mediterranean which relieves Gen. Eisenhower's armies of all responsibilities for the Dalmatian coast and the Balkans. These are assigned to Gen. Wilson, of the Middle East Command, but he does not possess the necessary forces. One command has the forces but not the responsibilities, the other the responsibilities but not the forces. This can hardly be considered an ideal arrangement. . . .*
>
> *Most unfortunate of all has been the Dodecanese and the Aegean . . . the Germans are now complete masters of the Eastern Aegean. Although already outmatched in the air in Italy, they have not hesitated to reduce their air-power there, and have transferred to the Aegean forces sufficient to dominate this theatre.*
>
> *Although the U.S. and British air forces in the Mediterranean have a front-line strength of over 4,000—i.e. practically equal to the whole of the German Air Force—the Germans have been able to reproduce in the Aegean theatre all the old technique of the days of our air nakedness, and with their Stuka dive-bombers have broken down the resistance of our best troops and sunk or damaged our ships. . . .*

Three months later he sent a message to the Partisans:[2]

[1] *The Second World War*, Vol. V, pp. 291-3.   [2] Ibid., p. 418.

Prime Minister to Marshal Tito 5 *February* 1944

. . . I have asked the Supreme Allied Commander in the Mediterranean to form immediately an amphibious force of Commandos, supported by air and flotillas, to attack, with your aid, the garrisons which the Germans have left in the islands they have taken along the Dalmatian coast. There is no reason why these garrisons should not be exterminated with forces which will shortly be available.

Meanwhile Doenitz had reported to his Feuhrer on the situation. At a conference at the Fuehrer's headquarters on 24th September 1943 he put forward his ideas:[1]

The C.-in-C., Navy, was present with Field-Marshal Baron von Weichs, who reported to the Feuhrer on the situation in the south-east and recommended the timely evacuation of our outposts on the islands in the Aegean, including Crete.

The C.-in-C., Navy, had intended to make the same proposal motivated by the following considerations:

(a) *The strategic moves of the enemy are evidently directed against the Balkans. . . .*

(b) *Our own position in Greece and the neighbouring areas of the Adriatic and the Aegean Sea is very precarious. Our forces on the peninsula are kept busy with the suppression of Partisan activities and are hardly in a position to prevent a landing attempt in force.[2] The naval forces assigned to coastal defence are likewise not of sufficient strength to prevent such a landing. They do not possess any fighting strength to speak of, except for the Aegean area.*

(c) *At sea we have only small vessels which are without military value once the enemy decides to bring his superior naval forces into play. . . .*

The Fuehrer agrees with the line of argument presented by Field-Marshal von Weichs and the C.-in-C., Navy. However, he cannot order the proposed evacuation of the islands, especially the Dodecanese and Crete, on account of the political repercussions which would necessarily follow. . . .

To avoid such a blow to our prestige we may even have to accept the eventual loss of our troops and material. The supply of the islands must be assured by the air force.

* * * * * *

[1] *Minutes of the Fuehrer's Naval Conferences*, 1943.
[2] See General Smuts' suggestion, given on pages 149–50.

So much for the strategic background. The more localised tactical situation, so far as the Germans and British are concerned, will be given later.

The first major move towards operating MTBs in the Adriatic was made on 23rd September 1943, when the Commander, Coastal Forces, Western Mediterranean (C.F.W.), Cdr. (later Capt.) A. E. P. Welman, D.S.O., D.S.C., R.N. visited the Flag Officer, Taranto, to investigate the possibility of Coastal Forces bases at Brindisi and Bari, using H.M.S. *Vienna* as a base ship.

Brindisi was selected and official records state that on the 28th September *Vienna* was ordered to sail in Convoy AH 1, and the 20th MTB Flotilla (under Lt. H. A. Barbary, R.N.) and the 24th (under Lt. David Scott, R.N.) were to join her at Brindisi. These two flotillas had been operating from Taranto, and three boats of the 20th and two of the 24th had already made a successful raid on Valona Bay, the port on the Albanian coast east of the heel of Italy.

Barbary had managed to get a chart from the Italian naval authorities showing the details of boom and net defences of the bay, which was being used by the enemy as an anchorage. With this information plans were made for an MTB attack. One boat was detailed to torpedo the net or boom to clear the way in for the rest.

The boats taking part were MTBs 89 (S/Lt. W. J. Archer), with the S.O., Lt. Scott, embarked, and 85 (Lt. K. C. Banks) of the 24th Flotilla, and 295 (S/Lt. F. N. Frenzell), with the S.O., Lt. Barbary, embarked, 290 (Lt. D. Austin) and 287 (Lt. J. D. Lancaster) of the 20th Flotilla.

The boats left Taranto together at 1500 on 21st September, and just over an hour later Scott in 89 sighted red smoke on the horizon and altered course to investigate, leaving 85 and the rest to proceed.

He found two rafts crowded with survivors from the S.S. *Almenara*, which had been torpedoed the night before with eighty people on board. Scott searched for more survivors, helped by an Italian flying-boat, and by 1700 he had fifty-two people on board his Vosper. He then sighted a landing-craft, LCI(L)6, and the fifty-two survivors were transferred. Scott then headed for the rendezvous, near Saseno Island, at full speed.

The other four boats had arrived at the rendezvous at the arranged time, 2300; but as there was no sign of Scott, Barbary decided that the boats would proceed as one division. At 0009/22nd they made their run up to the reported position of the boom, moving at 7 knots. Although they searched the area with their binoculars, there was no sign of a boom, and Barbary set a course for the reported position of the enemy shipping.

Five minutes later Scott rejoined. His Vosper had maintained its maximum speed, 1,600 revs, for seven hours. Banks, in 85, joined him, leaving Barbary with 295, 290 and 287.

There was still no signs of the boom and Scott took his two boats to search the northern end of the bay while Barbary started a sweep of the southern end.

At 0215, after one false alarm due to some houses on the beach looking, for a few moments, like vessels, Scott identified a group of shipping anchored close inshore inside Battery Point. He immediately turned the two boats to close and the unit was challenged twice from the beach. A machine-gun fired short bursts of tracer in the direction of the boats, perhaps as a warning to the other shipping.

Scott found the ships anchored close together—three reasonable targets, a floating crane, and a number of small craft. He ordered Banks to attack the left-hand of the three larger vessels while his own boat stopped and was pointed at the right-hand vessel, which was of about 1,500 tons. The range was too close to miss—about 250 yards. The starboard torpedo was fired. The boat then swung about twenty degrees to port and the port torpedo was fired at the big ship in the middle at about 400 yards' range. Banks fired two torpedoes from 300 yards.

At this moment both boats were fired on by several light guns at close range, but all were firing very high.

Scott's starboard torpedo was seen to pass right under the foremast of the right-hand ship, but was not seen or heard to explode (later Barbary reported seeing a hole in the bows). The ship in the middle, however, was evidently carrying ammunition, and Scott's port torpedo hit her. She blew up with a satisfactory explosion, and the action report says "a sheet of flame engulfed the whole vessel and debris was flung high into the air: MTB 89 was considerably shaken and her crew drenched with water".

Banks scored at least one hit on the left-hand target, a 1,500-tonner; and although she was not seen to sink because everyone was somewhat distracted by the ammunition ship disintegrating, she was considered to have been destroyed.

By this time the shore defences were well and truly awake and firing wildly. Scott's boat was suddenly caught in the blinding glare of a searchlight only 400 yards away and immediately became the main target. He dropped a smoke float, and the old trick worked: the enemy gunners hotly engaged it. With Banks in company, Scott withdrew, calling up Barbary by W/T to tell him that a torpedo target was still afloat.

Barbary's boats had swept the south end of the bay, keeping half a mile offshore, and then turned north. Several merchant ships were sighted. These were the ones that Scott was about to attack, although Barbary did not know this.

He was just preparing to fire torpedoes from 400 yards when Scott's two boats were seen to crash start and disengage. Barbary's proposed target then blew up. The smoke of the explosion drifted rapidly westwards with the wind, obscuring the other targets, and Barbary ordered the other two boats with him to keep clear while he went in with 295.

On emerging from the smoke, Barbary saw a ship 200 yards on the starboard beam. He made a wide turn to starboard, coming under fire from shore batteries, until his boat was almost stopped 150 yards from the target, slightly abaft its beam. The port torpedo was fired with a depth-setting of 4 feet. The torpedo porpoised once and ran at the target's bows and was thought to have hit.

Barbary then disengaged astern, but the ship was seen to be still afloat, so the starboard torpedo was fired from 100 yards. It porpoised twice and disappeared running five degrees to starboard of the course on which it was fired.

MTB 295 then disengaged to port, passing close under the largest ship's stern. Barbary then decided on a depth-charge attack and, turning to starboard, passed close up the side of the ship at 6 knots, releasing depth-charges set at 100 feet abreast of the ship's funnel. 295 then crash-started and crossed the target's bows at high speed—noticing a hole in the bow.

The depth of water on the Italian charts for this position was 24 metres, and there was no indication that the depth-charges exploded.

Barbary then swept eastwards for more targets, but did not find anything worth attacking. He returned to find the merchant ship still afloat and tried another depth-charge attack at high speed, dropping them set at 100 feet only four feet from the ship's bows. Again there was no explosion.

He disengaged southwards at 12 knots. At 0242 an under-water explosion was felt astern and seen in the area of the depth-charge attack.

Barbary continued southwards until, at 0244, his boat was caught by searchlights and shore batteries opened fire again. He then altered course north-westwards at high speed, under heavy and accurate fire, reducing speed to 25 knots at 0256.

Four minutes later the boat hit a submerged obstruction in the reported position of the boom. The whole boat vibrated and a diver was sent down to check up on damage. He found that the starboard and centre propellers were damaged, and at 0310 MTB 295 got under way on her port engine at 9 knots.

She rendezvoused with 290 (Austin) and 85 (Banks) at 0350, and Banks took her in tow. Later the boats met the destroyer *Ilex*, and the tow was transferred to her.

The C.-in-C., commenting on the action, said: "A well-executed operation, carried through with dash and determination, and reflecting credit on the C.O.s, officers and men of the flotillas involved."

The Captain, Coastal Forces, wrote: "MTB 295 carried out both her attacks at ranges less than the minimum recovery ranges of her torpedoes. Accordingly the probable hit she obtained with her port torpedo was very fortunate."

. . . . .

In October H.M.S. *Vienna*, the base ship, moved from Brindisi northwards to Bari, and a base was established there under Cdr. Welman. The C.F.W., one of the veterans of the coastal motor-boats of World War 1 days, had played a great part in starting and running the Coastal Forces training base at Fort William, in Scotland, where his forthright views on how the boats should operate had a considerable effect. He had later gone to the Mediterranean as C.F.W.

As soon as it was possible, he had obtained a lift from Messina with an American fighter squadron bound for Goya, a few miles south of Bari. With the help of another lift from a medical supplies lorry, he reached Taranto and then went on to Brindisi to arrange a berth for *Vienna*. That completed, he went up to Bari, which was clearly the MTBs' first advanced operational base.

A group of naval officers had been sent over to the islands from Bari to establish contact with the Partisans and arrange for the reception and turn-round of the convoys bringing in supplies.

Lt.-Cdr. Morgan Giles[1] had been given the task of setting up a gun-running organisation to supply Tito and was given two Special Service

[1] Now Capt. Morgan Giles, D.S.O., O.B.E., G.M., R.N.

MLs. With these he set off for Bari. There he soon found that Partisan schooners (and even two steamers which they had concealed from the Germans) had crossed the Adriatic and entered Bari and Brindisi in search of the large quantities of war materials of all kinds which they confidently hoped to get from the Allied authorities.

The Allied problem became, as Giles quickly discovered, not so much a question of smuggling across small quantities of arms and ammunition, but rather how to find and make available enough material, since they were fighting a not inconsiderable war (and occupation) of their own.

To ease the predicament, many of the Partisan schooners were sent to Sicily and loaded up with the so-called "Battlefield Clearance Stores"—i.e. ex-enemy equipment salvaged by the Allies after the fighting in Sicily. This was in fact more valuable to them at this time than Allied weapons and equipment, since much of the gear the Partisans were using was captured from the Germans and Italians.

One of the officers sent to the islands to "break the ice" was Lt.-Cdr. Merlin Minshall, R.N.V.R., a large man whose florid face was topped with red hair, and who had a highly-developed sense of humour and a gift for languages.

As mentioned earlier, it had been decided to increase supplies to Tito; but, as Minshall says in his report:[1] "In London no one knew quite how to do it and what supplies—'Guns or butter'—and how the supplies were to be landed and how distributed, seeing that the Germans held, in theory at any rate, the whole of the Dalmatian coastline.

"So when we landed in Cairo I wasn't sure if I was going to become a surreptitious cloak-and-dagger free-lance working with Partisan smugglers as a sort of nautical Lawrence, or the accredited Naval Attaché to the Allied Military Mission to the National Army of Liberation of Yugoslavia. Some people in authority told me the first, some the second. . . .

"On 12th October 1943 I left Bari on board ML 386 (Lt. 'Butch' Crossley) with Lt. Webb, R.N.R., coming as conducting officer, for the island of Korcula in Dalmatia. And such was the information available at that time that nobody on board knew for certain whether Korcula was held by the Germans or by the Partisans."

Minshall and Capt. Pears, an Army officer, landed surreptitiously on the island, and after meeting some Partisans they made their way to

[1] *Report of Proceedings, September 1943–February 1944, by British Naval Liaison Officer to the Partisans.*

the port of Velaluki, where none of the Partisans bothered to check their credentials. It was decided that they should see the Island Commander. An ancient lorry was produced for the journey to the headquarters. It was a curious vehicle, with three solid tyres and one pneumatic, and when once it was started various factors entered into the problem of stopping it, since it had no brakes.

"All this came as rather a shock," writes Minshall. "One tended immediately to jump to the conclusion that the whole of the vaunted Partisan military organisation was just a myth. It all seemed so desperately casual and apparently inefficient, especially when one realised that the highly-efficient Hun was hammering away at this very organisation only a few miles away.

"And yet in this very fact one saw that one could not be too hasty to judge these people. For this organisation of theirs that in English eyes looked so impossible, so lackadaisical, so utterly hopeless, *was* in fact succeeding in holding down whole German divisions."

At Blato, Minshall and Pears met Celenic, the Island Commander, who "treated Capt. Pears and me coldly and with the greatest suspicion as we had no proof of our identity".

After a good deal of argument Celenic asked why they had not come straight to Velaluki in the ML instead of landing secretly. Minshall was rather reluctant to admit that in Cairo it was not known who controlled the island.

"This convinced him conclusively that we were to be pitied," continues Minshall, "and, as such, ought to be put in touch with our own people. What people? Didn't we know that Brig. Maclean was in Korcula town? Further disastrous loss of face because we had been given to understand in Bari that he had been, and long ago returned inland. . . . So that afternoon Brig. Maclean held a conference in Korcula town to put Pears and myself into the picture.

"After the furtive landing of that morning and its dream-like anticlimax, the setting of this conference seemed quite in keeping. We had landed more or less expecting to have to live in the woods, and here we were sitting in the deepest of armchairs looking out over such a panorama as people save up to visit once in a lifetime.

"On one side of us the little mediaeval town of Korcula jutted out into the sea as ethereal as a miniature Mont St. Michel. Opposite us a deep-blue ribbon of sea no broader than a big river, one bank formed by the serpentine projections of our island, the other bank a soft etching of blue hills.

"And in those hills were the Germans."

Minshall's first task was to gain the confidence of the Partisans, which, "because we had promised so much and produced so little, was going to be, Brig. Maclean insisted, very very difficult".

The entry and distribution of supplies on the scale envisaged would have been a major problem in a familiar harbour. The British were starting with the flimsiest knowledge about local port facilities, capacities or storage possibilities. There was no information about the local shipping available, no contact with Dalmatia, and there was also the task of evacuating the Partisan wounded to Italy. And winter was well on its way.

Minshall left for Hvar Island to set up business as British Naval Liaison Officer at the Partisan Dalmatian headquarters. Pears was sent to Vis Island to find out some of the supply problems. By mid-December liaison with the Partisans was working well, and Minshall had managed to overcome the distrust with which the Partisans at first viewed his activities.

Before the year ends we had better return to the "legitimate" Coastal Forces activities, but before we do that it might be of interest to read Minshall's comments on the Partisans:

"Compared with most other troops, the Partisans certainly are tough. They certainly do keep going under conditions which most armies would give up immediately. They certainly have the ability to fight on the scantiest of rations, and the mere fact of having no boots, or wholly insufficient clothing in the depth of winter, is taken as the normal course of things. . . ."

Minshall refers to the wounded being carried on men's backs from the heart of Croatia at a temperature often below freezing point, and then adds: "And yet there is more than mere courage and toughness here. Here is an underlying spirit that bears them up through all adversity, an ardent belief in the rightness of their cause. This belief is kept alive by their well-organised propaganda system. . . .

"Men and women fight side by side in the front line, sharing equally all the dangers and all the hardships: men and women share the same hospital wards. . . . But perhaps the clearest proof of Partisan bravery is the fact that the Partisans are not awarded medals for bravery. It would never occur to a Partisan not to be consciously brave. . . .

"Their strength is in the attack, and it would never occur to a Partisan not to attack, but once put them in a defensive role and it is an altogether different story. They are far too volatile to be reliable in any static defence."

He gives a first-hand example of their courage: a German steamer was preparing to sail north from Dubrovnik with supplies. "Acting quite alone, the Partisans sent three small boats, each manned by six men, the largest was only 27 feet long and none of them was more than an open fishing boat, to lie in the narrow channel between the east end of the island of Hvar and the mainland."

For two nights they waited, spaced out across the channel in full range of the German shore defences. "Then on the third night, deep under the shadows of the high cliffs of the mainland, a ship appeared, hugging the coast.

"Silently from different directions crept the pigmy Partisan striking force. With five light-calibre machine-guns they opened fire simultaneously. The ship, although she mounted some ten machine-guns, responded as expected: she turned in towards the mainland and was promptly fired on by the German coastal batteries.

"In the ensuing confusion the Partisans boarded her, captured her without a single casualty to themselves, and sailed her back to Hvar with 90 prisoners and 130 tons of provisions.

"People, when told the story, say to me: 'Jolly fine, but that was just one of those lucky actions which occur once in a lifetime.' The following night the Partisans did exactly the same to a 140-ton German schooner."

      .   .   .   .   .

Included among the MLs which were sent to start the "gun-running" were 361, commanded by Lt. R. Young, R.C.N.V.R.; 386, Lt. Crossley; and 841, Lt. J. Weir. Other naval liaison officers—apart from Minshall—included Lt. D. R. ("Agony") Pain, R.N., on Brac, and Lt.-Cdr. K. J. ("Spider") Webb, R.N.R., on Korcula.

About this time Lt.-Cdr. Glen, whose job it was to live in a cave on the Albanian coast south of Valona and pass over intelligence reports, was surprised to hear from the Partisans inland that they were bringing a party of thirteen American nurses down from the mountains.

This news was quickly signalled across the Adriatic to Bari, and it was found that they were the survivors of an American plane which was missing after taking off from North Africa for an aerodrome at Brindisi.

Lt.-Cdr. Giles sent ML 361, the veteran Special Service craft, with her Canadian C.O., Bob Young, to fetch them from the enemy-held coast. In the meantime the American authorities were warned; and when Young, on his way back, signalled his estimated time of arrival, ambulances and a reception committee of what the Americans call "top brass" was waiting for the starving, bedraggled and probably badly injured girls to be carried ashore.

Young brought 361 alongside, and very shortly thirteen neatly-dressed girls, their cheeks freshly powdered, their lips newly-outlined in lipstick, stepped ashore. Bob Young, realising that psychology enters into modern warfare, had called in at the shops before sailing for Albania.

CHAPTER XXIV

THE WHITE HORSE AT VIS

THE problem for Coastal Forces was to find an advanced base
among the many islands. Bisevo and Vis were among those
proposed, and Cdr. Welman favoured the last-named, which
was already famous in naval history. Bisevo was to become a prison
camp where the Partisans kept the Germans permanently.

Vis (Lissa) is the outermost island of the Dalmatian archipelago, ten
and a half miles long and four and a half miles wide. The island is
said to have been settled originally by people from Lesbos, and the
Parians, helped by Dionysius the Elder, introduced a colony there in
400 B.C.

After various civilisations swept over the island, Velo Selo, then the
chief settlement, was destroyed by Ferdinand of Naples in 1483. After
it had been rebuilt the Turks ravaged it in 1571.

The present city rose up shortly afterwards. During the Napoleonic
wars the French held Lissa, as it was then called, until 1811, when the
British captured it. The Battle of Lissa was one of the series of British
naval battles which also included the Nile and Trafalgar, and was
fought on 13th March 1811, about three miles off the coast.

However, we must move forward in time, to Coastal Forces. Three
MTBs—242, with Cdr. Welman and Lt. David Scott, the S.O. of the
24th Flotilla, embarked, 81 and 97—left Bari at 1700 on 16th October
to investigate the islands.

The weather soon deteriorated (those "wine-dark seas" have a
certain vintage viciousness about them in winter, as will be seen later),
and the three boats made for the port of Vis. Fortunately a British
and an American officer had preceded the unit to warn the Partisans,
and the MTBs were warmly received (after a few shots from sentries
at the harbour entrance) by the commandant of the island. The boats
went round to the north of the island to moor up.

Next morning Cdr. Welman, firmly seated astride a large white
horse (see photograph facing p. 176), and David Scott rode northwards,

like two horsemen of the Apocalypse, to inspect the cache where the boats were moored. They found the local Partisans had already provided the crews with sardines, grapes and wine, and were full of sincere enthusiasm for their newly-arrived Allies.

The Captain, Coastal Forces' report on the visit to Vis says: "On the return of the C.F.W.'s party to the port of Vis an invitation was received to an official reception and dance. As the wind had reached Force 8, acceptance was possible, and was made."

The three MTBs later returned to Bari to make arrangements for establishing a base at Komiza Harbour. The only untoward incident during their visit to the island occurred just before they sailed, when a Yugoslav Royalist was found to have stowed away in Lt. Scott's boat. He hid himself in the officers' "heads" (toilet).

. . . . .

Describing the situation in a summary covering December 1943 and January 1944, Capt. Stevens, the C.C.F., writes:

> The operations of Coastal Forces among the islands off the Dalmatian coast have, I think, been unique. Experienced observers who have seen service in Home Waters before coming to the Mediterranean recall with amusement that at home they thought they were hard-worked if they were out three nights in a week, from an established base, at which, on their return, they retired to comfortable shore accommodation while base staff overhauled their boats.
>
> During recent weeks, boats spent sixteen days in the islands, during which they have carried out night patrols on thirteen nights, spent two of the other three nights refuelling by hand, and been called to action stations at least five times each day by air alarms.
>
> There have been sudden storms of great violence. Broken frames have been patched up with iron frames obtained from the local blacksmith, and any boat returning to the mainland has been robbed of parts.

Repairs to the boats in Komiza were done in a small boatyard used for repairing local craft. The Partisans had been using it for converting their schooners to warlike purposes, and it soon became well-known to Coastal Forces as "John Brown's". There was only a rudimentary slipway, and the only way of repairing underwater damage, providing it was near the stem, was to run the bows up on the beach.

At first, while operating from Vis and other islands nearby, few

targets presented themselves, and usually not more than two "Dogs"
and three short boats could operate from Vis and Hvar. In daylight
the Luftwaffe had their own way, and boats lying up had to be carefully camouflaged.

One of the first acts of violence in December occurred on the 12th/
13th when MTB 649, commanded by Lt. Peter Hughes, S.A.N.F.(V).,
bombarded Tranpanj and Crvice. He later sighted a ship leaving the
Neretva Channel and gave chase. He identified it as a two-funnelled
ex-Austrian steam torpedo-boat and engaged it with gunfire. The
enemy vessel escaped into Loviste and was later bombed by the R.A.F.
The torpedo-boats used by the enemy were, in fact, small destroyers,
and should not be confused with craft as small as MTBs and MGBs.

On the 18th/19th two MTBs, 297 (Lt. Lancaster, who was also
S.O.) and 637 (Lt. R. C. Davidson), supported a raid near Omis, on
the Dalmatian coast north of Brac, in which several hundred Partisans
were successfully protected in their crossing from Brac to the mainland. The two MTBs became separated during the operation, and
Davidson was carrying out a diversionary bombardment when he
met a force which he at first believed to be friendly.

Davidson immediately made the Partisan challenge, and as the
vessels did not reply, he increased speed to investigate more closely.
As he passed he saw a Siebel ferry and could clearly see drums of fuel,
and troops on board.

*The Siebel was SF.193, and with her were two small landing-craft of
20 tons, I.43 and I.55, and a motor-boat, M.24. They were transporting
cased petrol, supplies and troops from Trogir to Ploca. The SF.193 was
carrying 110 drums of petrol and 29 soldiers.*

*The convoy had left Trogir at 2000 on the 18th, and at 2215, when off
Omis, a ship was sighted at extreme range, but she disappeared. Shortly
afterwards a fast-moving craft came up astern flashing a green light and,
passing along the port side, disappeared.*

*At 2310 this craft again closed to about fifty yards from SF.193 and
hailed her in English, German and Italian, shouting "You'll never get
through". A few minutes later the Germans were attacked with machine-
gun fire, which they effectively returned until the enemy withdrew.*[1]

Davidson, in 637, had closed and opened fire with all guns, and the
enemy's heavy return fire scored hits forward, aft and in the engine-

[1] This and subsequent passages in italic type are taken from captured German documents.

room, and there were casualties among the men on the bridge. He broke off the engagement and moved round to gain bearing and to get inshore of the enemy convoy.

Eleven minutes later Davidson began his run in from SF.193's bow. He fired one torpedo—the other failing to leave the tube—and engaged the Siebel with all guns. Within half a minute the ferry blew up. The other craft were left in flames.

A second enemy vessel [this was in fact Davidson returning] closed on the port side and a gunnery duel ensued with hits on both sides. On SF.193 the petrol drums were set on fire and these started to explode as the crew started to abandon ship. There were about twenty casualties.

The burnt-out wreck of SF.193 drifted ashore at Brac. I.56 and M.24 also sustained damage from the gunfire, but succeeded in reaching Ploca. Two small vessels, AZ.09[1] and AZ.08, which left Zara the same night in connection with an island operation, were later reported missing and it was presumed they were sunk by MTBs.

Lancaster, in 297, after becoming separated from Davidson, had continued his patrol and sighted a shape under a cliff at Krilo Point. At first it was thought to be an eccentric rock formation, but later it proved to be a ship about 200 feet long and well camouflaged—possibly a patrol vessel or coastal defence ship. Lt. J. R. Woods, the C.O. of 297, fired two torpedoes at this "sitting bird" and she sank.

The Partisan raid the two MTBs were supporting is believed to have provoked the Germans into making plans for the occupation of several of the islands, described later. The trilingual threat made from Davidson's boat is explained by the fact that they were by this time carrying Partisans, who acted as interpreters and, when necessary, as pilots when their local knowledge of the coast could be of use.

. . . . .

Less than a week after he chased the ex-Austrian torpedo-boat, Peter Hughes, in 649, had a further success and intercepted two enemy schooners. He captured them and took them back to Hvar.

Two days later, on the 21st/22nd December, our forces in this area scored the most important success to date. The boats had made many dashes after the ex-German, ex-Yugoslav, ex-Italian, and now German cruiser *Niobe*, but each time they had missed her. The *Niobe* started

---

[1] "AZ" probably stood for "Adria(Zara)".

off her career before the Great War as the *Niobe*, in the German Navy. She passed to Yugoslavia after the German surrender and was renamed the *Dalmacija*. In 1941, after the Axis occupation of Yugoslavia, she was taken over by the Italians and renamed *Cattaro*. On 8th November 1943 she was commissioned by the Germans at Pola and four days later was renamed *Niobe*. Her wheel had turned a full circle and was about to stop.

German records (given in italic type in the following passages) say:

At 1900 on the 19th December, while on passage from the Pasman Island area to Pola in company with the torpedo-boats TA.21 and TA.22, Niobe ran aground at Arat di Ponente, on the south-west tip of Silba Island. Tugs were sent out to try to salvage the cruiser and it was while work was in progress that the MTBs attacked. . . .

The news that the cruiser was aground came through the Partisan grapevine to the MTBs in Hvar two days later. Immediately the S.O. of the 20th Flotilla, Lt. Lancaster, sailed in MTB 298 (Lt. the Hon. F. M. Shore) with 276 (Lt. Peter Hyslop). To reach the cruiser, attack and get back to Hvar before daylight brought swarms of angry air-craft buzzing round their heads meant the two boats had to make 25 knots. Hyslop had a struggle to keep up that speed because of leaks in the engine-room which needed emergency repairs.

The boats were off Silba Island just before 0100, and at that time the cruiser was sighted. Lancaster reduced speed to between 2 and 4 knots and crept in towards the stranded cruiser, the centre of a fussing band of tugs and E-boats.

Neither of the MTBs was sighted. At 400 yards both boats fired their torpedoes. Satisfactory explosions occurred, and enemy vessels then opened inaccurate fire on the two MTBs, who retired gracefully.

At about 0200 [the Germans kept different zone times] on 22nd December, without warning, Niobe was hit by two torpedoes. One hit her forward and the other aft. The torpedo which hit her forward exploded in an ammunition compartment which had previously been emptied in con-nection with the salvage operations. The damage was extensive and the Niobe became a total loss. The tug Parenzo, which had been alongside Niobe at the time of the attack, was hit by a third torpedo and was blown to pieces.

It was at first thought that a submarine had carried out the attack, but it was later reported that the noise of engines had been heard. This led to the conclusion that the torpedoes had been fired by MTBs.

Capt. Stevens wrote that the final elimination of "this hoary but agile cruiser, which had been responsible for so many fruitless patrols, was a fitting climax to the operations of Coastal Forces in the area in 1943".

· · · · ·

There was, however, another climax in the Adriatic. The large-scale Partisan raid mentioned earlier resulted in the Germans attacking and capturing the Partisan-held island of Korcula on 20th/21st December.

Merlin Minshall feared Lagosta would be the next island to fall and visited it in an MTB commanded by Lt. Ennis. In anticipation of a German assault on the island, Minshall and Ennis set about, with the somewhat limited means at their disposal, destroying the telephone exchange, dismantling the W/T station, and generally savaging the harbour installations and power station.

Minshall went as far as buying up a ship chandler's store on being assured by Ennis that it would be invaluable to Coastal Forces, and after he had given the owner all the money he had he gave an IOU for the balance of 93,000 lira[1] and carted his purchase down to the MTBs in three lorries.

The boats took scores of refugees with them when they left—women and children chosen from 700 or more people who clamoured and fought on the quayside to be evacuated. Minshall writes: "On the way back to Hvar we fought a spirited battle with two of our own destroyers. The refugees behaved with amazing calm; afterwards I discovered they believed we were just having a practice shoot."

A few days after this the Partisan Dalmatian headquarters moved to Vis, and both Brac and Hvar were left lightly defended. This decision to hold Vis in strength was largely at the instigation of Rear-Admiral McGrigor, the Flag Officer, Taranto, acting in concert, of course, with the Army and Air Force commanders.

The decision was agreed to by the Partisan authorities, and it was planned that an Allied garrison of Commandos supported by artillery should be installed to assist the Partisans, who provided the bulk of the troops.

The object of forming this base was:

[1] The payment of this claim led to repercussions which were still in progress with the British authorities in Trieste in 1949.

(a) To have a firmly-held terminal point for the delivery of Tito's supplies by sea.

(b) To provide a base for Coastal Forces operations against the enemy's sea-traffic along the coast; and for Commando raids against the enemy-held islands and coastline.

(c) To have a foothold on the eastern side of the Adriatic for use as a springboard for any large-scale operations which might be found necessary in the Balkans.

In Vis the problem of forming an advanced Coastal Forces base soon became an almost domestic one. There had to be a headquarters for Minshall, and a mess and sleeping quarters for S.O.s of each flotilla had to be found. This in itself was quite a problem, because not one house in 200 at Komiza had either running water or even an earth closet.

.   .   .   .   .

Before we go on to 1944 we must go back to the beginning of December in Bari, where, because of the delay in unloading one, there were two convoys of ships in the port. Just after darkness had fallen one night a force of twelve German bombers came in from seaward at almost wave-top height, thus preventing our radar from picking them up and giving a warning.

Within a matter of minutes they had completed one of the Luftwaffe's most successful attacks of the Mediterranean war: they left seventeen ships either sunk by bombs or destroyed by exploding cargoes of ammunition. There were more than 1,000 casualties. H.M.S. *Vienna*, the Coastal Force base ship, was straddled and damaged by blast, her bow warps being cut by bomb fragments. Several MTBs were damaged by blast and "fragments"—some of them four-feet-square pieces of plating—although fortunately none of them received a direct hit.

Every man available was set to work helping rescue survivors. The MTBs went round picking up men swimming in the water—which was contaminated by chemicals from the cargo of a ship which had sunk—and taking them off wrecks. Many officers acted as pilots to get undamaged ships out of the harbour to safety. Lt.-Cdr. Morgan Giles was among several people decorated for gallantry, receiving the George Medal.

Coastal Forces had suffered a double blow. The raid—which had formed an unwelcome reception committee for C.C.F. and his staff, who were visiting *Vienna*—had not only damaged boats but sunk a cargo ship carrying sixteen new Packard engines and most of the spares for the 20th MTB Flotilla.

With its strength in the Adriatic seriously depleted overnight, more boats were quickly brought round from the Bastia-Maddalena area, the first to go being four "Dog" boats which sailed on the 19th December.

CHAPTER XXV

GUNFIRE AND AMICI

AT the beginning of 1944 the Allied armies were having a grim struggle nearly halfway up the mainland of Italy. The 8th Army, on the Adriatic side, had crossed the Sangro river and reached Ortona, but the 5th Army was halted in front of Monte Cassino.

On the island of Vis Lt.-Cdr. Giles had arrived to take over command of naval operations. He had been appointed Senior Naval Officer, Vis (abbreviated to Snovis—in case the uninformed should mispronounce this title it should be pointed out that "Vis" rhymes with "peace"), and Cdr. Welman was running the Coastal Forces bases on the mainland of Italy. The main base was still Brindisi, but Bari was used as a mixed operating-administrative headquarters. Manfredonia, however, became a forward repair and working-up base.

With Giles went the Vis garrison, which was commanded by Brig. Tom Churchill.[1] The basic garrison[2] was the 2nd Commando Brigade under Brig. Churchill. This consisted of No. 2 (Army) Commando, commanded by Lt.-Col. J. M. T. F. Churchill, D.S.O., M.C., the brigadier's brother and better known as "Mad Jack"; and No. 40 (Royal Marine) Commando, under Lt.-Col. P. Manners, D.S.O., who was later to be killed in action on Brac beside Lt.-Col. Churchill, who was captured.

Giles set up his operations room in a cottage at Komiza and operated Coastal Forces under the general direction of Fotali (Flag Officer,

---

[1] Brig. T. B. L. Churchill, C.B.E., M.C.
[2] Elements of No. 9 (Army) and No. 43 (R.M.) Commando served in the island for certain periods. The brigade was supported by the Raiding Support Regiment and, later, by 111th Field Regiment, R.A., commanded by Lt.-Col. J. Elliott. The island was reinforced at different times by a Light A.A. Battery (Bofors) and a Heavy A.A. Battery (3.7-inch). Col. Hugo Meynell, O.B.E., looked after the administrative side of the garrison. Two surgical teams worked under Major Ricketts, R.A.M.C., who did outstanding work, especially in the early days when equipment had to be improvised. There were other ancillary units impossible to list here.

Taranto, and Liaison, Italy), who was then Rear-Admiral C. E. Morgan.

MTB and MGB operations continued in January as far as weather permitted. On the 13th/14th two MTBs sailed from Komiza to endeavour to intercept German troops invading Brac. The boats were 651, commanded by Lt. K. M. Horlock, with the S.O., Lt. Scott, embarked, and 226 (Lt. Hyslop).

Off the island they sighted a small merchant ship, and Hyslop chased it into Sumartin Harbour. He then patiently waited for her to secure alongside and then torpedoed her, killing two birds with one stone, since the sunken vessel prevented that section of the pier being used. The two boats then sighted a Siebel ferry. Horlock fired two torpedoes, but they failed to hit, and Scott ordered both boats to attack with gunfire. The ferry was damaged but not seen to sink.

A number of MTBs and MGBs were lying in Komiza towards the end of January, but there were not always enough Vospers or "Dogs" to make up homogeneous units and it was the practice for mixed patrols to go to sea—as in the case of the Sumartin Harbour attack.

There were some advantages in this, but for a variety of reasons (different operating speeds, engine silencers and gun armament) boats tended to prefer their own kind and the mixed marriage never caught on—certainly never when a like bed-fellow was disengaged for the night.

On the 29th January Bligh (662) and Bowyer (97) were sent out on patrol under instructions from Lt.-Cdr. Giles. They were to go to the area of the Drevnik Channel, some eighteen miles east of Split. It was the first time Bligh had led a unit in the Adriatic.

The boats left Komiza at 1750. It was always stirring to leave Komiza Harbour—at that time the sally port of an island besieged—on an offensive operation, but more so to do it by day, when the Partisans' oriflamme "Zivio Drug Tito" ("Long live leader Tito") was to be seen painted on the walls of the houses overlooking the harbour, than by night, when the Partisan sentry at the end of the jetty was liable to fire his loaded rifle at any boat under way, as all movement was to him potentially hostile, from whatever direction.

It was quite a good night for MTBs. Fine, wind from the north-west at 10 knots, a quarter moon, sea and swell slight. And, looking not unlike an elongated penny-farthing, the unit reached the patrol area at 1945.

German recognition cartridges were fired from the surface near

Drevnik Mali, and it seemed a fair guess that the boats had been sighted. But as the surface craft were more likely, at that time of night, to be E-boats than coastwise shipping, Bligh decided to use an old ruse to attract the enemy.

A small smoke-float was dropped and a calcium flare thrown on to the water underneath it, which from a distance gives a creditable impression of a small surface craft on fire. But no E-boats swallowed the bait, although a small, fast-moving boat appeared from behind Arkandjel and made towards the "fire". But this one was too elusive and disappeared when the boats gave chase.

Bligh withdrew a little to the westward of the "fire", which soon went out, and decided to lie stopped on hydrophone watch. None of 662's crew had any faith in this piece of apparatus, which, of archaic appearance and uncertain performance, had never even managed to pick up the trot-boat at 200 yards in broad daylight. But, thought Bligh, it gives the chaps something to do and need not detract from the night-vision of the bridge look-outs.

The boats were lying about three miles to the southward of Ploca Point. The moon had gone down, and it was dark. There was enough wind and sea to cause slapping and banging under the chine, and the boats were given a petulant irregular motion. The cocoa could not be put on the chart table. The telegraphist grew irritable in the W/T office. The coastline appeared to recede. Nothing would be seen. ("Just like a hundred other patrols," thought Bligh. "All that silly business," thought Bowyer). And then, in a voice full of disbelief, the hydrophone operator reported propeller noises ahead.

He had won. The bridge did not see "dark objects" until about a minute later. The hydrophone reported that the noises were moving from right to left. The bridge could now distinguish two shapes moving at slow speed from east to west. Enemy in sight. Green "Ns" to Bowyer. Start main engines. Up hydrophone. All guns on target. Enemy sighting report. Under way. "I's" to Bowyer. 16 knots.

As the range began to shorten the enemy could be distinguished as two vessels, the one astern looking like a small tanker. But no escort could be seen and it was clearly to be a gun action. The boats opened fire at just under half a mile, and ceased fire when the distance had closed to about fifty yards. There had been no evidence of any return fire. But, oh, the shouting. Bitter, aggrieved wailing that was intensely pathetic. "Italiani! Italiani! Italiani!" It was as if the mere statement of that fact not only excused them from participation in the war but at the same time accused their attackers of an excessive breach of proper behaviour. Bligh felt rather upset.

Both the enemy ships were lying stopped, with the tanker blowing off a lot of steam. Bowyer was sent alongside to investigate the situation and report. He later said: "I was ordered to close the enemy. I picked up three Italians from the water, leaving one dead whom we were unable to bring aboard. I then went alongside the tanker, and to my inquiry 'Sprechen sie Deutsch?' they continued to shout 'Italiani! Amici!'

"Their love for the Germans was only less than that for war. I took off five Italians, three of whom carried suitcases, apparently ready packed for such an emergency. The tanker was marked with a German cross. She was armed with what looked like a 3-inch aft and a 20-mm. forward. The after gun was surrounded with recumbent bodies, apparently the German gun's crew. The vessel was seriously damaged, but not sinking fast."

Bligh decided that the tanker had better be sunk. If 97 fired a torpedo she would have to return to the Italian mainland for a reload.[1] He thought it better to use gunfire. She was shelled for about five minutes and then her bows rose slowly in the air. The telegraphist was called up on to the bridge to be given visual proof that the struggle availed something. She slid stern first under the water at about 2330.

Attention was directed on to the other vessel, a schooner. She was damaged and, as far as could be seen, abandoned. MTB 97 dropped a depth-charge set to 50 feet underneath her, which immediately changed her silhouette. But as she did not settle very fast she was shelled for a few minutes and left well on fire, a total loss.

MTB 97 then came alongside 662 and transferred the eight survivors, of whom one was seriously wounded and six were slightly wounded. The master of the tanker was deeply grateful for being taken prisoner. Once the shooting had started he had expected death.

Bligh considered there had been enough disturbance to freeze any coastal shipping in the vicinity for some hours, that if any of the E-boats whose presence had been suspected earlier were coming to the rescue they would by then have arrived, and that early interrogation by a skilled questioner might elicit information of immediate operational interest. Accordingly the boats returned to Komiza, and after

[1] Spare torpedoes were not kept at Komiza.

running the gauntlet of Partisan sentries along the western shores of Vis they tied up alongside at 0145.

Merlin Minshall cheerfully got out of bed to question the prisoners. It was learnt that the tanker was the *Folgore*, of 330 gross tons, which had been manned by Italians, with Germans as guns' crews: these had all been killed in the shelling. The *Folgore* had been lying idle for many months in Durazzo and was, that night, on passage to Sibenik. Her survivors had no knowledge of any other shipping movements, north-wards or southwards, in the near future. Her consort on the last voyage had been an armed schooner.

It so happened that a week later Lancaster took some prisoners, among whom was one Normanno Penso. He had been on the schooner when she was sunk. She was the moto veliero *Roma*, of 120 tons net, carrying a cargo of 65 tons of cement. She had a crew of five Italians and one German (who looked after the gun). They had all rowed ashore soon after their vessel was damaged and had sat on the beach watching the two ships being sunk. They had salvaged from the *Roma* the upper half of one of her masts.

.   .   .   .   .   .

On the night of 31st January David Scott sailed with MTBs 85 (Hyslop), 297 (Woods) and 298 (Shore) and did a repeat performance near Silba Island, sinking a 120-ton and 40-ton schooner with gunfire and depth-charges. Both vessels were on passage from Zara to Fiume (now called Rijeka) and Scott took two German and six Italian prisoners, who were brought back to Komiza for Merlin Minshall's attention.

Two nights later Bligh (662) and Hughes (MTB 649) went among the islands to the north of Sibenik, and there let off the biggest firework they had ever seen.

Leaving Komiza after an early tea, the boats set off to patrol between Rogoznica (by this time called, inevitably, Rogers Knickers) and the Zlarin Channel. They passed close to Ploca Point and then inside Smokvica Island, pausing to look into Rogoznica on the way north.

At 1915 the unit stopped near Lukvenjak and Bligh ordered a small boat to close 662. Three fishermen were taken on board for questioning, and retention. They were, they said, Partisan sympathisers and alleged that there were no German ships south of Sibenik and that Rogoznica, which had run out of food, was daily expecting supplies. Their views were noted and their fishing licence, issued by Der Hafenkapitan

Rogoznica, was confiscated. They were sent below for a good meal.

The moon was bright and high in the eastern sky, the wind fitful, the sea like glass. There was no sea horizon anywhere round the compass. Nothing but islands. Little ones like haystacks, tiny ones like conning towers, long flat slabs like permanent smoke streaks, pyramids, cones and crouching animals. None friendly—they knew; none hostile—they hoped.

At 2030 the unit stopped very close to Obonjan and drifted towards Zmajan with the ancient hydrophone probing the water and picking up the swirl of the sea round the islands—an uncanny noise like vast breathing and superficially inexplicable since the surface looked so still. But no propellers, and after half an hour the boats went slowly towards Murter.

At 2130 Bill Darracott, the First Lieutenant of 662, said, from his seat on the wing of the bridge, and in the conversational tone he reserved for really important statements, "There's a three-masted vessel off the starboard bow."

Bligh flashed green "Ns" to Hughes and increased speed towards the enemy, who was steering south-east at about 8 knots. He aimed to open fire with the moon hanging like a well-fired star-shell over the enemy's masts, and then pass under her stern to seal off the gap between Tijat and Logorun.

The enemy sighted the boats after a minute and shot a bright white flare into the air—a recognition signal—which lit her guns' crews training round on to 662. Both sides opened fire together at about 150 yards, but the enemy did not fire for long. It is not difficult to hit at that range, and 662's gunners, who had recently had ample practice against the Folgore, were determined not to risk further rebukes for sluggishness.

The enemy was hit all along the hull and the deck, and 662, with everything firing—including the bridge Lugers—passed a few yards under the enemy's stern, warmed by a large fire burning on her after-structure. Hughes followed up with another close gun-run and started a fire on the fo'c'sle.

The enemy had swung round to port and was moving very slowly through the water. She was indisputably on fire. Some of her crew were seen jumping overboard. But it was unlikely that she was holed near the waterline, and both boats had another gun-run to put the matter beyond doubt. The boats then circled round to pick up survivors, including one very fine athlete who swam much faster than any of the others despite his great-coat, pack and leather boots. Twelve were saved.

Flares and tracer were rising from the burning ship. Her ready-use lockers seemed to be blowing up, and Bligh withdrew the unit to the westward to lie stopped on hydrophone watch. The enemy burned with heart-rending vigour (remember that the watchers themselves stood on wooden platforms on top of petrol tanks) and beauty.

The sea was a mirror. The outward curve of an exploding fragment grew upwards and downwards. Green, red and white signal flares were rising away and falling, falling away and rising, from the orange glow in the centre. It could not have been better contrived. And, like all fireworks before and since, too exciting to last.

At 2215 the enemy blew up with a really enormous explosion, smoke and flames going up to over 1,000 feet. All future November the Fifths had been used up that night—a prodigality born not of appetite but another's misfortune.

The unit resumed patrol, very reluctantly, in the southern part of the area and got back to Komiza rather late in a thick mist. It was learnt from questioning the prisoners that the ship destroyed had been called the *Francesca di Rimini*, of 350 tons. On her last voyage she had carried 320 tons of ammunition—mostly for 105-mm. guns—10 tons of stores, 15 tons of blankets, one lorry and a motor-cycle. She had had twenty-five German soldiers as passengers, who were all thought to have perished. The crew had consisted of five Germans to man the guns and nine Italians (including the master, Giovanni Belli).

Bligh's boat was hit by a few 20-mm. shells, but apart from a slight bruise on the lower right cheek of the Oerlikon loading number there were no casualties. MTB 649 had no damage or casualties.

For the first week in February the MTBs and MGBs were very busy. The sinking of the *Francesca di Rimini* on the 2nd/3rd was followed the next night by the sinking of the schooner *Amelia B* by MGB 643 (Hobday, S.O.) and MTB 667 (Jerram).

Jerram had arrived in the Adriatic with the boats sent from Bastia after the Bari air raid, and this was his first action in the area. The two boats sighted the *Amelia B* off Rogoznica, and a party from Hobday's boat boarded her, taking off ten Germans and four Italians. She was then sunk by gunfire.

On the same night two MTBs captured the biggest haul of prisoners the Adriatic had yielded so far. The MTBs were 298 (Shore) and 242, which was under the temporary command of S/Lt. R. P. M. Tonkin. Lancaster was the S.O. The two boats were off Silba Island when they sighted three vessels—two schooners and a large motor-boat. They took eighty-five prisoners, twenty of whom were Germans.

Hobday (643) and Bligh (662) sank a small tug with a 35-foot motor pinnace in tow some hundreds of yards off the entrance to Rogoznica on the 8th/9th; but from the 9th onwards the main Royal Navy activity off Vis was anti-invasion patrol, carried out mostly by destroyers and MLs.

But before we deal with the invasion threat to the island which Tito had ordered was to be the "Malta of the Adriatic" we must turn to the Aegean, where the Navy had been fighting a losing battle, mainly against their old enemy, the Luftwaffe.

CHAPTER XXVI

"ACCOLADE" AND AEGEAN NIGHTS

THE situation in the Aegean was, for the British, a frustrating one. In September, as mentioned earlier, Field-Marshal Baron von Weichs had recommended that the Germans withdraw from the Dodecanese, and Hitler had refused because of the psychological effect on Turkey and other neutrals.

The Allies were in a difficult position. The possibility of capturing Rhodes, the key island in the Dodecanese, and opening up the Aegean (Operation "Accolade") had been under consideration by the British since January 1943, and outline plans had been drawn up and later put back. Then, because of our unexpectedly light losses of assault shipping during the Sicily landings, an attempt was made to plan and mount "Accolade", using such forces as were available in the Middle East or earmarked for India.

"Once again," reported[1] Vice-Admiral Sir Algernon Willis, the C.-in-C., Levant, "it became necessary to call on Gen. Eisenhower to make up deficiencies, particularly in long-range fighters, and, as a result, 'Accolade' was cancelled by the decision of the Combined Chiefs of Staff at the Quadrant Conference.[2] The Commanders-in-Chief, Middle East, informed the Chiefs of Staff on 31st August that the only operations which could be mounted from the Middle East were:

(a) Small-scale raids.
(b) Sabotage and guerrilla operations by resistance groups.
(c) Unopposed 'walk-in' to areas evacuated by the enemy."

Before the Italian surrender, however, the Germans had planned to take over the entire military administration of Greece as from 6th September and had concentrated enough troops to carry it out. After

---

[1] Despatch to the Admiralty, 27th December 1943.
[2] The British-American conference at Quebec, August 1943.

the Italians did surrender, and the Germans had collected enough
vessels for seaborne operations, it became increasingly apparent to the
Allies that we had to have control of Rhodes. The Chiefs of Staff
finally gave permission for "Accolade" to be mounted before the end
of October.

Meanwhile the Germans were moving in large numbers of fighters
and bombers, calling in squadrons from France and—which shows the
importance they at least attached to the Aegean—the Russian front.
These planes caught the destroyers *Intrepid* and *Queen Olga* in Leros
Harbour on the night of 26th September and sank them both.

A number of special operations were being carried out by MLs and
the Levant Schooner Flotilla, and we were getting information about
enemy shipping and troop movements from agents in the Piraeus, and
from Long Range Desert Group patrols in the Cyclades, far to the
north.

From the end of September the battle took the all-too-familiar
pattern—the pattern of Dunkirk, Norway, Greece, Crete and Malta:
the Luftwaffe dominated everything. Opposing them were six Spitfires at Kos. Most of the other islands were out of range of aircraft
from Egypt and Cyprus, so Kos had to fall. This happened on 3rd
October.

Immediately cruisers and destroyers left Malta for the Aegean to
give much-needed help, and established patrols from 5th/6th November onwards. The next night they entered the Aegean after an enemy
report from the submarine *Unruly* and wiped out a convoy believed
to be carrying an invasion force to Leros.

For some days the Luftwaffe had been stepping up their attacks on
Leros, making many heavy attacks on the harbour with upwards of
forty Ju.88s and thirty Ju.87s (the vulture-like dive-bombers better
known as Stukas).

The experience of an ML gives an idea of what the situation was
like, and ML 835 has been chosen. She was commanded by an Aus-
tralian, Lt. Brian Close.[1] This officer had come out to the Mediterranean as First Lieutenant of ML 135 (Lt. E. Davies) with the 3rd ML
Flotilla.

In March 1941, shortly after the two boats of the 3rd Flotilla arrived
in Malta from Gibraltar, an attempt was made to pass two more of
them through to Malta, but they were lost (see page 44). The rest
of the 3rd Flotilla remained at Gibraltar, and in June 1942 MLs 121,

[1] Now Lt.-Cdr. B. Close, D.S.C., R.A.N.R.

135, 134, 168, 459 and 462 sailed to join the escort for Convoy WS 19Z as it passed through the Straits of Gibraltar for Malta (Operation "Harpoon") when only two of the merchant ships reached Malta.

The MLs, which had been fitted with Oropesa sweeps, then stayed at Malta minesweeping and were for a considerable time the only surface vessels at the island. Before Close left he had experienced 1,120 air raids and his flotilla had swept more than a hundred mines, ML 135 cutting thirty-five of them.

The 3rd Flotilla in 1943 took part in the Pantelleria, Sicily and Salerno landings—by which time Close had been appointed C.O. of 135. He left her to commission 835 at Cairo, and this was completed by August.

On 20th September, as the Luftwaffe was increasing its activities, Close was sent with 835 from Beirut to Casteloriso, the tiny island just off the south-western Turkish coast and most easterly of the Dodecanese.

Close writes: "We left Casteloriso at dusk on 21st September and hugged the Turkish coast, past enemy-held territory, to Leros. We were bombed an hour after arriving, and the bombing then went on, continuously.

"We fuelled at dusk and were sent on patrol at night, being told to hide as best we could during the day, using camouflage nets. The instructions were: 'No friendly ships in the vicinity—anything large, report; anything small, attack.' We were armed with Bofors and Oerlikons.

"Conditions were such that there were no reliefs, and therefore no nights off. Nor was there any rest during the day because of the bombers. First a search plane would locate us, and then about an hour later a bomber would attack.

"We found it necessary to keep a sentry continuously on deck, so that as soon as we were spotted by the search plane we could get under way before the bomber arrived. They found their 112-foot-long target, moving at 20 knots, very hard to hit; and although we had several near-misses (one ten feet away) which covered us with spray, very little damage was done apart from broken glass and crockery.

"Under the strain of waiting, watching and moving, our nerves got very frayed, and this strain was increasing all the time.

"On the 28th, while anchored in Turkish waters, a Ju.88 circled us and flashed a challenge. While hurriedly weighing anchor we flashed back with our lamp badly trained, and that delayed him long enough for us to get under way before he finally attacked. This was the day that the Army called for air assistance, and an R.A.F. Wellington appeared on the scene and dropped its bombs on us.

"On the night of 8th October, while patrolling in a reefy area east of Leros, we sighted and challenged a ship,[1] which was doing 4 knots. She did not reply, and increased speed to 14 knots, opening fire at the same time. We also increased speed and returned the fire, the ship being nicely silhouetted against the moon. Soon she caught fire and beached.

"As by this time the crew of 835 were on the verge of break-up because of the lack of sleep and general strain, I requested permission by radio to return to Alexandria, but was told to anchor 835, take all the crew ashore, and sleep for twenty-four hours.

"We did this, placing a sentry on a small hill, and turned in under a hedge. Soon a sentry brought in a 'Greek' who said he was Major Malley of the Irish Fusiliers. I did not believe him, but it turned out later that he was!

"After our rest we shot down a Ju.88 over Leros."

The ML had, apart from this brief rest, been almost continually on patrol for ten days. On the eleventh day she was finishing a patrol at dawn and heading for Levitha Island, where Close was going to hide up.

At 0625 the crew heard planes approaching. Within seconds they sighted them—six Ju.88s, which promptly attacked the ML as it weaved at high speed, trying to dodge the bursting bombs. Close managed to avoid any direct hits, but a near-miss put the port engine and the W/T out of action and riddled the dinghy with splinters. Within a very short time all the ready-use ammunition had been fired off at the attacking planes and Close ordered a smoke-screen to give the gunners time to reload.

Fifteen minutes later the attack started again. Eight more Ju.88s appeared, and with them were two single-engined Me.109 fighters. This time the Ju.88s attacked singly, with the Me.109s diving down to try to riddle the ML with cannon-fire.

In 835 the gunners fired hundreds of rounds trying to beat off the planes; but soon the craft was running dangerously short of ammunition. Several near-misses caused more damage and she took a list to port. Close "decided to make for a harbour and get the crew ashore

---

[1] This was the 1,200-ton Italian steamer *Volta*.

to safety, as the ship was in such a bad state I considered it was impossible to fight off a further attack".

Once in harbour he manœuvred 835 in close against and parallel to the shore. He had barely anchored when the Luftwaffe attacked again. He immediately ordered the crew to abandon ship and take shelter. All of them swam ashore safely; and finding an old observation post, they took shelter in it.

Later Close and his First Lieutenant, Lt. T. F. A. Winter, and the motor mechanic, Petty Officer Chandler, returned to 835 to inspect the damage. One engine was started, and using a system of makeshift telegraphs the craft was moved to a (relatively) safer position at the foot of some nearby cliffs.

This was hardly done when another bombing attack started. Close ordered both men to abandon ship, but Chandler stayed a moment to break the main switches. He was still on board when the first bomb dropped and was soon wounded, losing the use of a leg.

He tried to swim ashore after Close and Winter, but Winter had to swim out and help him in. The three men hid among the rocks, but blast from one of the bombs knocked Close unconscious and Winter was the only mobile man left. He went to get help.

The bombers and fighters kept on attacking, and for the next one and a half hours they periodically machine-gunned the rocks where Close and Chandler were hiding, Close having by this time regained consciousness. During a lull it was possible to get Chandler to a small farm, where a donkey was commandeered to carry him. With the assistance of two Italians sent along to help by Winter, Close and Chandler managed to get back to the observation post and rejoin the rest of the crew.

The air attacks on the ML kept up for the rest of the day, and towards the late afternoon Close decided to get ready to move her to a safer anchorage at dusk. The crew were gathered together for the attempt, but yet another air attack started—the fifty-seventh in less than ten hours—and either a bomb or bullet set the ML on fire, and within a few moments she was ablaze from stem to stern. Finally she blew up and then sank.

Close and his crew were rescued by another ML two days later.

．　　　．　　　．　　　．　　　．

On 9th October all Commanders-in-Chief in the Mediterranean met at Tunis to discuss the situation and finally decided there were not enough forces to mount "Accolade". We should, however, try to hold Leros (which was by now being supplied by submarines) and Samos as long as possible.

The island of Kalimno was captured by the Germans on the 8th, and on the 11th the small British garrison on Symi was evacuated after a heavy dive-bombing attack. Naxos and Levitha fell on the 12th, followed by Stampalia on the 24th.

. . . . .

The first successful MTB action in the Aegean during this period was fought on 19th/20th October by three boats of the 10th Flotilla. The boats were Elcos which, despite nearly two years' hard service, had made the thousand-mile trip from Messina to Alexandria without a hitch and moved up to operate from the island of Casteloriso.

The S.O. of the 10th Flotilla, Lt.-Cdr. C. P. Evenson, D.S.C., left the island at 1815 in MTB 315 (Lt. L. Newall, D.S.C., R.N.Z.N.V.R.) with 309 (Lt. R. Campbell, R.C.N.V.R.) and 307 (Lt. J. Muir). Deciding to get the full benefit of the moon, Evenson started to search the north coast of Kos. At 0045, off Cape Dephni, speed was reduced to 12 knots on silent engines, and with the shore a mile off he worked his unit eastwards. All was quiet.

He then crossed over to the south-west shore of Kalimno and again worked his way back to the north shore of Kos. Nothing was sighted. The islands, starkly beautiful in the moonlight, kept their secrets.

Then, at 0235, the outline of a ship was seen close in on the shore a mile away: red "Ns" to the other two boats, and they closed. As they got within 1,000 yards they could see it was an F-lighter with its bows inshore, like an alligator on a river's bank. At that moment a second vessel was spotted half a mile to the eastwards.

Evenson signalled Campbell, in the rear boat (309), to attack the F-lighter with torpedoes, while Evenson, after telling Muir, in 307, to stop, went off in 305 to attack the new target with torpedoes. It was a small coaster of 500–600 tons, and he closed to 600 yards. It was unwise to get any nearer because of the danger of his torpedoes hitting the shallow bottom.

Five minutes after sighting the F-lighter 315 fired her port torpedo at the coaster. It missed astern and blew up ashore. The starboard torpedo ran under the target and hit, apparently, an F-lighter which was probably unloading the steamer and inshore of it.

"This went up with a terrific explosion," Evenson reported, "with several succeeding detonations, and a large fire was started."

As 315 turned away, Evenson signalled 307 to attack the coaster with torpedoes. The target was nicely silhouetted against the burning F-lighter, and Muir fired his starboard torpedo, hitting the coaster's bow.

In the meantime Campbell had closed the F-lighter and fired both torpedoes, the starboard one set to run at 3 feet and the port at 5 feet. But he was unlucky. To his chagrin the starboard torpedo porpoised true but ran off at right angles. The port one passed under the target and ran up the beach without exploding.

• • • • •

Soon our forces in the Leros area started suffering casualties on a heavy scale. Three cruisers were hit and the destroyer *Panther* was sunk; while the *Hurworth*, the Greek destroyer *Adrias* and the *Eclipse* were mined.

Still the Coastal Forces patrols continued, and during the first few days of November more supplies were run into the hard-pressed island of Leros. The long-expected sea and airborne invasion started at 0100 on 12th November. All available British warships were sent up to the Leros area; and on the 14th/15th three MTBs left Casteloriso to patrol off the island. They were MTBs 315 (Newall, acting as S.O.), 266 (Broad) and 307. Unfortunately 307 developed a leak and had to return to Casteloriso.

As usual, the MTBs were fired on by our own coastal batteries at Leros, without damage; and then, at 0513, Newall spotted two R-boats 300 yards away, laying a thick smoke-screen close inshore north of Alinda Bay. He made an enemy report and closed the two boats. At that moment shore searchlights were switched on, and in their glare he saw about a dozen landing-craft of various types heading shore-wards. The nearest, similar to our own LCIs and full of troops, was 100 yards away.

The boats swung into the usual routine: Flag 5—gun attack—and close. At fifty yards Newall and Broad opened fire with all guns that would bear. The landing-craft started altering course violently, but the two MTBs kept station on it, pouring 2,000 rounds into the vessel at point-blank range. Fire broke out in several places and the enemy stopped.

As the two MTBs moved away the two R-boats opened fire at long range; but Newall was more interested in the landing-craft. He was preparing to attack a large power-driven barge when a destroyer was sighted in the searchlights. Ordering Broad to attack the barge, Newall prepared for a torpedo attack on the destroyer.

Broad cut in close to the barge and dropped depth-charges, which, as Newall wrote later, exploded and the barge "disintegrated satisfactorily, emptying her big load of troops into the water".

The destroyer then challenged and was identified as the *Echo*. She had just been into Leros, landed troops, and come out again. She also attacked landing-craft, and as daylight was fast approaching she and the two MTBs withdrew.

The next night the same three MTBs, 315, 366 and 307, took more troops to Leros, but the situation was critical. On the 16th the island surrendered, although the MTBs were busy for the next few nights evacuating small parties of men.

As the Germans had ample shipping to capture Samos, the British evacuated. This was followed by the evacuation of Casteloriso on 27th/28th November, although a party of fifty men was left on the island to simulate full occupation, as it was intended to continue to use it as an advanced MTB base.

It was hard for the sailors and soldiers fighting in the Aegean area during these eight desperate weeks to understand why a few fighter squadrons and several thousand men could not have moved over from Italy; and it may well be that future historians will deal harshly with this phase of the war.

.   .   .   .   .

For the next four months operations in the Aegean were of the "In, bash, and out" variety: raids by MTBs and MGBs, Commando landings from MLs and caïques, various raids by R.A.F. and U.S. planes, and patrols by submarines. For reasons of space it is not possible to follow the devious and widespread day-to-day operations of the boats.

Chapter XXVII

"THE F-LIGHTER BLEW UP"

AT the beginning of 1944 the Allied armies were still held many miles south of Rome by a stubborn Kesselring. The fighting was extremely bitter and a deadlock was almost reached. The Allies then decided to land a force at Anzio, thirty miles south of Rome, to cut the two main roads behind the German lines, and thus, it was hoped, force the Germans to withdraw. In actual fact Kesselring brought up more troops instead and the Anzio bridgehead had to be supplied from the sea for four months, not the planned fifteen or so days.

The "Dog" Flotillas had been re-formed and in the 56th MTB/MGB Flotilla every commanding officer was a Canadian. A Canadian, Doug Maitland, had been promoted to Lt.-Cdr. and made the S.O. The boats were 657 (Maitland), 658 (Burke), 663 (Ladner), 640 (Campbell McLachlan), 633 (Keefer) and 655 (Pickard). This Flotilla was at Maddalena.

Two German destroyers, or large torpedo-boats, were becoming a nuisance, and the MTBs and MGBs had had two or three encounters with them without securing any hits.

On 21st January the Anzio landing was to take place. Coastal Forces had many jobs to do, and it is impossible to cover them all in this book. The Maddalena boats, with four American PT-boats under Lt.-Cdr. Stan Barnes, had to create a diversion at the port of Civita-vecchia, some twenty miles north of Anzio, where the main landings were to take place. The diversion was the usual routine—loudspeakers playing "invasion fleet" records, fireworks to simulate the flashes of big guns firing, shouting, small arms being fired—to make it look as though a large-scale landing was about to take place.

At 1700 on the 21st six "Dogs" left Bastia to carry out their part of Operation "Lurcher 1"—the code name for the diversion for the Anzio landing. They were MGBs 657 (Maitland, S.O.), 658 (Corny Burke), 663 (Tommy Ladner), 640 (Cam McLachlan), 659 (Peter Barlow), and MTB 655 (Pickard).

By 2109 they were patrolling between Giglio Island and Giannutri Island, and at 2341 rendezvoused the American PT-boats under Stan Barnes (PTs 209, S.O. embarked; 203, 211 and 217) off Giglio. Forming up in two columns, the boats moved off towards Civitavecchia and the release position (i.e. the record-playing and firework-lighting position: had it been a real landing, the position where landing-craft would have been lowered from their parent ships).

Up to now the Senior Officer, Inshore Squadron's orders were being carried out to the letter; but since the enemy did not have a copy of the plans, he was not to know that the coast of Civitavecchia was a place to avoid, for the time being at least.

The two columns of boats were moving south-east at 13 knots and approaching the release position when at 0147 Stan Barnes, in PT 209 called up Maitland on the R/T and reported that his radar showed possible targets at Red 40,[1] distance 2,800 yards. He and Maitland decided that the "Dogs" should check up on these while the PT-boats went on to carry out the preordained part of "Lurcher 1".

The "Dogs" turned twenty-five degrees to port, increasing to 15 knots. Five minutes later the cruiser *Dido* joined in the diversion and started bombarding Civitavecchia, her shells whining over the "Dogs" to burst inshore, and Stan Barnes' PTs started their "large-scale landings".

It was a very dark night, with visibility about 500 yards. As the "Dogs" approached the target, the radar set on Maitland's boat was sweeping the horizon with its invisible eyes and at 0204 picked up a target 1,500 yards ahead and another at 1,700 yards Green 20,[2] both closing.

Maitland quickly flashed this news to the boats astern, signalling that he intended passing them to port. All guns trained on to the bearing. He followed this with "I's" and increased to 18 knots.

(From now on the wording in italic is taken from Maitland's action report.)

0207. *Target in sight ahead, one F-lighter escorted by two E-boats, on either beam. Enemy course S.45° E., speed 7 knots.*

The "Dogs", bows lifting as they cut through the waves at 18 knots, came down astern of the three enemy ships: there was no indication

---

[1] Forty degrees on the port bow. Green is to starboard, Red to port.
[2] Twenty degrees on the starboard bow.

that they knew five MGBs and an MTB were following up fast in their wake. Soon the range was 1,000 yards . . . 800 . . . 600 . . . 400 . . . 200.

> 0211. *F-lighter to port, range 200 yards. Unit in Order 1 engaged in succession, scoring many hits with 2-pounder, 20-mm. Oerlikon and 6-pounder.*

All the boats, which were in line ahead, opened fire at once, pouring a tremendous broadside into the F-lighter and E-boats. The enemy ships returned the fire for a few moments, but the gunfire from the MGBs cut down the enemy crews at their guns and sent others ducking for shelter. The five boats moved down the side of the enemy convoy. The two E-boats were heavily engaged by the last two boats in the line, 659 and 655.

> 0213. *Altered to reciprocal course of north-west to make second run. The F-lighter was again heavily hit, the E-boat stationed on the F-lighter's port beam was hit hard and set ablaze. During this run the E-boat stationed on the F-lighter's starboard beam had cut through our line between 659 and 655, the latter ship scoring many hits on this E-boat, which, however, made off and was not seen again.*

The E-boat remaining on the far flank had stopped. When the other E-boat cut loose and ran between 659 and 655, the MGBs did not know whether he regarded this as his only way to safety, if his steering was out of action, or he intended to ram.

> 0216. *Altered to reciprocal course of south-east, for third run. Both targets were again hit hard and left ablaze, both stationary and all gunfire from them ceased.*
> 0222. *MTB 655 signalled "Damaged, am disengaging to the west".*
> 0223. *Altered course towards F-lighter, reduced speed to 12 knots, range to 200 yards. The unit scored many more hits and left her well ablaze.*

From the time of firing until the F-lighter and remaining E-boat were stopped and blazing the action had lasted exactly five minutes. Two minutes after Maitland ceased firing, shore batteries opened up and the boats spent a short time evading the shells and then went off to search for Pickard and his damaged MTB. They were still doing this when . . .

> 0240. *F-lighter blew up, the multi-coloured flash and smoke rising 1,500 feet in the air. Altered course to west, increased speed to 18 knots.*

An hour later Pickard reported by R/T that his damage was repaired, and the boats joined up with him at daylight. Three boats—Maitland's, Burke's and Pickard's—had been superficially damaged by gunfire, 658 having had a burst of 20-mm. fire hit her pom-pom, wounding the gunner and fatally wounding a loading number. Another burst in the port waist had entered the wing petrol tank, but it was full and luckily did not catch fire.

The damage to Pickard's boat was caused by two 20-mm. shells which hit exhaust pipes, causing gas to escape into the engine-room, almost overpowering the mechanics.

When forwarding Maitland's action report to the Senior Officer, Inshore Squadron, the commanding officer at Bastia, Cdr. Bobby Allan, added the comment: " . . . this was the first time that the newly-constituted 56th Flotilla operated as such. After such a start it is satisfactory to note that their tails are nearly as high as the explosion they caused. The tactics were thoroughly aggressive and the results most satisfactory."

.   .   .   .   .   .

The next night Maitland, in 657, took out 663 (Ladner) and 659 (Barlow) to patrol farther north than the previous night's hunting-ground. Leaving at 1745, the three boats started their patrol at 2125, sweeping up and down the Italian coast. All was quiet until, as Maitland writes in his report:

> 2327. *Possible radar target Green 10, range 4,200 yards.*
> 2331. *MGB 663 also reported possible radar target Green 10, range 4,000 yards.*
> 2341. *Radar confirmed three or more targets, range 2,800 yards. Altered course to S.10° E., speed increased to 16 knots to close target.*

Maitland was happy: three targets. "I's" to the boats astern, hands moved down to turn the handle on the port side of the bridge to increase revolutions, · the boats surged forward, and the gunners checked over their guns and eased themselves into comfortable positions.

> 2347. *Three targets in sight Green 10, approximately 700 yards.*
>
> 2349. *Range closing, now observed six F-lighters in two columns of three with two or more E-boats dispersed on either side of starboard column. Altered course to starboard in order to pass astern of convoy and attack enemy's starboard column.*

This was a bigger convoy than Maitland had expected; but it was a welcome target for the 56th Flotilla's second outing. As 657 swung round to port the other two boats followed him round.

> 2351. *Altered course to port. Last F-lighter of starboard column fine on port bow, range 400 yards closing. Enemy's course south, speed 8 knots. Leading ship of starboard column commenced flashing us on a white lamp. This ship was observed to be much larger than the others and thought to be a destroyer or escort vessel. The leading ship of the port column was also larger than the F-lighters but indistinguishable.*

Maitland had only a few seconds to finally plan his attack. Over the R/T the other boats heard him: "Hullo, Tommy and Pete, this is Doug. We will each take the last F-lighter, then shift target after we pass him. Over."

When only 100 yards from the F-lighter all three MGBs fired, and at the same time every gun in the enemy convoy which could bear opened up. At such a range the MGBs could not miss and the F-lighter was ablaze in a few seconds.

An E-boat cut through the convoy's starboard column ahead of the blazing F-lighter, and 663 and 659 opened fire on it. Heavily hit with 6-pounder, 2-pounder and 20-mm. shells, the E-boat's guns were silenced, and after an internal explosion she vomited flames.

By this time the large escort was keeping up a heavy fire of 88-mm., 40-mm., Bofors and 20-mm. All three MGBs shifted fire to it and the F-lighter just astern. But 659 was hit and had to pull out of the line with one engine and her 2-pounder gun out of action.

With one boat short, any element of surprise lost, and in view of the large escorts (which completely outgunned the MGBs) Maitland decided the time had come to break off the action. With the score two nil for the Canadians, it was a sensible decision.

.   .   .   .   .

The next night, the third in a row, MGB 658 (Burke) and MTB 655 (Pickard) sailed with PT 217 to patrol off Capraia Island. As Maitland had been out two nights running and had little or no sleep, Burke was the S.O. and the PT-boat was to be used as a radar guide and a reserve unless torpedoes were wanted.

The three boats were on patrol by 1946, and one of Burke's officers describes the action:

"Some four hours later we got a signal from the Senior Officer, Inshore Squadron[1] to proceed much farther north and patrol from Vada Rocks to Piombino.

"It was 0230 before we got on this new patrol, but the excitement began when the R/T loudspeaker on the bridge gave its tell-tale 'click-click' and the C.O. of PT 217 reported a radar echo bearing 085 degrees, distance four miles, enemy course north, and speed 12 knots.

"Corny immediately altered course to the south-east and increased speed in order to gain bearing and get inshore of the target. It was a very dark night, and the sky in the north-east was particularly black with low-lying clouds.

"Unfortunately it soon became obvious that the nearness of the Vada Rocks would mean it was too late to make an inshore attack, so instead Corny swung out to the port (seaward) flank of the convoy. When the range was 500 yards the convoy appeared to consist of six F-lighters in two columns, and only one E-boat seemed to be screening astern.

"Corny therefore spread the unit up to port and ordered a torpedo attack. PT 217 fired one fish at 300 yards, and although it ran true no hit was observed, and Corny immediately deduced that these lighters were running light and therefore ordered 655 to rejoin. PT 217 disengaged to the south-east and almost immediately the E-boat opened fire on her.

"This gave us an excellent opportunity and, moving round the stern of the convoy, we were able to get within 100 yards of the E-boat on her 'blind' side. When we opened fire the enemy obviously had no idea of our presence, and consequently our first salvoes, all hitting,

[1] Capt. N. V. Dickinson, D.S.O., D.S.C., R.N. At this time the boats in this area were under his operational control.

immediately set the E-boat on fire and stopped her within thirty seconds. Her return fire, never very effective, fizzled out rapidly.

"The convoy had scattered very quickly and it was now difficult to visualise the enemy dispositions. Over to the south-west the PT had made a great deal of smoke while disengaging, and this now hid part of the convoy.

"The next target was another E-boat, the nearest of a group of three enemy ships which opened fire at us at about 200 yards. Once again the concentrated fire of two 'Ds' seemed—not unreasonably—too much for an E-boat and we quickly silenced it and concentrated on a bigger vessel (appearing rather like a large trawler) which was firing 88-mm., 40-mm. and 20-mm. shells in profusion.

"Once again A. B. Howe, at Y gun (the old 6-pounder) was very accurate and secured many hits. Fire became so heavy at this stage that we disengaged to the northward, and in doing so Pick in 655 lost contact.

"On discovering this, he reported by R/T that he was heading westward, switched on his recognition lights for a split second (enough to let us know where he was), and began attacking an F-lighter on his way out.

"Corny was still well in contact with the enemy by radar, and at 0433 we closed in again to resume the attack under cover of heavy cloud. We were able to tackle a single F-lighter at 100 yards and made two runs at him, leaving him with fire aboard but still with one 20-mm. in action.

"Contact was then made with yet another F-lighter, which also seemed bewildered by the attack and hardly replied; and although he altered course, we got in two runs before heavy fire was brought to bear on us from a larger ship. This had a considerably higher freeboard than we had previously noticed, and we were forced to disengage.

"We had suffered hits by 20-mm. shells about the waterline in the last run and were making water in the engine-room, so we set off to the westward to meet up with Pick and with Doyle in the PT.

"Behind us the enemy ships could be seen firing at each other occasionally, and obviously a great deal of confusion and fear existed among the scattered ships."

Next day an intelligence report reached the Senior Officer, Inshore Squadron, from the R.A.F. and other sources, that one F-lighter and one E-boat had been sunk, three others damaged, and a 900-ton minelayer was aground near Vada Rocks, inshore of the position of the action.

.   .   .   .   .

In February German opposition stiffened. His F-lighter convoys moving up and down the West Italian coast were strengthened with large landing-craft mounting more of the high-velocity 88-mm. guns as well as 40-mm. and 20-mm. These, acting as LCGs, sailed as extra escorts with the E-boats.

The MGBs and MTBs from Bastia first ran into these enemy LCGs on the 7th/8th February ten miles off Giglio Island. Maitland was embarked in 658 as C.O. (Burke was ill) and S.O. of the unit, and with 659 and 640 slipped at 1800.

By 2207, with a full moon overhead robbing them of any chance of surprising an enemy, they were moving along in a calm sea at 11 knots.

Ten miles off the island the boats sighted an enemy convoy down-moon, about four miles away. It was impossible for the enemy to miss seeing the three boats silhouetted by the moon like moorhens on a mill-pond.

Four minutes later the convoy was seen to be two columns of F-lighters, six in all, escorted by a 2,000-ton "flak" ship ahead and a 1,500-ton "flak" ship close astern.

Maitland quietly changed positions so that the enemy was up-moon and approached them from astern. The "flak" ship astern of the convoy flashed a challenge on a white lamp and thirty seconds later both "flak" ships opened up with 88-mm. guns. Almost immediately all the F-lighters joined in with their 88s, 40-mm. and 20-mm. The 88-mm. guns were the same type that did so much damage to our tanks in the Western Desert, and were some of the most effective artillery produced in World War II.

A minute later shore batteries added their quota of shells and the fire from the convoy became very accurate, forcing the MGBs and MTBs to increase to 22 knots and withdraw under a smoke-screen, using the old dodge of dropping calcium flares. A little while later three of the F-lighters again opened fire with 88s.

It was hopeless for the boats to attempt to attack again, and after shooting up a lighthouse and watching the enemy convoy enter Porto San Stefano the boats returned to Bastia.

On the 13th/14th it was the same story again: this time MGBs 658 (S.O.) and 659, and PTs 215 and 203 sailed to patrol north of the Piombino Channel to Leghorn. For amorous couples in gondolas on the Venetian canals and for lovers walking the wide streets of Rome it was a wonderful night—no wind, a bright moon, extremely good visibility, and only a slight swell. For the MGBs it was the promise of the kiss of death.

Shortly after reaching the patrol area PT 215 developed a major engine defect and returned to base, and an hour later PT 203 reported possible radar target at Green 30, range 4,500 yards.

Two minutes later the boats sighted a convoy moving southwards, looking like beetles on a horizontal sheet of frosted glass. This is how Maitland described the next few minutes in his action report:

2305. *Convoy observed to be several F-lighters. PT 203 fired two torpedoes (range 2,000 yards plus), both running very erratic and missed well astern. PT 203 retired to seaward.*

2308. *Convoy abeam, seven F-lighters, one E-boat, distance by radar 2,200 yards. MGBs 658 and 659 turned to starboard coming on the convoy course of South 5° East. Unit reduced to 7 knots (convoy speed). Convoy plainly visible up in the path of the full moon.*

2311. *Observed two F-lighters had separated from convoy, placing themselves between us and the convoy, approximately 300 yards from the latter. For the following twenty minutes we stalked the convoy, but whenever we endeavoured to approach the convoy from astern or gain bearing on the beam the two F-lighters mentioned always placed themselves between us and the convoy. (They were obviously German LCGs.)*

2338. *. . . The two LCGs directly in the moon path bearing Red 50, range by radar 2,100 yards. We selected the leading LCG as target and opened fire with 6-pounder and 2-pounder.*

2338. *We had observed two hits with 6-pounder and several with 2-pounder. By this time the enemy fire from the LCGs and F-lighters in convoy (using 88-, 40- and 20-mm.) was beginning to get very accurate and concentrated. The unit disengaged to seaward under cover of smoke and calcium flares. . . .*

0050. *South of Leghorn, full moon overhead drawing to westward, visibility extreme. Decided it was useless to continue patrol as we could easily be observed from the shore. . . .*

Maitland, in his action report, added: "Under bright moonlight conditions with extreme visibility it was considered suicidal to close this convoy. . . ."

And Cdr. Allan added: "The fact that these aggressively-designed boats manned by remarkably aggressively-minded officers and men

N

cannot get to grips with the enemy is giving rise to a sense of frustration. It is, however, believed that the situation is fully appreciated and you[1] are aware of the various tactics and devices with which we are hoping to discomfort the enemy."

The "various tactics and devices" will be described later.

.   .   .   .   .

The PT-boats at Bastia were equipped with rockets during February, and their S.O. regarded them, according to a report by the C.C.F., "as weapons of extremely limited effectiveness which can only be used in smooth water and which are dangerous unless handled with extreme caution.

"The accuracy of the weapon is, of course, extremely limited. . . ." He tersely describes the terrifying effect of the rocket discharge as very nearly duplicating that of the rocket explosion.

"It is necessary for all hands to take cover when firing. Finally, once it has been decided to carry out a rocket attack and the rockets have been placed and armed, the boat is virtually committed to firing them, to free herself of her dangerous cargo."

.   .   .   .   .

By the beginning of March there were on the average twelve "Dog" boats in Bastia, with about eight operational at any one time. The problem of the enemy F-lighters along the coast was becoming a tough one, and a disappointing feature of the previous two months was the failure of torpedo attacks.

Having found the heavily-gunned enemy convoys all too responsive to gun attacks by the MGBs, every opportunity had been taken to attack with torpedoes. But although they were generally set at zero and two feet, of sixteen torpedoes fired there was only one "possible" hit.

With the enemy F-lighter convoys virtually immune from attacks by the guns of the MGBs and the torpedoes of the MTBs the position could have become serious; but Cdr. Allan, in conjunction with the Senior Officer, Inshore Squadron, worked out a method of attack using LCGs, MTBs, MGBs, and PT-boats.

In effect, Allan's plan was to form a "Battle Squadron"[2] in which

---

[1] The S.O., Inshore Squadron, to whom the action report was forwarded.

[2] In Home Waters a parallel though dissimilar method was later adopted. To trap E-boats with slower MGBs and MTBs, two or more divisions of boats were vectored on to targets by a control frigate which used its own radar and frequently had the use of aircraft.

the battleships would be the LCGs, each mounting two 4.7-inch guns, and the MTBs, MGBs and PTs would be the scouting forces. He proposed directing the attack from the radar screen of one of the PT-boats, rather like a fast-moving, complicated and dangerous game of chess in which mating was, so to speak, carried out with high-explosive.

The operation could be likened to a full-scale action between opposing fleets—except events moved a great deal faster—with Bobby Allan as the Allied admiral.

The immediate task, as Mrs. Beeton might well have laid it down, was first get your LCGs. Three were eventually forthcoming, and escorted by four MTBs and four PT-boats, Bobby Allan's "Battle Squadron" sailed on 27th March on Operation "Gun".

South of the Vada Rocks it found a convoy of six F-lighters escorted by two ex-Italian destroyers. From his radar screen Allan manœuvred his craft, illuminated the convoy with star-shell, engaged and totally destroyed all six F-lighters.

The Royal Marine gunners, using flashless ammunition, had only needed one sighting salvo, and in some cases hit with their first shell after shifting target.

The action has not been described in detail because Allan was, a month later, to fight an even more brilliant action, Operation "Newt", using the same tactics.

Bad weather stopped operations two nights after "Gun" and the LCGs retired for a refit during the full-moon period.

.   .   .   .   .

On 10th April an Italian boat, MAS 505, one of the many ships which were working with the Royal Navy after the surrender, left Maddalena bound for Bastia. She never arrived and was thought to have been mined.

In fact German naval records subsequently captured and translated at the Admiralty show that during the passage the crew shot the three officers and, deserting to the Germans, took the boat into San Stefano.

They were promptly interrogated by German Intelligence officers and revealed, among other things, the radio wavelengths used by Allied MTBs during operations, their patrol areas, convoy traffic in the area, the state of Maddalena Harbour, the number and type of British and American boats operating, and troop movements in Sardinia.

Chapter XXVIII

A STING IN THE NEWT'S TAIL

O N 24th/25th April Bobby Allan took his "Battle Squadron" to sea again, this time for Operation "Newt", the most successful action of its type ever fought. The "Battle Squadron" consisted of:

LCGs   14 (S.O., LCGs embarked), 19, 20.
MGBs 657 (S.O., MGB Escort embarked), 662, 660.
MTBs 640 (S.O., MTB Escort embarked), 633, 655.
PTs   218 (S.O., Operation, Cdr. Allan, embarked), 209 (Deputy Controller).
PTs   202 (S.O., Escorting Force), 212, 213.
PTs   211 (S.O., Close Radar Screen), 216.

The plan was that Bobby Allan, embarked in PT 218, would stay at the radar screen throughout the whole of the action, directing the various craft by R/T. It was to be, in fact, a vast game of chess played on a screen, with no restrictions (except speed) on the moves. His boat would stay with the main force, while PTs 202, 212 and 213 would be the Scouting Force, and are referred to in the narrative by that title.

Because of the great differences in speed of this motley force, the units sailed from Bastia at different times, the LCGs leaving at 1500, the MGBs under Maitland and MTBs under Bligh at 1800, and the PTs half an hour later.

The sea was calm, and what little breeze there was came from no specific direction, attaining the official description of "light variable airs". The whole force rendezvoused at 2000, formed up and moved off at 7 knots.

The following passages[1] in italic type are taken from German records:

[1] These captured German documents are at the Admiralty and were among many translated for this account. The Germans say they lost a total of eight ships, one less than we claimed. In night actions it is always difficult to accurately assess enemy losses.

At 2000 [the same time that the "Battle Squadron" rendezvoused] *three F-lighters, F.515, F.423 and F.621, and the tug* Tebessa, *left Leghorn with supplies for San Stefano, farther south down the coast. Also at sea in the area were three armed F-lighters* [this is the German description: they are almost certainly referring to their equivalent of our LCGs], *F.610, F.350 and F.589. Fifteen minutes later yet another convoy sailed for the area, to arrive in time for the action. This consisted of two patrol vessels, M.7607 and Vp.7013,[1] each of which was towing a barge. They left Porto Ferraio for Leghorn.*

At 2125 Allan detached his Scouting Force of three PT-boats in the Vada Rocks area, and at 2205 they reported a southbound convoy a mile from Vada Rocks.

Two minutes later Allan, in PT 218, picked up another radar contact off Piombino Point, well to the south of Vada. Within a short while he could also see on his own screen the convoy reported by the Scouting Force.

His "Battle Squadron" kept a steady course at 7 knots while he carefully plotted the two targets which he could, by now, see quite clearly on the screen. He wrote:

"Examination of the plot led me to believe that the target off Piombino, which was northbound and opening the coast, formed an escort group[2] which was probably going to rendezvous with the southbound convoy. I decided to attempt to cross the bows of this group, getting between it and the convoy. Course was therefore altered to the northward at 2300.

"It soon became evident that it was not going to be possible to pass ahead of the escort and still intercept the convoy, which, by now, was very close inshore.

"With the intention of passing under the escort group's stern, I altered course at 2320 to the southward, but shortly after this the enemy (i.e. the escort group) appeared to increase speed and alter course to the west, making interception almost inevitable.

"As any further alteration of course was likely to prejudice our chances of making contact with the convoy, I was very loath to take further avoiding action with regard to the escort and so maintained course and speed.

"By 2300 the escort group was three miles distant on a collision

---

[1] The former French fishing vessel *Louise Elise*.
[2] Allan's deduction was correct: these were F.610, F.350 and F.589.

bearing, and I decided that the enemy was aware of our presence and was determined to engage. As I considered that this engagement should be fought under conditions as favourable to us as possible, I altered course to steam parallel and reduced speed.

"At 2340 the enemy bore Green 30, range two miles, and a look-out bearing was passed to the LCGs."

Carefully Allan watched the three glowworm-like blobs on the radar screen which represented the enemy steering towards his own force. Then, a minute later, they seemed to alter course to starboard. He saw that if they stayed on their new course they would miss his "Battle Squadron".

This gave him his last chance of intercepting the convoy, which was the most important target, so as soon as it was clear the escort group could be avoided he ordered his own force to alter course to port. By stages he swung round 180 degrees and by R/T ordered the LCGs to make their maximum speed. Still the three blobs on the radar screen kept their course: the enemy escort group was not following, and gradually the range opened.

Allan then set a course to intercept the convoy.

He continues: "The first engagement then ensued. At 0001 the enemy bore Red 20, range 3,000 yards. Course was altered to starboard and an alarm bearing of Red 40 was passed. At 0005 the order was given to open fire."

As soon as Allan's alarm bearing was passed to the LCGs the Royal Marines swung their guns round in the darkness on to the targets. Some of the guns were loaded with star-shell fused to burst at 2,000 yards. Immediately the order was given to fire, star-shell arced across the sky, bursting to light up two F-lighters. Many of the shells landed among trees perched on the hills ashore and started fires.

The three ferry barges, F.515, F.423 and F.621, and the tug Tebessa, *were off San Vicenzo when attacked by MTBs and destroyers or torpedo boats. . . .*[1]

Allan reported: "At 0008 the LCGs appeared to check their fire. I immediately informed them there were many more targets and ordered them to search left. This they did, and a large ocean-going tug and more F-lighters were illuminated. The tug was hit repeatedly and sank, one F-lighter blew up, and another, which was seen by many, burned furiously before blowing up with a less spectacular explosion.

[1] The Germans did not realise they had been engaged by LCGs.

"As smoke from the fires (which were seen at Bastia) and the exploded and burning F-lighters obscured any further targets, course was altered away from the beach to intercept a further radar contact which had appeared to seaward."

> . . . *Two of the barges were set on fire and blew up. The third barge and tug were also sunk. . . . About 0020 star-shell and gunfire were observed by the three armed barges, F.610, F.350 and F.589* [the escort group nearly intercepted earlier], *and, realising that the southbound convoy was being attacked, proceeded to join in the battle. . . .*

In the meantime Allan ordered the MGB escort under Maitland (657, 662 and 660) to close the beach and dispose of any F-lighters there remained. One entirely undamaged F-lighter was found, abandoned except for a few hands. The MGBs engaged it with all guns and set it on fire. After blazing for some time it blew up with a great explosion.

The MGBs then closed to pick up survivors and found twelve. Six of them were Dutchmen who had earlier been picked up after the *Tebessa* sank.[1] Allan then ordered the MGBs to return independently to Bastia.

While the MGBs were detached, the other radar contact, the escort group, was being closed. Allan, still at his radar screen, saw that they had sheered off the coast when the firing stopped and were steering north. Setting an intercepting course, he ordered the LCGs to make their maximum speed so that he could intercept from landwards.

He continued: "The second action commenced by the firing of star-shell only. I had assumed that this force was the escort force previously encountered, and before engaging so heavily armed a unit I was anxious that its composition and position should be clearly established for all, and that the guns' crews should have a chance of sighting it.

"Immediately our star-shell burst the enemy fired a five-red-star recognition and I ordered cease-fire. Two minutes later, having informed the LCGs that the first rounds would count, I ordered them to open fire with all guns.

---

[1] These prisoners said that in addition to the three F-lighters of their convoy, two other F-lighters had joined later and were the first two to be sunk. Since no survivors returned to German hands, this accounts for the German admitted losses and British claims. Thus five F-lighters and the tug were sunk in this convoy—three definitely claimed by the LCGs, one by the MGBs, and the fifth, though not definitely claimed by the British, by the LCGs.

"The first salvoes hit two F-lighters and they never returned our fire. The third was not hit for two minutes, during which time it maintained a high rate of fire. PT 218 [the boat in which Allan was embarked] increased speed ahead of the LCGs, thus drawing the majority of the fire, but there were several near-misses on the LCGs.

"Many rounds passed close over PT 218, and at least two shells landed within ten yards; however, no casualties or damage were reported from any of our craft."

. . . *They were immediately engaged by the Allied force, and the leading barge, F.610, was repeatedly hit by large-calibre shells. At the same time F.350 received a direct hit and went up in flames. On F.610 a fire was started and ammunition began to explode, so an order was given to abandon ship. The barge developed a heavy list and finally sank with a loud explosion.*

The remaining barge, F.589, tried to escape behind a smoke-screen, but she was hit and severely damaged and two of her guns put out of action. A fire started in the ammunition, but this was extinguished by the crew. In a panic some of the men had jumped overboard. . . .

Allan, after describing how the first two F-lighters were set ablaze, goes on: "The third, which was hit and on fire, withdrew under a heavy smoke-screen. The W/T set in LCG 14 (the S.O., LCGs' vessel) was out of action, and as I feared the F-lighter was in danger of escaping I gave the order at 0110 to cease fire, and detached the Deputy Controller (PT 209) to lead the MTB force in to attack and destroy. This they eventually did, although it took some time, and they lost contact with the main force."

. . . *The enemy remained in the area illuminating with star-shell, and after about twenty minutes again contacted F.589 and inflicted further damage. The barge did not sink and was finally beached south of San Vicenzo. . . .*[1]

The Scouting Force, at 0120, then reported northbound targets ten miles to the northward. As the LCGs were too far away to intercept, Allan gave permission for the Scouting Force to attack with torpedoes. In this, the third action of the night, the enemy—another escort group —opened fire before the PT-boats were in a firing position. PT 202

---

[1] From this, it seems the PT-boats were somewhat over-optimistic.

fired a five-red-star recognition cartridge which happened to be aboard, and the enemy obligingly ceased fire.

This allowed the two boats (the third had returned with underwater damage) to make an unopposed final run-in, and each fired two torpedoes. One of the F-lighters blew up, sinking almost immediately. Heavy and accurate fire was opened by the other two lighters and the PTs withdrew under a smoke-screen.

There is no German report of this action; but they reported that at 0120—the time the Scouting Force reported the convoy—two patrol vessels, the M.7607 and Vp.7013, were each towing a barge in the Vada Rocks area when suddenly Vp.7013 blew up and sank. The Germans later concluded she had been hit with a mine or torpedo. It is hard to reconcile this with the gunfire the PTs reported, so there may have been yet another convoy in the area.

Earlier this convoy had seen the attack on the first convoy, and they reported that their barges had been brightly lit by the star-shell from the LCGs.

Allan then ordered the whole of his "Battle Squadron" to return to Bastia. The Scouting Force, after their attack, were told to proceed at slow speed well to the north, as the Deputy Controller (in PT 209) and the MTBs had been detached with orders to keep well astern, and with the MGBs returning independently, there remained as escort only the Close Radar Screen, PTs 211 and 216. These two boats were kept along the starboard beam of the LCGs, while Allan, in PT 218, remained close alongside, keeping a radar watch to port.

Continuing his description of the action, Allan wrote: "At 0400, Bastia's signal that an unknown enemy was stopped in a position three miles due west of Capraia was received. The time being what it was, I considered that this must be an E-boat force probably lying in wait for us returning.

"I was unable to get in touch with the MGBs which I expected might be in the area, and requested that Bastia should pass the signal to them. This was done, but the MGBs were already entering Bastia by the time they could receive it.

"I warned the LCGs at 0525 that I suspected the presence of E-boats, and gave them a look-out bearing to starboard, at the same time altering course to port. The Scouting Force were also informed of the enemy position and ordered to proceed round the north of Capraia, while the Close Radar Screen was ordered to intercept round the south of the island."

In order to follow the next part of the proceedings we must go back a few nights, to 10th/11th April. On that night the Italian torpedo-boat *Sirio*, escorted by British MGBs and American PT-boats, successfully laid a minefield south-west of Capraia, using Italian mines. Capraia was an island due west of the mid-point of a line running north-south joining Vada to Port Baratti, so that the "Battle Squadron's" actions had all been fought well inshore of the island.

Now we must turn to German reports. On the night of Bobby Allan's Operation "Newt", three German torpedo-boats (small destroyers), TA.26, TA.23 and TA.29, sailed to lay mines off Capraia.

At 0145 TA.23 hit what was believed to be a mine. There were no indications of the presence of enemy units in the immediate vicinity. TA.23 was severely damaged and slowly sinking. She was taken in tow by one of the other two vessels in an attempt to reach the nearest German-held port. Porto Ferraio. . . .

"Further reports were then received from Bastia," writes Allan, "indicating that the enemy was moving north. I passed this information on to the Scouting Force, which, at 0440, reported that they were in contact and about to attack.

"They challenged at 2,500 yards, and at 2,000 yards they were illuminated by star-shell and heavily engaged. When the range was 1,700 yards they fired their remaining four torpedoes and withdrew at speed under smoke. An under-water explosion was felt by all forces, including the LCGs, at this time. In view of this and the subsequent discovery of oil in the area, a probable hit was claimed."

. . . At about 0446 silhouettes were sighted and the Germans immediately illuminated and engaged the MTBs. Six torpedoes were fired at TA.26, TA.23 and TA.29, but they were all avoided.

When it became clear that the damaged TA.23 could not be saved, she was torpedoed and sunk by TA.29 at 0645.

Allan goes on: "It was not until I saw the star-shells that I realised the enemy force was other than E-boats. I immediately ordered the Radar Screen PTs to proceed to the attack and told the S.O., MTB Escort, that there were enemy ships, presumably destroyers, to the east of Capraia and that, if possible, he was to attack."

He replied that he had only one boat with torpedoes, and that she was being detached. But she failed to intercept.

In Bastia the three enemy ships had been picked up on the radar plot as they came down the west coast of Capraia, just missing the mine-field laid by the *Sirio*. They were then seen to turn north and cross the minefield. The radar showed that they stopped for some time—this would be when TA.23 hit the mine.

For Allan it was a triumph—achieved at the age of twenty-nine.

· · · · ·

In May the 7th MTB Flotilla started operating from Bastia with their new Vospers and American-designed and built Higgins boats. They had been working up at Malta under their S.O., Lt. A. C. B. Blomfield, D.S.C., R.N.

The first attacks by this flotilla coincided with the arrival of the first Mark VIII torpedoes with magnetic pistols. It was the introduction of these pistols (the mechanism which explodes the torpedo) which revolutionised torpedo attacks on shallow-draught targets such as F-lighters.

Ever since the designers of warships thirty years before this had realised the menace of the torpedo and added bulges to the sides of their vessels, torpedo designers had been trying to increase the menace by developing a non-contact pistol.

Previously torpedoes exploded on impact with the often-armoured side of the target. A non-contact pistol would give the torpedo these advantages: it could easily break the back of a ship; hit vital regions—such as engines and magazines—innaccessible through the sides; allow the torpedo to run deeper and thus reduce the effect of surface waves; the torpedo left a less-visible track; and running deeper, allowed it to get well ahead of what track it did leave.

These advantages were sufficient to set most of the world's leading navies trying to design such a pistol; and only the Japs failed. The obvious method was to use the magnetism of the target ship to actuate the pistol's mechanism, and the first British one was the Duplex pistol.

This was used for a few years in aircraft torpedoes, but in wartime its success was short-lived because its effectiveness was reduced so much by degaussing[1] that it would only operate at a maximum distance of two to three feet under the hull. It was also so sensitive to the earth's magnetism that it would explode if the torpedo deviated sharply from a straight course—as it might when running near the surface in bad weather.

[1] A device used on ships to counter the effect of magnetic mines.

In the war the Germans were using three types of non-contact pistol —their own version of the Duplex, the Italian S.I.C., and another one designed to reduce the chances of counter-measures being used by the Allies. Our own pistol, coming into use with Coastal Forces at this time, was far more effective than any enemy type.

These new torpedoes were first used by MTBs in the Mediterranean on 9th/10th May when the 7th Flotilla's 378 (Lt. N. Ilett, with Lt. R. Varvill embarked as S.O.), 377 (S/Lt. R. Aitchison) and 376 (S/Lt. G. Masters), with PT 203, attacked two F-lighters. They torpedoed one, which blew up, and almost certainly hit the second.

The next night Blomfield was S.O. in 420, and he had with him 421 (Varvill), 375 (Lt. R. A. Johnson) and PT 214. He found a merchant ship escorted by five R-boats in the vicinity of Vada Rocks and scored one certain and one probable hit on the merchantman and one probable on an escort. He left the enemy ships firing at each other in a fratricidal fashion.

The 7th Flotilla's most spectacular attack of the month was on 27th/28th May off Spezia. The boats, MTBs 421 (Varvill, S.O.), 419 (Lt. A. H. Moore), 420 (Lt. E. S. Good) and PT 218, left Bastia to patrol off Misco Point, north of Spezia.

Like most of the previous nights during the month (on the thirty-six nights between 26th April and 31st May boats were out on twenty-six nights, making contact with the enemy on thirteen of them) the weather was good—wind light, sea calm, visibility good, phosphorescence negligible, and a half-moon to westward until 0115.

At five minutes past midnight a convoy of five F-lighters was sighted one and a half miles away and only half a mile off Misco Point. They were escorted by a single E-boat. The radar on the PT-boat did not pick them up.

Varvill ordered independent attacks and the boats closed at 10 knots. The convoy apparently sighted the MTBs, because the F-lighters immediately swung in towards the shore, but the E-boat kept the same course and speed.

Varvill (421) closed to within 400 yards and, using a target speed of 9 knots, fired both torpedoes. Two F-lighters blew up with considerable explosions. 419 (Moore) fired one torpedo from the same range, but missed astern. PT 218 also fired two torpedoes and claimed a hit, although this was not seen by the rest of the unit. A minute later

Good (420) fired his port torpedo at a stopped F-lighter which disintegrated in a sheet of flame.

These attacks provoked the E-boat into ineffectual fire with 20-mm. guns. An F-lighter which had beached herself then started firing tracer in the E-boat's direction and put up a four-red-star cartridge for good measure. The MTBs were not hit and resumed their patrol.

An hour later, four miles to the northward, PT 218 reported a radar contact one and three-quarter miles ahead, apparently closing, and two minutes later two vessels were sighted close inshore at 1,000 yards, steering south-east at 15 knots.

At this time Moore (419) and Good (420) each had a torpedo left, and PT 218 had two (the PT-boats carried four each). Varvill again ordered independent torpedo attacks and hauled off to seaward to keep out of their way.

On the run-in the MTBs saw that the two ships seemed to be a sloop or small destroyer escorting a KT (war transport) ship of about 1,500 tons. The escort challenged with a single letter "S" but did not open fire until Moore had closed the KT ship to 500 yards and launched his remaining torpedo. This hit and apparently broke the vessel in half, and the remains sank rapidly.

The escort, now thoroughly roused in defence of its late ward, scored hits on the bridge and charthouse of Good's boat. Two of his engines cut out and he tried to disengage, firing a four-red-star cartridge to try to bluff the escort. This worked, making the enemy hold his fire for about a minute. During this time Good's motor mechanic, Petty Officer Joseph, repaired two electrical faults and Good managed to get his boat under way in time.

PT 218 had fired her two torpedoes and missed astern. All the boats then converged on the damaged 420 and escorted her to seaward.

When Varvill's action report finally reached the Admiralty, the Deputy Director, Operations Division, noted: "According to the rules 419 and 420 should have fired both torpedoes at their first target, in which case they would have had nothing left for the merchant vessel. Thus do the wicked prosper!"

The 7th Flotilla's bag for the night was three F-lighters and one KT ship for the expenditure of five British torpedoes, and Capt. Stevens, C.C.F., with the fairness that made him liked and respected by every member of Coastal Forces in the Mediterranean, wrote: ". . . But no matter how good the weapon, attacks will fail if they are not well executed. Pleasure . . . should not, therefore, be allowed to obscure the fact that these successes were the fruits of well-conducted attacks, resolutely and accurately pressed home."

.   .   .   .   .

In the Corsica-Sardinia area big movements of craft were made during May and June. The 57th MTB/MGB Flotilla was sent to the Adriatic at the end of May, to be followed by the 56th ("all-Canadian commanding officers") at the beginning of July.

At the beginning of May there was a large-scale movement of MLs to the area in preparation for a landing on the island of Elba. The 31st Flotilla, fitted for minesweeping, moved from Ischia to Maddalena. The 28th, also minesweeping, moved from Algiers to join the 3rd sweeping along the west coast of Italy. The 8th, fitted for minelaying, went to Bastia; and the 22nd, rearmed with Bofors guns, joined the Corsica force. The 24th Flotilla moved from the Eastern Mediterranean to take over the 31st's anti-submarine work, based on Ischia.

All these moves threw a heavy load on the base staff at both Maddalena and Ischia. The total number of craft in the area at this time was about fifty. Thirty-nine took part in the Elba landings, the 22nd Flotilla having by then moved to the Adriatic.

.   .   .   .   .

In June the 7th MTB Flotilla continued its run of successes, joining other boats in patrols off Elba, where the enemy might have attempted an evacuation. Tim Bligh had taken his boats to the Adriatic, and the 56th was preparing for its part in Operation "Brassard", the Elba landing, before following him. On the eve of "Brassard" we must move east.

CHAPTER XXIX

THE OVERTURE *DER FREISCHUTZ*

IN February 1944 the British base on the island of Vis faced the danger of invasion. As early as September 1943, when the war in the Adriatic was warming up, Vice-Admiral Lietsmann, the German Admiral-in-command, Adriatic, realised the importance of the German occupation of the Dalmatian islands, especially Vis and Lagosta.[1]

Partisan operations were a considerable embarrassment to the Germans (the German N.O.I.C., Split, plaintively reported in October: "Railway communications are cut and land transport . . . is further hampered by the continuous activities of Partisans who completely surround Split to landward").

As reports from agents came in week after week about British and Partisan activities among the islands, Vice-Admiral Lietsmann, convinced of the necessity to occupy the islands, suggested early in December 1943 that all available forces should attempt the operation.

By 11th December the German Naval Staff agreed, and shipping was concentrated for the occupation of Korcula, Hvar and Brac. This was to be followed by the capture of Lagosta and Vis.

On 21st December the Germans, hearing reports that the British were in Vis and Lagosta, feared that landings on Korcula and Brac were imminent, and therefore occupied Korcula on 23rd December (see p. 166).

German plans for the capture of Vis, Operation "Freischutz", ("Freeshooter") began on 1st January 1944. Eighteen days later the Partisans evacuated Hvar and the Germans moved in. According to the Army, this satisfied the Navy's needs for a sea route from Dubrovnik to Cattaro. To stamp out supplies to the Partisans, the Wehrmacht said, they were prepared to clear Vis and use it as a base. However, the Navy would have to provide a garrison of at least one battalion and three coastal batteries. This was impossible, the Navy said, and a quarrel began between the two Services.

[1] All references to German plans are taken from captured German documents.

207

At a noisy two-day conference in the third week of February, "Freischutz" was postponed to 17th March; and later, at the Army's request, to 4th April. After a subsequent conference at the H.Q. of the 2nd Panzer Army, Vice-Admiral Lietsmann outlined the plan for the attack on Vis:

> Our attack forces would approach between 0000 and 0200, steering to the north of Korcula so as to evade observation from Lagosta. Landings would be made on the south-east of Vis. The chief difficulty is the length of the passage in relation to the speed of our ships, and it is therefore advisable to take as much material as possible over in the first wave of the attack.

Finally, the arguments—by then extremely bitter—were put before Hitler. Coastal Forces based on Vis were seriously affecting German sea traffic, capturing[1] eight ships and sinking three in the first eight days of April alone. Doenitz, the C.-in-C., Navy, wanted the island liquidated, and put up a plan to Hitler:[2]

NAVAL STAFF

Minutes of the conference on 12th and 13th April 1944.

. . . *General Jodl informs the Fuehrer that the seizure of Vis was purely a naval matter. There is a difference of opinion between the Navy on the one hand the Army and the Air Force on the other. The latter believes that the Navy is too weak to carry out the seizure. Moreover, it is doubtful whether Vis is worth the commitment of so many valuable forces, since it is a question whether we shall be able to hold it afterwards.*

The C.-in-C., Navy, points out that Vis is a vulnerable spot on the Dalmatian coast. Infiltration of enemy troops and weapons is easier through Vis than straight across the Adriatic and Italy. Therefore it is important to seize Vis. . . .

The Reichsmarschall[3] is against the operation.

General Jodl says that he and the Army also consider the risk too great. The Fuehrer tends to agree with the C.-in-C., Navy. . . .

General impression: The Fuehrer is inclined to agree with the C.-in-C., Navy, but agrees with us as follows: "If the Army is opposed to begin with and the inner conviction is lacking, then nothing will come of it anyway."

·   ·   ·   ·   ·   ·

---

[1] These actions, mostly by Lt.-Cdr. Tom Fuller, D.S.C.*, apparently had a great bearing on Doenitz's decision. They won Fuller a second Bar to his D.S.C.
[2] *Minutes of the Fuehrer's Naval Conferences, 1944.*
[3] Hermann Goering, head of the Luftwaffe.

Although the final notes of Operation "Freischutz" given here have taken us rather far ahead in our narrative, it is interesting to compare the co-operation (*sic*) between the three Services which dominates the German planning, and the co-operation between the three British Services; and also to see how a short series of MTB-MGB actions such as Fuller's can have a decisive effect on a campaign such as this.

However, we must return to the Coastal Forces narrative.

In Brindisi *Miraglia* was operating as the Coastal Forces base in place of H.M.S. *Vienna*, which had been damaged in the great air raid on Bari. The situation regarding *Miraglia* was unique: she was a seaplane tender belonging to the Italian Navy, and although still commanded by an Italian captain she was run by British officers as a base ship.

In the islands the boats were involved in several successful actions against schooners. The first of these, on the 8th/9th, was by MGB 674 (Davidson, S.O.) and MTB 651 (Horlock). They intercepted an 80-ton schooner off Gradac Light, carried out three gun attacks—despite shore-battery fire—and left it ablaze.

This was followed two nights later with another attack by Davidson in 674 with MTB 85 (Hyslop). They stopped a 120-ton schooner, boarded it, took off twenty-seven Germans and one Italian, and set it on fire.

A 200-ton schooner was destroyed on the 13th/14th by MGB 645 (Martin, with Lt.-Cdr. Basil Bourne embarked as S.O.) and MTB 649 (Hughes).

April started badly, with the loss of one of the Senior Officers. Lt. J. B. Sturgeon, D.S.C., was S.O. in MTB 242 (Lt. C. R. Holloway), and with MTB 81 (Lt. L. V. Strong) in company sighted an I-boat. Sturgeon immediately engaged in a series of gun attacks, and the I-boat was last seen damaged and close inshore. A stray shot killed Sturgeon, who was the only casualty. He had done fine work for many months and was a great loss.

During the first week of April the boats began a new technique—capturing schooners instead of destroying them. This, mentioned earlier because of its effect on the German Naval Staff's attitude, was started by a Canadian, Lt.-Cdr. Tom Fuller, D.S.C., on 2nd/3rd April, when he was S.O. in MTB 651 (Horlock). With MGB 647 (Mountstephens), Fuller intercepted a 30-ton schooner. Deciding it would be a pity to sink her when she was carrying stores which would be useful at Vis, Fuller crashed his boat alongside, put a party aboard,

captured the crew, and towed the vessel back to Vis. She was loaded
with explosives and mail.

The next night Fuller, with the same two boats, went one better and
captured two schooners off Prisnjak Island and towed them back to
Vis. The night after that Horlock—who had commanded the boat in
which Fuller had been embarked the two previous nights—was S.O.
in 651, and he took MGB 661 (Lt. R. Cole) out to the Murter Island
area and captured the schooner *S. Nicola*, loaded with a cargo of wheat.
She, too, joined the prize fleet at Vis.

On 6th/7th Tom Fuller was out again, embarked in MGB 661
(Cole). With 647 (Mountstephens) he captured a 400-ton schooner,
the *Libecchio*, off Murter Island. Loaded with foodstuffs, she was
towed fifty-two miles back to base.

Very soon a new Coastal Forces target was set up in the Adriatic—
to achieve the minimum time required to board, capture, take in tow
and have under way at 10 knots a vessel in prize. Tom Fuller held the
record—twelve minutes.

The MTBs and MGBs had for some time been carrying Partisans
with them on operations. These men were useful in many ways
because, apart from knowing the islands, they could question or
threaten suspicious craft by using the loud-hailer. As soon as taking
vessels in prize became a popular feature, small Commando parties
were also embarked in the boats to form boarding parties.

The usual technique for capturing schooners was to lie close inshore
and then, when a schooner passed, suddenly swoop down from astern.
Sometimes, at the last minute, blood-curdling threats would be made
in German and Italian over the loud-hailers. The boats would then
come alongside and put a party on board. Back in Vis the captured
vessels were welcomed by the Partisans, who promptly put in more
armament and added them to their "Tiger" fleet.

The Partisan ships had for many long months been doing remarkable
work among the islands. They were usually schooners—many of
them captured—which fairly bristled with captured German and
Italian guns. The Partisans protected their craft by putting sand-
bags and slabs of concrete round the bulwarks.

Three nights after capturing the *Libecchio* Fuller took the same two
boats, 661 (Cole) and 647 (Mountstephens), and destroyed a schooner
and an I-boat with gunfire, sank a motor-boat by ramming, and
captured two schooners and a motor-boat.

He followed that up two nights later, the 14th/15th April, by taking out 661 (Cole) and 646 (Knight-Lacklen) and destroying a 100-ton tug and the 400-ton tanker it was towing by gunfire, and capturing a 250-ton lighter. The two boats took thirty-five German prisoners, and forty-three others of the various crews were reported missing. For this brilliant series of actions Fuller was awarded a second Bar to his D.S.C., Cole a D.S.C. and Mountstephens was mentioned in dispatches.

In Vis itself the Allied hold on the island was strengthened during the month by the provision of an airfield, which was built in nine days by a U.S. Construction Unit. In the previous month various raids had been successfully carried out by Commandos against some of the small islands.

.   .   .   .

There was better weather in May, but enemy craft were harder to find. However, two boats from Vis had a brisk action against some I-boats on the 1st/2nd.

They were MGB 645 (Martin, with Basil Bourne embarked as S.O.) and MTB 667 (Jerram), and they sailed from Komiza Harbour on a cloudy night, with a brisk wind, to patrol between the port of Makarska, on the mainland, and the islands of Brac and Hvar.

After an hour the wind eased up. Bourne planned to approach Makarska from the south to avoid being spotted by any possible enemy shipping, and then lie stopped as close to the port as possible. This would put him in a good position to intercept ships approaching the port from any direction.

To get into this position he had to risk being sighted from some part of the coast; and at 2350, with the shore one and a quarter miles away on the starboard beam, the unit was challenged.

They watched a light flashing the letter "K" for several minutes. Bourne headed the boats seawards and then turned south. Still the flashing continued, so he headed seaward again. Suddenly two green flares arcked up and hung in the sky—one from where the signal lamp was, and the other two miles farther down the coast.

Bourne then decided to withdraw to five miles off the coast and wait for a while and perhaps allay the coast-watchers' fears. He also knew that ML 361 was farther south, and guessed that if it was spotted the enemy would think it was the MGB and MTB.

When the two boats were lying stopped, but with engines running, they could see a long message being flashed from the challenge point on the shore. But nothing else was sighted for another hour.

The visibility—which had been about four miles—gradually closed down to about a mile, with slight haze, and at 0152 Bourne moved off for another sweep to the south-east of Brac.

At 0235 two ships were sighted a mile away, close inshore. Bourne and Jerram tried to identify them, but they were against the dark land background. The leading vessel seemed to be a lighter, about 100 feet long, followed by a smaller craft of about 60 feet.

Not knowing their maximum speed and as they were already very close inshore, Bourne decided to attack at once from seaward, and he turned the unit on to a parallel course. Both boats opened fire with all guns on the leading ship at a range of 125 yards.

Bourne, describing the action at the time, wrote:

"Immediate hits were observed, including 6-pounder, and no fire was returned. Having drawn ahead, the unit was turned to port and the target was re-engaged to starboard, both boats again scoring many hits, and the target was left in a sinking condition, gunwales awash and one on fire.

"Cease-fire was ordered over the W/T and guns were reloaded and the unit turned again on to an easterly course to find another target. Almost at once another shape was seen heading for the shore in the direction of Sumartin and was finally headed off when within 100 yards of the coast.

"Fire was opened by 645, hits again being observed, range 100 yards. and the target [was] now identified as an I-lighter turning to port, 645 [was] coming up from astern and a figure was seen facing us with hand raised in surrender. I told the Partisan interpreter whom I had with me on 645 to hail them, which he did unfortunately in Croat, and immediately the I-lighter opened fire with what appeared to be two 20-mm. guns at a range which had closed to about ten yards as the lighter had apparently stopped.

"645 returned fire with all guns except 6-pounder at full depression, and at this range could not miss. The lighter scored many hits on 645's port side forward of the bridge before fire was stopped, and 645 drew ahead, leaving the lighter completely wrecked and nearly cut in half.

"667, following astern, finished it off with Oerlikon fire and had the satisfaction of seeing it turn over on its side and sink."

Bourne's boat had been hit many times. The pom-pom and both 0.5-inch turrets had been put out of action, and one of the turrets was blazing fiercely. This fire was put out by the gunner and a couple of ratings.

For the next eleven nights, however, the boats could not find any targets. It fell to two Special Service MLs, 361 (Lt. R. N. Young, D.S.C., R.C.N.V.R.) and 841 (Lt. J. H. Weir), to end the blank period by sinking an I-boat on the 13th/14th by gunfire.

Tom Fuller ended the blank periods as far as the MTBs and MGBs were concerned on 18th/19th May. After being briefed at Komiza by Morgan Giles, MGB 661 (Cole, with Tom Fuller embarked as S.O.) and MTB 667 (Jerram) headed up to the Peljesac Peninsula in a calm sea, with no moon or phosphorescence.

Arriving at the south-western tip of the peninsula at 2330, Fuller tried to seek the protection of the land by lying about ten feet from the shore, in a slight indentation. This would have given him a clear view of the Peljesac Channel and any shipping proceeding westwards at Cape Loviste. However, the ground was low-lying and Fuller moved off.

Shortly afterwards vessels were seen rounding Cape Loviste, moving south-west. There was nothing gained by letting them proceed, because shortly they would come under the protection of shore batteries on Korcula, so Fuller signalled green "Ns" to Jerram and moved off north-east at 10 knots. Fuller's boat had only three engines, giving a maximum speed of 17 knots.

As the boats closed the range the enemy craft were identified as a large coaster, estimated at about 700 tons, escorted by a large R-boat and two small craft which were presumed to be I-boats.

The action from then on is described by Tom Fuller: "The intention at this period was to clean up the escort before they escaped and then look after the slow-moving larger craft, which we considered had not sufficient speed to get far away.

"Owing to the lack of shadow from the poor background we were unable to close the convoy to any short range unobserved. . . . At 0052, at a range of approximately 600 to 700 yards, the enemy opened fire with a multiplicity of 20-mm. At the same time their convoy proceeded to disperse. Speed was increased and an attack angle shaped on the R-boat, which we singled out for her heavy amount of fire. The time lag from the enemy opening fire until both our craft were hitting was only a matter of a split second.

"It was unfortunate at this stage that 661 received a hit with incendiary ammunition on her port turret, causing a fire of considerable brilliance which attracted all the enemy's fire like flies to a honey-pot.

"It was also unfortunate that we had to, at this stage, cease fire and

make our display signal to make certain that the craft we were attacking
was not 667, who might have turned inside our radius. Receiving a
reply display from 667 well astern of us, we then proceeded to close
the R-boat.

"At this period the motor mechanic on 661 reported to the bridge
that there was a fire in the engine-room and it was out of control. We
were able to ascertain from him that all the engine-room personnel
were then on deck before he collapsed.

"Range was then decreased to some fifty yards and it was my
pleasure to witness the finest display of gunnery under heavy fire. In
over a minute and a half continuous pom-pom gunfire was delivered
in the most systematic manner against this R-boat, and not one single
shell was seen to miss but just splattered her from stem to gudgeon.

"The tenacity and fanatical ability of the German gunners to stand
up under this punishment was something to be marvelled at, but their
life was short-lived.

"667 during this period was delivering considerable heavy fire into
the larger coaster, and glows of fire within it were seen through the
scuttles. 667 also administered a good dusting to one of the I-boats.

"The escort now appeared to be somewhat silenced, and it was my
intention to signal 667 to torpedo the coaster. Unfortunately the
never-reliable generators had both fallen over and there were no
serviceable V/S lamps on the bridge.

"The fire in the engine-room of 661 was then well out of hand and
all fire-extinguishers had been expended and the methyl-bromides
pulled. The heat was becoming terrific and almost forcing the personnel off the bridge.

"The steering was jammed, fortunately amidships, on a course of a
safe direction, and the fact that with no other choice we were proceeding at 14 knots made it impossible to use even buckets to fight the
fire.

"I therefore told the captain to remove all the wounded to the
foredeck[1] and suggested that if he had any personal knick-knacks he
wished to salvage, now was the time. C.B.s [confidential books]
were collected and brought on deck to scupper.

"A lone flashlight was then produced and 'Cs'[2] were made astern
in the hopes that 667 would see them. It was presumed she was
following, as there was no further evidence of a battle astern.

---

[1] There were five. A sixth had died of wounds.
[2] The signal to close.

"Leading-telegraphist Pegler continued single-handed to fight the fire with the dribs and drabs from extinguishers and half-used bromides which appeared to be a most futile and hopeless effort.

"667 came alongside and secured, slowing down to take some of the way of us, a feat which was a perfect display of seamanship. In no time her wash deck hose was run over to 661, and with that additional ammunition Pegler was able to get results. . . .

"Immediately 667 was secured, owing to the possibility of 661 blowing up and the presence of methyl-bromide fumes, the wounded personnel were transferred to 667. At 0130 the fire was well under control and at 0200 Motor Mechanic J. A. Lacey (667) was given permission to enter the engine-room because, as he so ably stated in his request, 'It would spoil the engines if they continued to run.' At 0225 I gave the order 'Up Spirits'. . . ."

.   .   .   .   .

The only other action during May was on the 20th/21st, when MGB 646 (Knight-Lacklen, with Bourne embarked as S.O.), MGB 674 (Bowyer) and MTB 656 (Masson) intercepted a 250-ton oil barge off Curzola Island and drove it ashore in flames.

At the end of May Bligh's flotilla arrived in the Adriatic from Bastia: they sailed via Malta—an inevitable detour, but even so some of the boats were operating from Komiza by the middle of June.

CHAPTER XXX

BIG GUNS AND LITTLE SHIPS

JUNE, with its shorter nights, produced only three actions of note in the Adriatic. On the 9th/10th, MGB 674 (Mountstephens) and MTB 656 (Masson) sank an 80-ton "flak" lighter by gunfire and damaged an I-boat.

On the evening of 24th June V.57[1] (Tim Bligh) went on patrol in MGB 662, with MGB 659 (Barlow) and MTB 670 (Hewitt) in company. The night was fine, with a breeze off the mainland and a crescent moon that gave little light after midnight. The unit steered well clear of Rogoznica and passed close to Blitvenica Light before turning to enter the string of islands.

A two-masted schooner was sighted and closed hard by Bacvica Rock (a small rock three feet high—as far as is known the only solid object in the Mediterranean which was immune to American radar, and another motor minesweeper in the dry dock), but this was identified after the usual rifle fire and "stoying" as Partisan. Her intelligence—"Nothing German south of Zara for months"—was treated with some reserve, although it was only too probable.

The unit sailed on at 20 knots, identifying the little islands with the long names as they passed quickly down either beam: Raparasnjak, Samograd, Vrtlic, Zgrizanj, Mertovjnak, Babinoguisica, Tetvisnjak, and Cavlin—more scope for the imagination than Harwich to Grimsby —and finally closed Murter at 8 knots, about twelve miles north of Sibenik.

The boats steered south-eastwards on one engine at about 100 yards from the shore. Just after 2200 a large patch of smoke was seen to the south, and soon after a two-funnelled steamship of low freeboard was sighted steering a north-westerly course at about 12–14 knots. Bligh decided that this was a warship, probably the T.7, a long-standing and much-discussed inhabitant of Sibenik with a reported speed of 25 knots.

---

[1] The title of the S.O. of the 57th Flotilla.

As this was one of the few genuine torpedo targets south of Pola, he ordered 670 to carry out a torpedo attack. The enemy appeared to be unaccompanied and she steamed serenely on, the target of a copybook exercise: an unobserved, unopposed run-in on a ship steering a steady course and speed, with a firing position some 500 yards broad on the enemy's bow.

But what was described in the subsequent report as a "personal sighting error by the commanding officer" prevented the perfect attack from having the perfect ending, and the two torpedoes exploded on Kukuljari Island, some way astern of the enemy. The "human factor" was unfortunate, though 670 was, under more difficult conditions seven weeks later, to make amends for this error. But at the time it left Bligh with an unpleasant decision—whether or not to carry out a gun attack.

Such an attack would have been pursued under the worst tactical conditions. A long run up the enemy's wash under full observation the whole time, with no chance of developing the "A" arcs of the unit's gun armament (the MGBs' main weapon was aft), with very restricted water in which to manoeuvre, and only a limited amount of time before the enemy could slip behind Pasman Island. Further, the T.7's speed was thought to be equal to the "Dogs'" best. And in addition it was assumed that the enemy would have seen the torpedoes miss astern, and that on the guess that these were the "Dogs'" main weapon he might well adopt offensive or obstructive tactics.

There was yet one more consideration, another manifestation of the "human factor". 662 had on board that night a Partisan officer from Tito's staff to act as interpreter and observer. He had applauded the idea of the torpedo attack, but when this failed and it emerged that a gun attack was contemplated he clutched Bligh round the waist and begged him to realise that the T.7 was too big to be sunk by little guns and that she carried big guns that would sink the British boats.

Notwithstanding all these considerations and the skilled and no doubt accurate local comment, "Dogs" swung round to the northwards, increased speed to over 20 knots and began the chase.

The T.7 was throwing out a lot of smoke and sparks (what an ex-destroyer rating called "cooking on the front burner"). The range closed faster than had been hoped; but still no star-shell, no flashes and splashes. The "Dogs" were steering to pass the enemy on his inshore beam, and Bligh decided to hold fire until the German started. There was no point in trying to achieve surprise and small-calibre guns are always more effective when fired at short range.

The "Dogs" were disposed in a slight quarterline to port, with 670 in the enemy's wake. At about 150 yards the T.7 opened fire at 662 with her after gun. The "Dogs" let fly with everything, and in half a minute the T.7, in a wretched state, burning and blowing off jets of steam and her guns silenced, altered course sharply to starboard and steered straight for the beach, missing 662 by about five feet and giving occasion for her identity to be confirmed by the eye. Good work here by Petty Officer Briddon, the coxswain of 662.

The boats slowed down and came on to a parallel course, continuing to fire at the enemy's waterline, but the T.7 struck Murter at something over 12 knots. There seemed to be a possibility of bursting boilers and exploding magazines, so 659 lay off a few cables while the other boats searched along the track for survivors. 662 picked up one Ustachi member of the crew, but his references to two escorting E-boats seemed to be too vague to attract credibility.

Meanwhile the T.7 had quietened down and 662 went alongside. A thorough search was made all over her. Three wounded men were found and taken into custody. Water was heard entering every compartment of the ship and from time to time she settled over to port. The first lieutenant, S/Lt. W. Darracott, landed on Murter with a small armed party and found five more of her crew ashore, of whom four were seriously wounded.

But before he could arrange for these men to be carried over the T.7 and on to 662 the three wounded prisoners had confirmed that there had been two escorting craft and both the gunboats were withdrawn to seaward, leaving 670 to try and bring home the other prisoners. But the change in arrangements evidently encouraged the Germans ashore, for the four wounded men could not subsequently be found.

All three boats fired a few rounds into the waterline and left for Komiza, leaving the T.7 firmly aground, filling up with water and on fire above decks. Her hull was subsequently given final treatment by an Army demolition party.

The T.7 was 185 feet long and of some 250 tons displacement. She was said to be armed with two 50-mm. Bredas, a number of machine-guns and four torpedo tubes, but inspection showed that her after gun was of a heavier calibre. She had been on passage to Fiume to be refitted and rearmed, and her loss must have been a blow to the

German Naval Command. On our side 662 had some very slight damage and one casualty, Stoker W. Abbot, who had a gunshot wound.

.   .   .   .   .

The third action of the month, on the 29th/30th, was a success for the MLs. 449 (Lt. J. D. Kelleher, with Lt. D. R. A. Romain embarked as S.O.) and 468 (Lt. F. A. Scott) engaged a convoy east of Korcula and sank a lighter, with a second possible, and damaged a Siebel ferry and an F-lighter. These two were driven into Zuljana Bay, where the F-lighter found the Siebel and destroyed it.

More raids were made during June. On the 1st/2nd an assault force of 1,000 British, 100 Americans and 2,500 Partisans were landed on the island of Brac (Operation "Flounced"). Cover was given by two destroyers and boats of Coastal Forces.

The object was to try and ease the German pressure on the Partisans in the Bosnia area, which had grown acute. The Allied force was involved in bitter fighting and withdrew on the 4th/5th, the British having lost eleven officers and forty-nine other ranks killed, and nine officers and sixty-four other ranks wounded. The Americans had one man wounded and the Partisans lost about sixty killed and two hundred wounded.

One of the British officers lost was Lt.-Col. P. Manners, D.S.O. He was killed while fighting beside Lt.-Col. Jack Churchill, who was captured by the Germans. In a matter of minutes Brig. Churchill had lost the commanders of his main units—his brother's No. 2 Commando, and Lt.-Col. Manners' No. 40 Commando.

CHAPTER XXXI

A DROP IN THE BUCKET

IN July the MTBs and MGBs kept up their heavy attacks, and
although there were fewer actions they were mostly successful
ones. The first of the month was on the 17th/18th and was fought
by MGB 659 (Barlow, S.O.) and MTBs 649 (Hughes) and 670
(Hewitt).

They found a convoy in the Mljet Channel consisting of a large and
a small lighter with several I- and E-boats. Barlow's unit attacked "in
almost Stygian darkness", sinking two I- or E-boats and badly damaging a Siebel ferry. Hughes' boat was hit in the forward tank space and
the crew had to fight a dangerous fire. Four of his men were wounded.

Tom Fuller fought one of his most successful actions in the Adriatic
on the 25th/26th. He was embarked in MTB 651 (Ennis), and the
other boats were 667 (Jerram) and 670 (Hewitt).

The three boats sailed from Komiza in a flat calm, reaching their
patrol area at 2309 and stopping twenty yards from the shore in a
small cove. At 0013 a small craft was sighted a mile to the northwards
and the three boats moved out after it. Almost immediately a large
schooner[1] of 400 tons, without masts or bowsprit, was sighted. Ahead
and to seaward of it were five E-boats, and two I-boats[2] were astern.

Fuller, describing the action, wrote: "At 0024 MTB 670, at a range
of 200 yards, and at the time the enemy opened fire, was ordered to
fire star-shell. This she did, and of three rounds fired at the schooner
the first landed in a bucket of petrol on deck, exploding, and instantaneously the 'flak' schooner was ablaze her entire length, her crew
jumping overboard after firing but a few rounds.

"The blazing ship showed up the two I-boats, and 651 (Ennis) was
detailed to part company and attack these, on a course in opposite
direction to our other two MTBs. Both these I-boats were silenced
and 651 stopped in the immediate vicinity, put on recognition display
and ordered the other two boats to re-form.

---

[1] This was the "flak" schooner *Vega*.   [2] I. 302 and I. 309.

"Difficulty was experienced in preventing the rejoining boats from shooting up the two prizes. MTB 670 (Hewitt), in passing the wreck (of the schooner), was able to destroy one E-boat perfectly silhouetted.

"MTB 667, which was reduced in speed, was ordered to board the I-boat and secure prisoners from those in the water, and to keep her display signal continuously on.

"A small boat was observed pulling to the shore, and 651 [Ennis, with Fuller aboard] obtained two prisoners from it. During this time 670 also rescued some survivors.

"651 and 670 then proceeded due south to the coast and turned east and steamed 28 knots a hundred yards from the shore. 667 (Jerram) was beautifully silhouetted by the fire, and the four E-boats whose duty it was to escort (which had, in the initial stages, steamed off to the eastward at full speed) could not resist the target that 667 afforded them.

"These E-boats returned to attack 667, and 651 (Fuller) and 670 (Hewitt) were able to rush from the concealment of the coast and have the E-boats silhouetted by the fire. 667 saw the E-boats approaching and manoeuvred her prize as a shield. At this time she was busy taking in charge some fifty prisoners and attempting to put out a fire on the I-boat.

"Three torpedoes were fired (by the E-boats), one passing astern and two directly under 667. The E-boats further delayed their escape by again attempting to fire surface torpedoes. Two passed astern of 651 and two astern of 670.

"The range was then able to be closed to 150 yards. The third-in-line E-boat was hit by pom-pom from 670 and there was a loud explosion. The fourth in line was repeatedly hit by 651.

"At 0115 MTB 651 (Fuller) was hit and engines stopped, disabled and without guns. It appeared that the leading two E-boats would make good their escape, but they very obligingly turned on each other and carried out a spirited gun action as we lay in a grandstand seat. The crew cheered as they watched the bits and pieces fly from both E-boats.

"670 took MTB 651 in tow and passed the Peljesac side of the burning wreck. The 105-mm. gun batteries on the eastern tip of Hvar let off about a dozen rounds during the initial stages of the action. These shells inconvenienced the hundreds of Germans swimming more than our own forces, the nearest shell dropping some twenty yards astern of MTB 670.

"The burning wreck, in exploding ammunition, sent up a lone two-star signal cartridge, which evidently was the correct one, as the shore batteries ceased and did not reopen."

The navigator in Jerram's boat, S/Lt. John Dean, R.N.V.R., was killed in this action. In boarding an I-boat he either slipped or was wounded by exploding ammunition and fell between 667 and the I-boat. A twenty-minute search was made for him, but without success.

·   ·   ·   ·   ·

Before this action, on the 23rd/24th, three short boats, 372, 81 and 297, found a convoy of four or five E-boats and other vessels and attacked. The enemy immediately opened fire and one of their first bursts hit 372 in the engine-room, disabling her. Astern 81 was increasing to full speed and rammed her.

The Germans did not follow up their advantage, and 81, quickly coming alongside, was able to rescue all but one of 372's crew. With 297 she withdrew, leaving 372 with her engine-room blazing. Unfortunately she did not sink immediately and a Spitfire was sent out next day to finish her off. (See picture on p. 113).

The missing man from 372 had managed to swim to a nearby island, where he was found by the Partisans. He eventually was brought back to Vis.

·   ·   ·   ·   ·

The month was nicely rounded off by the sinking of the schooner *Tritone*. On the 29th/30th MGBs 662 (Tim Bligh, S.O.), and 660 (Lt. A. H. Robinson) and MTB 634 (Lt. Walter Blount) were ordered by Morgan Giles to patrol north of Zara, and they sailed from Komiza in a brisk wind with moderate sea and swell.

The three boats passed through the Maknare Channel at 17 knots and steered close to Vir Island. For four hours—apart from a sweep round the island to the inner channel—the three boats were lying stopped fifty yards off the north-western point of Vir.

Then at 0155, through binoculars, they saw a ship three-quarters of a mile away to the eastwards. Bligh ordered the boats to close at 14 knots, and soon the ship was identified as a two-masted schooner of between 150 and 200 feet long. Bligh was intrigued by some rather odd superstructure fitted both forward and aft, and suspected that she might be a so-called "Q-schooner".

He could not get into an inshore position and closed the range to about 600 yards to carry out an orthodox gun attack, opening fire at

0211. All three boats scored many hits, but the enemy returned fire from aft in what Bligh later called "a most half-hearted and irresponsible fashion" for about thirty seconds.

Robinson, in 660, was then ordered to close and destroy the schooner. For about five minutes all his guns poured fire into the vessel, but she stubbornly refused to burst into flames. As she seemed to have drifted ashore, Bligh ordered 660 to stand clear while Walter Blount, in 634, fired one torpedo. This was neatly done at 0224, and falling debris hit Robinson's boat, damaging her charthouse. (See picture on p. 208.)

Bligh then closed in 662 to look for survivors and identify the schooner. He found a couple of German marines clinging to a dinghy and they were dragged aboard. The schooner, blown in half by the torpedo, was seen to have been carrying flour and fodder. (See picture on p. 144.)

When the two Germans were interrogated it was discovered that the schooner was the 390-ton *Tritone*, a brand-new ship on her maiden voyage. Incidentally, the two Germans provided the explanation why the forward gun—a 20-mm.—never opened fire. They were the crew for it, and they said there was never any intention on their part to fight three British "cannon-boats". They jumped over the side immediately the boats opened fire, and they appeared to be the only survivors of the crew of eleven who lived to avoid fighting another day.

Bligh, who was rapidly establishing a reputation for being one of Coastal Forces' finest gunboat leaders, wrote in his action report: "When engaging schooners in the Adriatic the previous policy has been to close the range to point-blank before opening fire. This is considered to be uneconomical with single comparatively heavily-armed targets. A five-second burst from a quadruple 20-mm. may easily put a 'D' boat out of action for three months, and if the schooner sees only a single 'D' at a time it might well decide to put up a fight; whereas the concentrated fire from three boats at a range compatible with accuracy but safe from any but considered return fire will have a discouraging as well as purely physical effect on the enemy. It is not suggested to employ these tactics on convoys, but only on single targets which can be assumed to have some armament."

.   .   .   .   .

Commando and Partisan landings on the islands were continued during July. For the boats, August opened with an attack on F-lighters

in which Tim Bligh's own boat,[1] 662, was badly damaged. With
MTBs 670 (Eric Hewitt) and 667 (Jerram) in company, the boats
left Komiza at tea-time on 7th August.

They went northwards up the Adriatic to pass well clear of the
islands south of Dugi, and then to arrive on the Zara-Fiume inshore
shipping lane by passing through the Maknare Channel and thence
right up to the coast of Vir Island (where 662, 634 and 660 had sunk
the *Tritone*).

It was a fine, clear, dark night, with little wind and a flat sea. Visibility was a mile and a half. Just as the nine o'clock news started,
vertical tracer and flares were seen to the southwards and it was
confidently expected that a convoy northbound from Zara (about
thirteen miles away) would be passing by Vir that night. The boats
lay stopped, waiting, 200 yards off the shore.

A few minutes after 2200 dark shapes were sighted through the
binoculars to the southwards. After six or seven minutes the characteristic silhouette of F-lighters could be distinguished and the enemy
was seen to be two F-lighters and a smaller vessel.

The darkness and land background encouraged Bligh to believe that
a gun attack offered the best chance of success (while operating from
Bastia he had seen over twenty of the torpedoes then being used fired
at F-lighters without a hit).

The enemy was in arrowhead formation with a large F-lighter
nearest the "Dogs", the small vessel leading and the other F-lighter on
the far side. At 2212 they altered course to starboard to close the coast;
and as it was essential for the "Dogs" to keep the inshore position,
Bligh started up and moved towards the enemy's inshore beam at
about 6 knots, telling 667 to be ready to illuminate with 2-lb. star-shell
and warning 670 to be ready to carry out a snap torpedo attack.

Two minutes later, when the range was about 350 yards, the enemy
opened fire at 662, scoring immediate hits and putting two engines out
of action. The boats immediately returned fire, concentrating on the
nearest F-lighter. Both groups reduced speed, 662 because she had to and
the F-lighters by choice, and they shot it out at close range, moving very
slowly on opposite courses. For minutes the battle hung in the balance.

MGB 662 was hit again and again and had one man killed and nine
wounded; the engine-room was on fire, the upper deck was covered

---

[1] Bligh was one of the S.O.s who kept his own boat. Some S.O.s preferred not to
have their own boat, embarking in one of their flotillas for a patrol. Each system had its
advantages, and individuals pleased themselves which they did.

with small fires from phosphorous ammunition, and two Oerlikon ammunition lockers were burning; in addition the pom-pom was out of action. But the large F-lighter was also burning fiercely all along the deck, and her gunnery, unlike that of the "Dogs", was faltering. Anything might have happened.

At this point the second F-lighter, which had not deployed her armament very skilfully, altered course and got under way to pass ahead of 662 and then down the boats' inshore beam, and the inference was that she was about to open fire from the disengaged side. This would have been a good move and must have resulted in the sinking of one of our boats. Bligh had only one Oerlikon that could fire on the second F-lighter and did not want to detach 667, which was engaged on the original target, so he ordered 670 to attack with torpedoes.

And then the enemy's morale wilted. The burning F-lighter, which had been giving all the trouble, ceased to fire effectively. And the second F-lighter turned right round to the southwards again and started to steal away with no guns firing. This was very strange and subjected 670 to some rapid manoeuvring. And at twenty-six minutes past ten Eric Hewitt sank his target with one torpedo and became the first Mediterranean "Dog" to sink a moving F-lighter with a Mark IV torpedo: an excellent shot most timeously contrived, especially as 670 was, at the time of firing, doing a "short turn" with engines revolving in opposite directions. And so the excitement ebbed away.

Meanwhile the position in 662 was still not under control. Phosphorous fires were coming to light all over the ship and the fires in the engine-room had been put out only by using the comprehensive methyl-bromide extinguishers, so that the engine-room staff could not stay down below for any length of time (according to the regulations they should not have gone down below at all).

But there were a number of heavy-calibre shell splashes falling round the boats which were believed to come from shore batteries on Vir, so 662 slowly withdrew a little to the eastwards, leaving 667 and 670 to sink the burning F-lighter, lying stopped and silent, with torpedoes. But the providence that guarded those unsightly craft from the ravages of underwater weapons again became operative and all three torpedoes failed to hit, 667's second exploding on a piece of floating wreckage a few yards from the enemy's side.

The two MTBs then searched for survivors and 667 picked up twelve Germans, including the captain of the torpedoed F-lighter, while 670 picked up five. They gave more close-range bursts to the

F-lighter, which turned over and sank at five minutes past midnight, and then rejoined the S.O.

MGB 662 had been carrying a passenger, Capt. B. Keefe, R.A.M.C., who came along in case he could be useful. He certainly earned his passage. He had given treatment during the action to the man who died of wounds and to the nine wounded. He subsequently treated the two motor mechanics who had been overcome by methyl-bromide fumes. And when the MTBs rejoined 662 he was transferred to them in succession to treat the wounded Germans.

The 6-pounder gun's crew on 662 will always remember the calm way he said "Is it always like this?" as he knelt on the deck amid the unpleasantness giving succour and help.

The two ships sunk were the F.963, armed with one dual-purpose 88-mm., one quadruple 20-mm. cannon, one twin 20-mm., two single 20-mm., and some machine-guns; and the F.968, armed with a similar 88-mm., two single 20-mm. and some machine-guns.

Commenting on the action afterwards, the S.O. said that if the second F-lighter had shown a little more spirit, the hitting power of an 88-mm. was such that the tide of battle would have gone completely the other way.

Notwithstanding this, and that the German gun positions were heavily protected with armour and reinforced concrete, he would continue to think that the best way for "Dogs" to attack F-lighters in landlocked waters was to attack with guns, getting as close as possible before opening fire, and that this was not foolhardy. It often seemed that at a certain stage in a gun battle the Germans suddenly realised that they were surrounded by sea, not land, for they would lose confidence in themselves with no reason at all. It was certainly so on that night.

.   .   .   .   .

By this time the 56th Flotilla had arrived in the Adriatic from Bastia, and on the 17th/18th the "Three Musketeers", as the Canadian C.O.s called themselves, went out on patrol in the Mljet Channel— Doug Maitland, the S.O., in 657, Cornelius Burke in 658 and Tommy Ladner in 653.

Burke's First Lieutenant, Reynolds, describes the action: "Since we had arrived in Dalmatian waters we had carried out nine patrols without any enemy contact at all, and the greatest danger was to become careless and take unjustifiable chances because of a false sense of security. . . .

"It was with great jubilation that we heard our R/T loudspeaker click twice, and Doug's 'Hello, Dogs, this is Wimpey. I have possible target. Four small ships moving fast up Mljet Channel. Am steering to intercept. . . .' "

The three boats chased after the enemy, but they were too fast and Maitland returned to the patrol area. The boats stopped under the cliffs of Peljesac. But they had been there only twenty-five minutes when Maitland hailed 658 by megaphone with: "Say, Corny, I think we're in luck. There's three targets at range three miles just coming into the Channel and running down towards us. Start up and get into fine 'Seven Order' [en echelon to starboard]. I shall hold on as long as I can."

Once engines were started, Maitland passed his reports by R/T. "Hello, Dogs, this is Wimpey. Target range two and a half miles, three ships surrounded by several smaller ones. Course 115, speed 6 knots."

Reynolds continues: "Suddenly Corny said: 'Here they are—three in sight, right ahead.' I murmured this information into the loud-hailer, and the gun barrels moved slightly as if in acknowledgement.

"At last came Doug's signal. 'Speed 8 knots, fine Seven Order. Attacking on port bow. Tommy—light please. Range is 500 yards.' As prearranged and rehearsed, Tommy Ladner—the third boat—obediently opened fire at high elevation with pom-pom star-shell, and at once we had a clear picture of what was going on.

"Running down the coast about 800 yards offshore was a convoy of two large schooners and an F-lighter (these three in line ahead) followed by two columns of smaller vessels, landing-craft, E-boats and lighters.

"Our first run was made inshore of them, running on an opposite course and engaging five of the enemy at a range of 300 yards. As we passed the last in line—a Pil-boat—we all gave it concentrated fire and in a matter of seconds it was sunk.

"In the excitement and noisy confusion of continuous firing for four minutes it had not gone unobserved that the answering fire was immediate and heavy, at least from the first three targets. But the majority had been high and erratic. I had not noticed any tell-tale thuds, but as soon as we ceased fire at the end of the run and followed Doug out astern and to seaward of the convoy it was obvious that the engine-room had suffered.

"The 'fruit-machine' clanged and showed that only the starboard outer engine was functioning, and soon after the inspiring figure of

Bill Last, the chief motor mechanic, appeared on the bridge. He was stripped to the waist and his tanned body glistened with perspiration and was covered with oil and grease.

" 'We've got a brick through the port side, sir, and the cooling system's all to pieces. I think I can get the starboard inner going, but the other two are out for the night,' he said. With that he ripped up the bridge deckboards, opened the hatch to the storage space under the bridge, and rigged a hose to pass water through the cooling system by an emergency method.

"Within ten minutes we were able to report two engines running, two permanently disabled. Doug had had a fire under his twin Oerlikon platform and this was now safely extinguished.

"During this interval Doug's radar had held all the ships of the enemy convoy, and as we began the second run, this time from astern, reports came to us giving range, position, course and speed of all the vessels.

"Doug had intended to attack from inshore again, partly to gain the advantage of background but also to give the starboard gunners a chance. However, it became increasingly obvious that the fire of the enemy ships during our first run had set light to all the dry bushes on the Peljesac shore, and these were burning fiercely and giving a first-class illumination to silhouette the enemy for an attack from seaward.

"We sighted the rear of the convoy, still struggling on, and as we overtook the last in line, an E-boat, we pasted it hard until it appeared to be sinking, and at 200 yards set both the small landing-craft accompanying it on fire.

"Only one gun from these three craft offered any resistance, but the schooners were now getting unpleasant. As we passed the three larger ships (the F-lighter held its fire until we were close) we hit them hard, whereas their fire was again high and we breathed again as we moved out ahead of the convoy and disengaged.

"Doug immediately ordered fastest possible speed and put two and a half miles between us and the convoy so that we should have a fair margin of time to prepare for the next run."

Rapidly more ammunition was brought on deck for the pom-poms; Oerlikon pans were reloaded; and Maitland, over the R/T, described the scene astern. One of the large units had stopped. The other two and one of the smaller craft were maintaining the same course and speed. As this was now the main part of the convoy Maitland decided to attack from ahead and slightly to seaward, again making use of the bush fire to silhouette the ships.

"We moved in at 8 knots," Reynolds continues, "and this time the leading schooner challenged us with the letter 'H'. We wondered why she had by this time any doubts that we were hostile. At 400 yards she opened fire on us, and we immediately replied. We could see the pom-pom and Oerlikon shells ripping into her, and after a few seconds she swung away to port towards the near shore.

"We shifted target to the second schooner, and soon were rewarded by the sight of fire spouting up from her high poop-deck. However, the fire from both ships was still quite accurate, and we turned to starboard and withdrew ahead of the convoy again in order to keep clear of the illumination.

"No sooner had we put ourselves about a mile ahead of the convoy than there was a startling explosion. It was the schooner we had left on fire."

At this point Last, the chief motor mechanic came to the bridge and reported that he could not keep the starboard inner engine going. When Burke reported to Maitland that he had only one main engine, Maitland told him to take up "Fleet Number Three", and Ladner, in 663, edged up ahead while 658 dropped astern.

Soon Maitland's voice came over the R/T again: "Hello, Dogs, this is Wimpey. Two of these jokers are still holding course, so we'll wait inshore of them until they come up." The boats moved into an attacking position and a quarter of an hour later the first schooner hove in sight, with a smaller vessel tagging on astern.

"At 300 yards we opened fire and it was returned heavily," Reynolds writes, "but they had by no means our accuracy or fire-power by now and shortly they were both silenced. The smaller boat was set well ablaze and stopped, and the larger schooner had a deck fire and turned sharply inshore under our stern."

Maitland then decided to go back along the Channel for some mopping-up operations. The large schooner was found close inshore and finally blown up. The "Dogs" then found an abandoned oil tanker and sank it with gunfire. After trying to winkle out a craft which was hiding inshore in the smoke, like a hot chestnut in a bonfire, they headed back for Komiza.

Their total score was two schooners, one E-boat, one oil-lighter and one Pil-boat sunk; and at least four other vessels (including the F-lighter, which was not seen again after the first attack) damaged.

Partisans later brought in fourteen prisoners, who revealed that the schooners were each of about 300 tons. One carried ammunition and the other food. Both were sunk on their first voyage after a refit at Split.

.   .   .   .   .

Some weeks earlier the Coastal Forces base had made its way up the east coast of Italy in the rear of the advancing armies. It started from Manfredonia on 23rd June, but had to pause at Guilianova while the Army captured Ancona. Eventually, after an epic journey over bad roads, worse diversions and deep fords it reached Ancona and reported, on 8th August, that all facilities were working and the shop was open for customers.

Chapter XXXII

THE FIRE-EATERS

IN the Aegean at the beginning of the year Coastal Forces continued their task of harassing the enemy shipping. At the same time the R.A.F. and the Americans made various bombing raids on the islands, mainly directed at harbours.

Lt.-Cdr. Peter Evenson's 10th MTB Flotilla was maintaining a two-boat patrol in the approaches to Rhodes. MTBs 260 and 309 were hiding up among the islands nearby from Christmas Day 1943 until 20th January, when they were relieved by 305 and 307, which stayed there for sixteen days. This turn-and-turn-about continued for many weeks.

All three types of Coastal Forces craft were operating among the islands—MTBs/MGBs, MLs and HDMLs—and with them were the vessels of the Levant Schooner Force. Although the latter seemed the odd men out, they were soon "one of the family" as far as Coastal Forces were concerned.

It was in the Aegean that the HDMLs really came into their own. With Diesel engines requiring far less maintenance than petrol engines, these boats did a great deal of patrol work among the islands. Yet they had originally been designed solely to patrol off harbours, as their name implied. In a way they fulfilled this role in the Aegean, except the harbours were enemy-held. . . .

For the first few months of the year there was a shortage of targets, which was very galling for the 10th Flotilla when they heard of the success of the other flotillas in the Adriatic and off the west coast of Italy.

Apart from the three actions at the beginning of January, described earlier, the first five weeks were unproductive: the boats patrolled night after night without finding a target. On the 8th/9th February, however, MLs 836 (Lt. A. E. Clarke, S.O.) and 357 (Lt. A. H. Doughay) captured and then sank a 30-ton caïque.

By March the 10th Flotilla, still working from advanced anchorages, were getting somewhat irritated by the lack of targets, but on the

3rd/4th two MTBs, 307 and 309, managed to find three destroyers and attacked them. Unfortunately there was excessive discharge-flash when they fired their torpedoes, and the enemy were able to take avoiding action.

On the 9th/10th MTBs 266 and 260 made a gun attack on three schooners, a caïque, F-lighter and R-boat. They were completely outgunned and the enemy return fire was heavy. 266's bridge was badly hit and the C.O. and coxswain were killed.

The MLs and HDMLs, greatly heartened by the Bofors guns which had been fitted, were by now penetrating far into the Aegean, often lying up in Turkish waters. One of the successful HDMLs was 1252, which captured several schooners and armed caïques south of Mitylene by boarding.

On the 7th/8th March, HDML 1226 (S/Lt. J. E. Hickford) was on passage with wounded German prisoners, as stretcher cases, laid on deck. Crowded on the craft's tiny wardroom was a refugee mayor and his family of six adults and one child.

Thus burdened, Hickford sighted three enemy lighters and a schooner. He promptly ran 1226 alongside one lighter and put a prize crew on board. The enemy crew of eight were driven into the bows and held up by a couple of ratings. Just as 1226 sheered off to attend to the other vessels, they opened fire. Hickford's gunners immediately replied, but the small craft was soon badly hit. With ammunition on deck exploding and on fire, her forward gun's crew and some of the Germans on stretchers killed, and her decks a shambles, Hickford had to break off the action.

There were still two of his ratings aboard the lighter, but he could not collect them. The enemy crew, seeing the way the action had turned, put up a fight and both ratings had to jump over the side, where the Germans machine-gunned them in the water. One of them was killed.

The other man, however, managed to reach the shore, where he went into hiding. He was later picked up by a Greek caïque and eventually managed to get back to the base at Casteloriso.

The enemy was also being harassed ashore on the islands. There was a series of successful raids during the month by detachments of the Special Boat Squadron and the Long Range Desert Group, transported by Coastal Forces craft and vessels of the Levant Schooner Force.

·   ·   ·   ·   ·

May was a quiet month in the Aegean as far as Coastal Forces were concerned, and the only loss we suffered was HDML 1380, which foundered in bad weather after her engines were put out of action by flooding. Two officers and five ratings were lost.

In June another adversary made itself unpleasant—maintenance. The MTBs had reached the stage where they needed, according to a report to C.C.F., "terrific care and supervision: quite a few, after a refit, managing to get only as far as Casteloriso before breaking down".

MLs were operating in the far north of the sector with "commendable determination and resource" on anti-shipping patrols and also landing raiding parties. On one expedition they destroyed 160-ton, 70-ton and 30-ton caïques, demolished a slipway and set fire to an olive-oil factory.

The next month, July, saw the same pattern of attacks, and many more reconnaissance and offensive raids were made in the Dodecanese, the most important of them being Operation "Tenement". This was a raid on the island of Symi on the 13th/14th when a force of about 220 officers and men brought about the complete surrender of the island garrison.

There were signs in August that the enemy was attempting to build up his forces in the eastern islands of the Aegean in order to be able to fight strong delaying actions. Many of these islands were reconnoitred by Coastal Forces and schooners.

However, there were happenings elsewhere which were to have a vast effect on the Aegean. The month of August saw the first defection by a German satellite: Roumania, after the Red Army had crossed the River Prouth, was disinclined to continue the fight, and on 23rd August, after secret negotiations lasting several weeks, decided it would perhaps be wise to come to terms with the Allies.

This was publicly proclaimed by Michael and a new government was formed. On the 25th, two days later, the government decided to prove they could have their cake and eat it too, and announced that a state of war existed between Roumania and their ex-ally Germany.

Bulgaria, too, had found the wind had veered and was conducting secret negotiations. A proclamation of neutrality was made by Sofia Radio on the 26th. Bulgaria was not then at war with Russia, but on 5th September the Russians declared war on her. Bulgaria promptly asked for an armistice and the next day declared war on Germany.

Hungary was just getting ready to follow suit when the Germans played an ace: they were in a better position to take action against their now-reluctant ally, and when Horthy, the regent, sought an armistice with the Allies in October he was interned in Germany.

All this, following the successful Normandy landings and then the assault on Southern France on 15th August, forced the Germans to start evacuating the Aegean islands.

This was apparent by the early part of September. At the same time more Coastal Forces craft were brought into the Aegean to undertake operations in a new area—the south-western sector. The 60th MGB Flotilla and the 29th ML Flotilla sailed from Brindisi, bound for the island of Kithera. They escorted their own supplies of petrol, stores and water, which were loaded in an LCT and an LCI.

British forces landed on Kithera on 16th September, and the Coastal Forces base was set up at Kapsali. This was the first liberation of Greek territory since the Germans overran the Balkans so many months before.

On the other side of the Aegean another advanced operating base was set up at Khios, and MTBs of the 10th/27th Flotilla and MLs moved up to operate from there. All the boats, especially the MLs and HDMLs, were kept busy mounting raiding force sorties to speed up the enemy evacuation of the islands. As the islands were cleared and Athens was liberated they changed their role to food relief ships.

The Coastal Forces activities leading up to the fall of Athens have been only reported briefly here. It has not been possible to go into any great detail because of the shortage of space, and this is thought to have been justified by the fact that many ML and HDML operations, for instance, have been "false-nose jobs" which fall into a rather special category not completely within the scope of this book.

Chapter XXXIII

OFF TO THE RIVIERA

WE left the west coast of Italy on the eve of the assault on Elba, the mountainous island eight miles off the Tuscan coast which for a year, more than a century before, had been the home of Napoleon. Eighty-five square miles in area, the island has a rugged, deeply indented coastline, with its main port at Portoferraio.

Between 9th and 15th June MGB and MTB patrols were out every night in the Elba area watching for signs of an enemy evacuation, but they did not find any.

The minesweeping MLs were busy. Beginning with the attack on Elba on 17th June (Operation "Brassard") the 3rd and 31st ML Flotillas embarked in a competition to be the first to sweep 100 mines. By 27th July they were both in the nineties.

It is not proposed to describe the actual Elba landing here, since it has been fully described elsewhere; but there are some Coastal Forces activities which we shall record.

The first of these was on the second night after the landings, when Doug Maitland took four boats out for a patrol in the Piombino Channel, between Elba and the mainland. Maitland was embarked in MTB 655 (Pickard) and had MGBs 663 (Tommy Ladner), 633 (Steve Rendall) and 658, which was commanded by "Woj" Bate, as Burke was away on sick leave.

At 0100 the four boats had passed along the south side of Elba and were making a run up the eastern coast when a radar report came over the R/T that there were three targets close inshore "of an appreciable size".

Maitland's voice—"Hello, Dogs, this is Wimpey . . ."—over the R/T warned that he was going in close to fire torpedoes and that all boats should stand by to follow up with a sharp gun attack.

One of the officers in 658 writes: "As we closed in the target became visible as a large destroyer, a corvette or torpedo-boat, and an F-lighter

—either moored or standing close off a small harbour. It certainly looked like an evacuation.

"We were in quarterline to starboard, and almost before we realised what was happening we heard the swish of Pick's torpedoes and Doug's curt order to Steve to fire when on. Trying to focus the targets in my glasses, I saw that almost as the fish were fired the destroyer seemed to gather way and turn towards us.

"We swung into line ahead and turned to port and heard Doug's order 'Open fire'. As I pressed the gun buzzer every one of our guns—and, indeed, all those of the unit—opened up simultaneously and, as if by magic, tracer from the destroyer joined with ours to make a fascinating criss-cross pattern.

"Our old goose-gun (6-pounder) was banging away, and we soon realised that even heavier stuff (as we might have expected) was coming our way. One never has much time to analyse a situation when the boats are moving fast on different bearings, but it had just flashed through my mind that the fish must have missed when there was an explosion from inshore; this hardly interested me as at the same time my glasses told me that the destroyer was really creaming along now and was getting alarmingly close.

"I yelled out: 'He's trying to ram us, I think', and every one of our guns on the port side was still pouring all it could into him. Putting down my glasses, I had a vivid picture of this long sleek craft with a characteristically streamlined funnel (she was an ex-Italian ship) hurtling across our stern. 'Woj' was desperately keeping station on the boat ahead, and I was concerned only with gunnery, so nothing could be done about the grave disadvantage we were at.

"Tracer from the German's 20-mm. had been hitting and flicking over us for some time, but as he passed right astern—and I am convinced he was only thirty or forty yards off—a whole shower of tracer ripped along our decks and there was a blinding flash on the bridge.

"For a few moments there was utter confusion—no noise, but complete bewilderment. I found myself on the deck and struggled to my feet, trying hard to collect my thoughts.

"I still had the loud-hailer 'mike' in my hand, but I had felt a heavy blow on my back and when I put a hand to my face it came away wet and sticky. I looked around. There was a sudden commotion at the wheel, where Hodges, the coxswain, was muttering: 'For Pete's sake the wheel's jammed—I can't turn it.'

"What he didn't say was that he was in a kneeling position, having found it impossible to get up. I called: 'Are you all right, Woj?' and a faint voice answered: 'I think I've got it in the leg—can you fix the wheel?'

"At last (although in fact it was only a matter of seconds) I realised what was wrong. One of the shells had brought down the wireless aerials and recognition lights from the mast and they were festooning the wheel and jamming it.

"I soon pulled these away and yelled for Mike (the pilot) to come and help. At the time of the burst he had been in the charthouse, but he soon scrambled out and began to take in the situation. 'What's the course, Mike?' I asked. We were spinning (or so it seemed) and for nearly a minute we may have been veering madly about the ocean.

"He had an approximate course ready, and as soon as I had got the ship's head round I handed the wheel to Mike and began to scan the blackness ahead for any signs of the other boats.

"As I did so I heard a voice on the R/T loudspeaker calling: 'Hello, Woj, this is Tommy. Are you all right?' I picked up the 'mike' and replied: 'Hello, Tommy, this is Rover—yes, I think so. We're a bit shaken but would like to pick you up. Over.' Back he came with: 'I am making smoke and can see you—can you see me now?'

"I then picked up a smudge of white on the inky horizon and breathed a sigh of relief. 'O.K., Tommy, I can see you—will rejoin fast.' "

The boats then returned to base. Three men had been killed in 658, Bate had been hit with shrapnel, the coxswain wounded in the leg, and three other men had been badly hurt.

. . . . .

A week later Campbell McLachlan's boat was mined. Three boats had gone out from Bastia to try to intercept some minelayers reputed to be busy off San Vicenzo. The boats did not find them and were preparing to return when 640 blew up.

Apparently 658, immediately ahead of her, had set off an acoustic mine which exploded under McLachlan's boat. 658 immediately turned to pick up survivors and found the boat still afloat—although her bows were blown off up to the charthouse. The survivors were picked up by 658 and a PT-boat. Five men were reported missing.

Later, in the Adriatic, Coastal Forces lost more boats through mining, and in almost every case it was the second or third boat in line which blew up.

. . . . .

The first fortnight of August was occupied mainly with preparations for Operation "Dragoon", the Allied assault on Southern France. The Coastal Forces bases had to put in much hard work to equip and prepare boats for the landings.

The 29th ML Flotilla were all fitted with Bofors guns at Algiers, while the 24th were equipped with a number of special radar devices at Ischia. The minesweeping gear of the 3rd and 31st Flotillas was overhauled.

All four flotillas, the 31st being reinforced by three boats of the 8th Flotilla, together with three Special Service HDMLs, assembled at or passed through Maddalena, so that the base handled a total of forty-eight craft. Sixteen were slipped and twenty had engines changed.

The tasks of the MTBs and MLs in "Dragoon" were: the 3rd and 31st Flotillas swept mines ahead of the convoys; the 24th, fitted with their strange radar devices, trailed their coats and waved their magic wands; while the 29th included Air/Sea Rescue among their tasks. The 7th MTB Flotilla was allotted the unspectacular task of guarding the right flank of the landings against seaborne attacks from Genoa and Spezia.

Operation "Dragoon" started on 15th August. It was a complete success and was achieved at a very small cost. Since the landing has been described fully elsewhere, it is proposed to describe it as seen from an ML—556 commanded by the S.O. of the 31st Flotilla, Lt.-Cdr. Ivester Lloyd.

His eight boats were fitted with captured German minesweeping gear, designed for "small, fast craft". When it was first fitted the work-up took the form of experiments, since the only handbooks on how to use the gear were written in Italian. The light German gear had many good points, the most important one being that it allowed the MLs to sweep at surprising speeds: they could do 11 knots with a single sweep and 9 knots with double sweeps.

There was one drawback, however: the craft could not stop without recovering the kites. There was no hydraulic system to get the sweeping gear aboard again: it all had to be hauled in on a hand-winch and lifted inboard with a hand-derrick.

The first division of Ivester Lloyd's flotilla—Lloyd himself, Coleridge, Waugh, Wilmot and Blair—were to sweep ahead of the American assault force on the coast near St. Tropez. The second division, Edelsten-Pope, Head, Binnie and Holloway, worked off Toulon. The 31st moved up from Ischia to Ajaccio, in Corsica, before D-Day.

The assault convoys mostly sailed from Naples, and gunfire support groups sailed from Malta and Taranto.

Two diversionary operations were staged—one off Nice and the other off La Ciotat—on the 14th/15th by groups consisting of gunboats, destroyers, MLs and PT-boats. There were more than 800 vessels flying the White Ensign in the whole operation.

The big convoy which had assembled left Ajaccio bound for the French coast. Lloyd writes: "Standing on the bridge of 556, looking over a placid, oily sea, I was depressed; I could not get the secret chart out of my mind, with its peculiar markings showing heavy and light gun batteries dotted along the shore. It was hoped that *some* of these had been put out of action by bombing, but in any case we had to go right in and try to come out again. . . .

"I slept quite well that night, until a seaman woke me at 0300 and I went on the bridge again. Everything was very dark and very quiet except for the hum of our engines, the churning of screws and the hiss of the water. I gave the order to draw ahead of the convoy, knowing that the other boats would follow, and when we had put enough distance between the convoy and ourselves we started to stream our sweeps.

"This rather complicated evolution had, by this time, become almost automatic with the crew, and we worked each phase of it according to a time-table, flashing a blue light astern to mark the conclusion of each. At last we had all streamed sweeps and the boats astern of 556 were taking up their stations as we moved slowly towards the French coast, which was showing up in the first glow of dawn. . . .

"Excitement was mounting within me, my pulse was quickening.

" 'We're on the sweeping course now,' said Alex.

" 'Increase to full sweeping speed,' I told him.

"Daylight seemed to be coming very quickly—too quickly, it seemed. To the watcher ashore our boats must stand out like a dollar on a negro's back, or so it seemed. I swung the binoculars along the coast.

" 'There's the lighthouse!' I cried. 'You can get a fix on that and the cape to the eastward.'

"There was so much to think about that the shore batteries marked on a chart became only one piece in the pattern. In any case, if the gunners knew their job, they'd spot us for sweepers and hold their fire until we started to turn. I could see the silver ripple of the Oropesa's bow wave and, not far astern of it, the bigger bow wave of the following ML. Less light would have made things more difficult for the shore gunners; more light would help us to see any floating or surface-laid mines. Sweeping conditions were perfect, with no wind, a flat sea and little current to worry about.

"We went right in until our gear was nearly sweeping the sea-bed, and then I started to turn. Until that time not a shot had been fired by either side. We were halfway in our turn when there were flashes ashore and bursts over our heads.

" 'Open up with the 3-pounder, and tell 'em to aim at the gun-flashes,' I told Alex, and blew a defiant blast on my hunting horn.

"The crew were shouting with delight, the little ship was shuddering with the old saluting gun's kick and the drag of the heavy sweeping gear being towed at brisk speed. Our battle ensign was fluttering from a yardarm, and as we swung in our turn to port the roar of the bombardment smashed the morning quiet.

"To seaward was a line of flashes where the big guns were opening up with all their heavy stuff. Closer inshore were occasional skyward waves of fire, terrifying in their unexpectedness, as the LCRs sent up their rockets to descend on the defences and blow them to dust.

"A shoal of small, fast craft, low in the water, darted past us like a spiteful swarm of roused wasps—the assault landing-craft going in to the beaches, along the channel which we had swept. I slapped Alex on the shoulder.

" 'At last Farmer's Boys have done something worth-while!' I shouted. . . ."

Allied shipping losses were negligible. Coastal Forces losses included ML 563, which went to try to save survivors from a ship which had hit a mine and fell victim to one herself (the S.O. of the 3rd Flotilla and a rating being severely hurt); ML 562, damaged by shellfire from a shore battery; ML 559, damaged by two mines exploding close ahead; and three PT-boats, all mine victims.

. . . . .

The Vosper MTBs of the 7th Flotilla and American PT-boats maintained their patrols, and September saw the operations of Blomfield's 7th MTB Flotilla reach the highest level yet, and enemy coastal traffic between Genoa and Spezia suffered. In a series of eight remarkable actions seven F-lighters, four large barges, one large merchant ship and a corvette were sunk; and one merchant vessel and six F-lighters were claimed as "probables".

The C.C.F.'s summary noted: ". . . On every occasion, so well was the approach carried out, that the torpedo attack was delivered unobserved; only when withdrawing did our boats come under fire."

In one of these operations, on the 26th/27th, off Sestri Levanti, the S.O. was Steve Moore embarked in PT 559 (Lt. R. Nagle, U.S.N.R.), with MTBs 377 (Aitchison) and 376 (S/Lt. G. R. Masters).

As usual the PT-boat was the only one with effective search radar, although the British radar in the MTBs was capable of detecting a target given previous information of its whereabouts and from then on giving accurate ranges.

The PT-boat had picked up a target, plotted it and relayed the information to the other two boats. The attack started with the MTBs approaching in port quarterline on the PT-boat. Lt. Aitchison, D.S.C., C.O. of 377, describes the rest of the operation:

"The night was an extremely dark one, and the convoy was close inshore. With the additional disadvantage of having the S.O.'s boat between myself and the target, I had great difficulty in sighting the target. In fact I had still seen nothing at all when Bob Nagle dropped two fish and turned away to starboard.

"The voice of the radar operator, continually calling ranges, was coming clearly up the voice-pipe, and already these ranges were well under 2,000 yards and I could see nothing at all. If I didn't soon get those fish off, 376 would have small chance of a shot; but then, to my immense relief, there came a whoosh and splash from her. From the corner of my eye I caught the splash of a fish right alongside, and then heard the anxious voice of A.B. Harry King on the port tube—'376 has fired, sir! Just missed us!'

"Now I could carry on with an easy mind until I really could see what we were shooting at. At last, with the range at somewhere about 1,000 yards, I did make out a dark shape, but as soon as I put the binoculars down it was gone. Holding the glasses close to the sights and as near as possible in line with them, I searched again.

"There it is: down glasses: adjust the enemy bar a fraction.

" 'Port a bit, 'swain—steady.'

"Even now it would be exaggerating to say I can see it without glasses, but we are on line, I am sure. The coxswain has his nose almost inside the compass cover, the soft red glow of the compass light reveals the intensity of his expression, both hands reaching down in front of him as he moves the spokes of the wheel swiftly to and fro, only an inch or two at a time but keeping the boat as steady as a train on railway lines.

"The only sound is the radar operator's voices calling the ranges from below; a note of excitement creeps in as he calls '800'. I can see the target now—at least, I see a spot that's blacker than the rest and moving into the line of sight.

" '700 yards . . .' She's coming along nicely.

" '600 yards . . .' Must fire now or we'll be too close by the time the fish are in the water.

"I move my eye closer to the sight and at once lose the enemy, but there's something moving out there, the darkness is changing! That's it. Fire, quickly!

"The boat seems to miss a step as the fish lurch out of the tubes. The coxswain straightens up and the voices of the torpedomen come unnecessarily from the stern reporting that the fish are away. A moment to let them get away and then 'Starboard wheel, 'swain'.

"We swing slowly away and I reach for the throttles to push them gently upwards. The boat has hardly begun to gather way when there comes the indescribable roaring crash of a huge explosion. A brilliant flash lights the sea as though the sun has been switched on, and the boat receives a savage kick along her flat bottom.

"The instant of light leaves an impression of a bay full of ships, almost upon us—R-boats, F-lighters, a corvette-like vessel and a large tug just ahead of the explosion. Time we weren't here. My thumb is already on the engine-room buzzer. Three short pips, and then I push the throttles right back to their limit.

"The boat's stern sinks as she gathers way rapidly, the silencers come out with a roar that seems somehow to change the scene. But they still do not see us because streams of tracer are snaking out in all directions. Star-shell go up, and the tracer swings towards us, all converging as the gunners sight us.

"I reach across and wrench a small calcium float from its rack alongside the bridge and hurl it over the starboard side. By the time it shows clear of us and our wash we shall be well past. A tiny flame breaks clear into smooth water well astern and the tracer all swings towards it. The gunners soon realise their mistake and swing back again, but in those few moments we've covered a lot of ground and they'll be lucky to hit us now.

"As we retreat to seawards, coming on to a steady course as we get out of range, we look back towards the shore, and there a straight column of smoke rises up high into the sky, well clear of the land silhouette.

"Presently Steve's voice comes over the R/T giving us a course to rejoin and then, a little later, ordering us to stop and giving a bearing, from us, on which he will approach. We're soon together again and close with silenced engines to compare notes before getting under way and falling once more into line."

·   ·   ·   ·   ·

The Coastal Force base at Bastia closed down on 29th September; and the following week the entire base staff, equipment and transport was transferred to Leghorn by LSTs and the Italian depot ship *Paccinotti*.

After their fine run of actions in September, October was an anti-climax. Weather went against the boats, although Leghorn was more sheltered than Bastia. Stung, no doubt, by his losses in September, the enemy greatly increased the fire-power of the convoys he sent to sea. He did this either by including destroyers or corvettes as escorts, or putting even heavier gun armament on craft like F-lighters. The convoys clung even closer to the coastline; and both the ships in the convoy and shore batteries were very much more on the alert and prepared to light up the night sky with star-shells at the slightest provocation. The result was that MTBs, on the two or three occasions that contact was made during the month, were driven off by heavy gunfire or unable to get into an attacking position.

Chapter XXXIV

"FLAP" PATROL

OVER in the Adriatic September produced a record number of patrols for any area; but more important, the Germans started to evacuate the southern Dalmatian islands. By the end of the month they had left most of the major islands; and this withdrawal was linked with the withdrawal of enemy troops in Greece and the Aegean islands, referred to in earlier chapters. The process was accelerated and rendered unpleasant by boats operating from Vis, and British and Partisan troops were landed.

On 6th September they landed on the south coast of Hvar Island and on the 11th at Brac. Supplies and reinforcements were ferried from Vis by Coastal Forces and landing-craft until the 18th, by which time both islands were under Allied or Partisan control.

The MTBs and MGBs had a successful month. On the 7th/8th two boats, 667 (Jerram) and 674 (Bowyer), under Basil Bourne sank a small E- or MAS-boat in the Hvar Channel, and this was followed on the 13th/14th by an action off Sumartin by three boats led by Davidson—637, 634 (Walter Blount) and 674 (Bowyer)—when four Pil-boats were sunk. The longest Coastal Forces patrol of the Mediterranean war took place on the 3rd/4th, when 662 (Bligh), 674 (Bowyer), 637 (Davidson) and 634 (Blount) sank seven craft and took eighteen prisoners in an action off Cephalonia. The boats were under way for forty-seven hours and covered 535 miles.

The next night Davidson, Blount and Bowyer carried out gun attacks which resulted in the sinking or destruction of three more Pil-boats and a large landing-craft. The latter, loaded with ammunition, blew up, and as the Senior Naval Officer, Vis, remarked, "definitely sealed the fate of the enemy forces surrounded by Partisans in the Sumartin area".

By 20th September the only enemy force remaining in these islands was being attacked from the land on Sulet Island, and on the 22nd/23rd their final attempt at evacuation was ruthlessly dealt with by two "Dogs" under Corny Burke, who by now was a lieutenant-commander.

The operation started with the Staff Officer. Operations at Komiza appearing in 657 with: "How soon can you get a unit out? We need two boats on a 'flap patrol'."

Burke left in 655 (McLachlan) with 633 (Rendall) and headed north at full speed to Sulet Island, where the 43rd Royal Marine Commando, involved in heavy fighting with the enemy, had signalled that a German evacuation was likely that night.

Arriving off Rogac Cove, the most likely point of departure for the Germans, Burke almost immediately sighted three I-boats leaving the beach. Realising this was the one time when they would be least expecting trouble from seaward, he attacked immediately. Both boats opened fire together and all three of the German craft were hit. They replied with sporadic 20-mm. fire, but at the end of the run (with the range 200 yards) all were on fire and silenced.

Burke then turned round and made another run, opening fire from fifty yards. Almost at once one of the enemy blew up with a double explosion, showering the two MTBs with debris. Since the bay was quite small, Burke ordered Rendell to stand off, then he searched the beach for the remaining two I-boats. But they had disappeared—sunk, he subsequently discovered.

Later Lt.-Cdr. Morgan Giles, the Senior Naval Officer, Vis, was able to confirm what had happened. The whole of the German garrison on Solta, about 200 men, had embarked in the three I-boats with their mules, equipment, guns and ammunition. Two of the I-boats blew up and the third had sunk rapidly, some of the survivors managing to reach the shore.

. . . . .

About this time several changes in command were made in the Mediterranean which affected Coastal Forces. Bobby Allan had become the Senior Officer, Inshore Squadron, in place of Capt. Dickinson, who had become Senior Naval Officer, Northern Adriatic. Doug Maitland, who had been V.56 (Senior Officer, 56th Flotilla), was appointed Capt. Dickinson's Staff Officer, Operations. Cornelius Burke was then appointed Senior Officer of the 56th.

. . . . .

September had seen a big increase in enemy minelaying, mainly by E-boats, in the swept channels. The first victim was MGB 657, which had her stern blown off about sixty miles north of Ancona. The after part of the boat had been sliced off up to the after bulkhead of the petrol space. The deck had been curled up by the explosion like a large shaving from a smoothing plane. Five men were killed. The damaged boat was towed back to base.

The next mine victim was ML 258, which had her bows blown off back to the bridge. This occurred on the 15th/16th, and she too was towed back to base.

In the Northern Adriatic during this month Vospers of Lancaster's 20th Flotilla worked hard to find targets off the Istrian Peninsula, but there were no large rewards being offered. Ten patrols were made without sighting anything hostile or warlike. Peter Hyslop was out in 374 on the 10th/11th with 295 (Cassidy) when they captured and scuttled a 300-ton barge.

The next month, October, was also not very productive in the Northern Adriatic: in the Gulf of Venice and Trieste there were numerous patrols off Rimini, Maestro Point, Chioggia, Tagliamento Point, Parenzo and Cittanova, but very few contacts.

Smyth (642) and McLachlan (655) had a successful night off Maestro Point on the 8th/9th when, with gun attacks, they managed to sink two schooners, probably sunk a third and damaged a fourth before the escort, a destroyer, fired star-shell and rudely interrupted the proceedings, wounding some men and damaging Smyth's boat.

The next night the minefields scored another victory. MGB 663, commanded by Lt. W. R. Darracott, D.S.C. and Bar (both won as a first lieutenant), who had been Tim Bligh's Number One blew up while returning from patrol off Venice. The unit was being led by Basil Bourne, followed by 649 (Hughes) and 663.

The boats were doing 18 knots when the mine exploded beneath Darracott's boat. The explosion blew him out of the bridge and doubled him over a guard-rail. Derick Brown, the First Lieutenant, was tossed out and landed up on an Oerlikon ammunition locker, and Nicholl, the coxswain, finished up above him on the depression rails. Altogether three men were killed and eight wounded.

CHAPTER XXXV

GUN ATTACK

THE main interest was among the islands north of Zara. On the last two nights of September four "Dogs" had lain up at Ist, but very bad weather had prevented them from operating. On 10th October four boats left Komiza to patrol off Zara and then lie up at Ist. They fought one of the most brilliant and successful Coastal Forces actions of the Mediterranean, and probably of any other theatre of operations.

The boats, under V.57, Tim Bligh, were his own 662, and MTBs 634 (Walter Blount), 637 (Davidson), and 638 (Lummis). The weather was fine—a light breeze from the north-east, no swell, and visibility 1,000 yards until moonrise at 0114.

They left Komiza at 1300 on the 10th, heading northwards at 17 knots in arrowhead formation. Walter Blount, who had been to Ist before, was sent ahead at 19 knots to contact a Long Range Desert Group officer and the Partisans to get the latest naval intelligence.

From now on the narrative is taken from Bligh's action report, which also included the reports of the three C.O.s. Blount "reported that the intelligence he had been given was as follows. A northbound convoy of some four or five ships (mostly F-boats) had been seen by L.R.D.G. to enter Zara some three or four days ago and it was to be expected that they would endeavour to proceed northwards as soon as possible.

"Further, no shipping had been seen either northbound or southbound for three days and there was a certainty of something passing near Vir Island during the night. In addition, three Partisan 'Tigers' were patrolling the Maon Channel to the northwards (where they had recently sunk one and captured another enemy schooner), and a Ju.88 had machine-gunned a small ship in Ist Bay at dawn two days previously.

"Accordingly the unit was led between Ist and Mulat (a very narrow but deep channel) at 1945 and course was set to close Vir Island on

247

silent engines, the three 'Tigers' being sighted on the port beam, forming up into their cruising formation as the leading boat left the channel.

"At 2040 the unit closed the coast of Vir and lay stopped, in wait for the promised northbound convoy. The weather was very dark and thundery, with vivid flashes of lightning to the southwards; but apart from two panics caused by the spire of Zara church, all was quiet.

"At 2245 three white flares were seen over Mulat.

"At 2347 much tracer was seen coming from Ist, in what appeared to be a land battle, but the L.R.D.G. representatives on board 634 considered that a low-flying air attack was being made on the harbour. I myself thought this unlikely, and was of the opinion that an E-boat was firing irresponsibly for some obscure reason known only to the enemy. (I had seen this happen before, in the same place, on the night of 26th June, this year.)

"The firing then ceased, but ten minutes later broke out farther south, near Mulat. This time there were some flares (or star-shell) being used, and some large flashes were seen on the land, and the air-craft theory seemed possible: however, some 88-mm. tracer was identified from the eastern side of Mulat and its was obvious something was taking place.

"In view of the intelligence reports received earlier in the evening, I was averse to leaving the patrol area—in fact the firing may have been a diversion to draw our craft away from the eastern side of the channel —but it did seem possible that there was at least one F-lighter or Siebel ferry over on that side, so at 0039 MTB 634 was detached to go to Ist to contact the L.R.D.G. or Partisans and find out what was happening, whilst the remainder of the unit stayed in the patrol area.

"At 0223 MTB 634 made R/T contact with MTB 637 and reported that there had been two destroyers in position 206 degrees four and a half miles Veli Rat Light, having previously sent a W/T signal to me to the effect that there was heavy firing to seaward, and broadcasting an enemy report. MTB 634 also reported that an F-lighter had been seen by the Partisans in amongst the islands, but was southbound.

"The unit at once proceeded to Kok Point to rendezvous MTB 634, torpedoes were set to 3 feet and 5 feet, radar switched on and a course set to pass between Skarda and Ist, to carry out a sweep outside the islands to try to find the two destroyers. Search was abandoned at 0345, and as there was a rising wind and sea the unit returned to Ist.

"It seemed probable that the destroyers had proceeded northward at high speed directly after the bombardment, and the chance of catching them was remote. My opinion is that I was justified in staying off Vir and not leaving my area, but that I should have detached MTB 634 earlier, when I might have been able to have contacted the enemy.

"At 0900 a Partisan reported a large warship with two funnels in a cove on the east side of Mulat, a moderately alarming report to have received at any time, but this dwindled to an F-lighter by 1000, an E-boat by 1100 and a 'trick of the light' by 1200.

"At 1730 a conference was held with the local authorities and it was decided to repeat the previous night's patrol, with the additional proviso that if any shipping at all was sighted near Ist a prearranged pyrotechnic signal would be made from the Partisan look-out post.

"Having thus secured the rear, the unit proceeded to Vir at 1825.

"It had been decided that the big demonstration put up by the enemy the previous night (which included torpedoes fired by E-boats at Mulat breakwater) was aimed at eliminating some 'Tigers' and/or MGBs and that it was probable that he would try and run a big convoy north this night. Hence the unit closed Vir Island and was disposed along the coast to meet a northbound convoy.

"Some flares were seen to the southwards, and there were some lights and flickerings in the sky over Nin—all appeared to be set. At 2215 some vertical tracer was seen off Zara.

"At about 2220 MTB 634's starboard outer engine pushed a con-rod through the crank case and most of the engine-room crew were overcome by fumes.

"At about 2245 all the boats started rolling, as if a lot of ships had passed to seawards, so at 2300 the unit proceeded northwards, a guess that eventually proved correct.

"The visibility was now very low, due to widely-scattered low cloud, but I was not prepared for the shock of suddenly seeing enemy ships on the port bow, at about 400 yards' range.

"The unit was at once stopped and the boats headed into the shore just north of Vir Light. The targets were now seen to be four F-lighters, of which one was altering course towards us: he appeared to be higher out of the water than the others and was possibly an escorting 'flak' lighter: he had probably sighted one or more of the unit and was closing to drive us off.

"MTB 634 was ordered to try and carry out a snap torpedo attack on this target, whilst MGB 662 ordered 'Single line ahead, speed 8 knots' and went ahead in order to engage the remainder by gunfire.

"The 'flak' boat opened fire on MGB 662 at 2306, at once killing one of the pom-pom loading numbers. Fire was returned from all guns, and MTB 638 illuminated with star-shell.

"It is scarcely possible to describe the next ten minutes. The visibility was such that the leading boat in the line had a completely different picture from the fourth boat, and the slight offshore breeze was blowing smoke from MGB 662's gunfire across the line of sight of our ships and the enemy convoy, which was, of course, much more of an advantage to us than them, as we had the inshore position and knew where to expect them, while the only ship that they could see was MGB 662.

"But it will, in fact, be easier to give the impressions of each boat during this phase of the action and try to paint the picture that each one saw than to give a coherent account of what the unit did."

MGB 662's Narrative

"MGB 662 had drawn ahead of MTB 634, who had manoeuvred for a torpedo attack, and was engaging many targets on the port side, including F-lighters, Pil-boats and E-boats. Very heavy 88-mm. and 20-mm. was coming our way, all high, from a variety of vessels, and this fire had a strong blinding effect on my bridge. Nevertheless I saw a Pil-boat hit by the 6-pounder and blow up, starting a petrol fire on the surface of the water.

"In the light of MTB 638's star-shell ahead, I saw F-lighters being hit by my pom-pom and Oerlikon. I saw an E-boat in the light of the petrol fire hit, set alight and blow up—a victory achieved by the bridge .303-inch Vickers, and on the port quarter I witnessed an inspiring display of 6-pounder gunnery. An F-lighter, at about 400 yards, was steering away from us, unilluminated and almost invisible, even through binoculars, yet the 6-pounder fired nearly thirty rounds that scored hits in about a minute. The 6-pounder also hit and sank a Pil-boat with an inert cargo.

"Meanwhile MGB 662 had crossed the northern end of the convoys and was lying stopped, waiting for the other boats to rejoin, and trying to ensure that no enemy got away.

"It had been intended to work round to the west of the enemy immediately and engage them against the fires of their burning vessels, but this was not possible until all the boats had come round.

"Everywhere on the port side there were burning ships and explosions. There were visible many more ships than the original four F-lighters. The sight was fantastic."

MTB 634's Narrative[1]

"The Senior Officer signalled 'Single line ahead, speed 8 knots' and opened fire on the enemy, which now appeared clearly as four F-lighters, three of which were stopped or proceeding slowly northwards in single port cruising line. One was closing.

"I prepared to attack the 'flak'-lighter with torpedoes, but the range had closed to 100 yards by the time the sight was on, and I decided it was too close, so I altered back to starboard and opened up with all guns on the 'flak'-lighter who was firing at MGB 662.

"As I turned, less than fifty yards from the 'flak'-lighter, MTB 634 was hit in the port pom-pom ready-use locker, which exploded and went up in flames. The fire was promptly extinguished.

"All our guns continued to pour an intense fire into the 'flak'-lighter, which burst into flames from stem to stern, by the light of which every detail of her could be discerned. She appeared to have an 88-mm. amidships, a quadruple 20-mm. aft and many 20-mm. in sponsons down the starboard side.

"Her bridge collapsed and she appeared to be breaking in two. I steered parallel to the enemy, who was turning slowly to port, at less than forty yards. Then another F-lighter, followed by two more, appeared very close to seaward of the burning 'flak'-lighter.

"They were well lit up by the flames and steering southwards in single line ahead. All my guns fired on the middle one and then the last one, and fires were started on both. All three were seen to be engaged by MTBs 637 and 638. Astern of the south-going F-lighters, what looked like an E-boat, bows on to us, appeared. This was engaged by the port 0.5-inch turret and was seen by me to explode and disappear.

"On rejoining, the 'flak'-lighter of the northbound group was seen to sink in a cloud of smoke and steam half a mile to seaward of the engagement and all the remaining F-lighters appear to have been driven south by MGB 662."

MTB 637's Narrative[2]

"At 2306 the enemy opened fire and MTB 634 altered course to port to attack with torpedoes. The Senior Officer and MTB 634 were

[1] Lt. W. E. A. Blount, D.S.C.   [2] Lt. R. C. Davidson, D.S.C.

engaging targets unseen by us, but fires could be seen breaking out. My pom-pom was engaging a northbound F-lighter, but as MTB 638 was on the port beam no other guns could fire. (This was due to the fact that I was manoeuvring to keep station on MTB 634's gun-flashes.)

"However, in a few seconds I opened fire with all guns on a target which was headed northwards. It was bows-on to another burning F-lighter. The range of the target was about seventy-five yards and every detail of the vessel was discerned. At this range none of our guns could miss. She immediately caught fire. The after superstructure resembled Wembley Stadium on a dark night, except for the Nazi flag. The gunners reduced it to a blazing wreck, and another large target seen abeam of this blaze was being engaged by MTB 638 with accurate fire.

"At 2317 two large objects were observed on the port beam and turned out to be upturned vessels."

MTB 638's Narrative[1]

"At 2305 the Senior Officer signalled enemy ahead. They were invisible to us at this moment. The boats ahead opened fire. My pom-pom illuminated with star-shell as previously arranged. An F-lighter was set on fire, fine on my port bow, and this illuminated two F-lighters, a Pil-boat and an E-boat on my port beam, steering southwards.

"We sank the Pil-boat with Oerlikon and concentrated on an F-lighter at 200 yards. Shells could be seen ripping open her side. This target was left burning fiercely, and fire was directed on another F-lighter which was hit with all guns and set on fire. An E-boat appeared on the starboard quarter and was hit with Oerlikon. We sustained one 20-mm. hit in this engagement."

Bligh's report then continues: "At 2314 the situation was resolving itself and a sweep was carried out round to the west and south to discourage any of the enemy from returning to Zara. An active F-lighter could be seen to seaward of the scene of the action, steering south, but he turned inshore, and I was confident that we would easily find him again: I somehow felt that none of the enemy would try and push any further north, and was mostly concerned with the southern flank.

[1] Lt. D. Lummis.

"At 2346, when about one mile from Vir Light, an F-lighter was seen close inshore; it was turned over and submerged, and was thought to be the one that had been damaged by MGB 662's 6-pounder. There was another possible small target here also, but I was looking for the other F-lighters and decided not to investigate. It was probably a wreck anyhow.

"At 2353 targets were sighted at Green 20, and MTB 637 was ordered to illuminate with star-shell. This was done well, and MGB 662 opened fire with all guns on an F-lighter and a Pil-boat or E-boat lying close inshore, near Vir Point. The F-lighter was seen to sink; the smaller craft was also hit.

"The enemy now opened heavy fire from a position abaft the beam, almost certainly one of the F-lighters lying very close to the beach, well north of Vir Light and completely invisible. All boats returned fire at the flashes, and some damage may have been inflicted, as the enemy craft ceased fire until we were going away to the northward, when they fired vigorously at nothing to the south-west.

"It was thus decided to go away and lie off until the moon got up and the light improved, and then come back and torpedo the remaining enemy. This entailed some risk of losing the enemy if he crept close to the coast, but I decided to place complete confidence and reliance in my radar set and its experienced operator, and to lie off, stopped at about 4,000 yards.

"I felt certain that we should be able to pick up any F-lighters that tried to move, but had to admit that if a Pil-boat wanted to get away—well, then it could; but I did not want to risk losing any boats by taking them into a dark coast with a belligerent group of well-armed vessels lying on the beach, when there was a big improvement of visibility due in two hours' time.

"Various echoes were plotted during the next two hours, but they turned out to be ghost or aircraft echoes in the centre of the channel.

"It was now planned to approach the coast just north of Vir Light in very broad single line abreast to starboard, on a north-easterly course with torpedoes ready for immediate firing. MGB 662 was to illuminate the coastline with star-shell, and the first MTB to sight an F-lighter was to fire torpedoes and say so at once on the intercommunication; no other MTB was to fire torpedoes until the result of the first attack was observed. By spreading out the unit danger from enemy fire was reduced, and perfect intercommunication ensured that good control could be maintained.

"It is at this point worth noting that during the waiting period there were several little explosions from two positions on the coast between Vir Point and Vir Light.

"At 0151 the moon was giving moderate light and it was decided to carry out the third attack of the night. All went according to plan until 0221 when MGB 662 opened fire with star-shell. Then the first hitch occurred in that, under the light of the shells that did illuminate, nothing of any size could be seen.

"After twenty minutes' searching with star-shell by both MGB 662 and MTB 634, and some pom-pom fire from all boats, at the two small objects north of Vir Light that had been seen, and nothing having happened from the beach, it was decided to close very near the coast and run down to the southward.

"At 0251, when about fifty yards off the coastline, the unit was brought round to south-west and set off down the coast in single line ahead at 8 knots.

"At 0254 a very large F-lighter was sighted dead ahead, at about 450 yards, with bows into the beach, a perfect torpedo target. MGB 662 at once altered course to starboard, ordering MTB 634 to sink the target with torpedoes and lay off ready to engage with covering gun-fire. MTB 634 fired at 0256, scoring hits with both torpedoes, and the unit, in loose formation, was stopped to the eastward of the smoking wreckage. (See picture on p. 128.)

"At 0310 MGB 662 decided to close the small piece of F-lighter still visible to try and identify it. Smoke was being carried away from the shore by a light breeze and MGB 662 went through this 'screen' to the southwards at 0314. At that moment I found myself only fifty yards from a beached convoy of two F-lighters and some small craft.

"Fire was at once opened with all guns and the unit called to close me with despatch. These beached craft were heavily damaged by gunfire from all boats, and the one F-lighter that was not burning was sunk by a torpedo from MTB 637 at 0337.

"During the whole of this third attack the enemy could not have fired more than twenty rounds in all. . . ."

In one night the four boats had, it was considered, sunk six F-lighters, four Pil-boats and one E-boat; probably sunk another F-lighter; possibly sunk another E-boat, and damaged two E-boats by gunfire.

Bligh, in concluding his action report, wrote: "This was the first really decisive victory of D-boats over the old enemy, F-lighters, and was made possible due to low visibility, land background, uncertainty of identification, absurdly close ranges, excellent gunnery and admirable coolness on the part of the following commanding officers."

Captain Stevens, the C.C.F., commenting on the action, wrote: "To the factors which made victory possible must unquestionably be added brilliant and inspiring leadership. . . ."

CHAPTER XXXVI

STABLING THE HORSE

B Y the middle of October the enemy had moved so far north that Vis was no longer an effective base for operations, and Snovis, Lt.-Cdr. Morgan Giles, planned to use a landing-craft as a mobile headquarters among the islands.

This LCH (Landing Craft, Headquarters) arrived at Vis and was promptly spotted by Cerni, Tito's naval commander-in-chief. He went along to Giles with the request: "Can we borrow your Landing Craft, Horse?"

Giles, somewhat puzzled by this request, asked for more details. Cerni explained that he had seen a landing-craft outside with a structure on top resembling a stable, and on the side was painted "LCH 282". What could be clearer?

On 20th October Giles moved his headquarters to the island of Ist, and on the 21st, Trafalgar Day, five boats of the 57th Flotilla were ordered to join him from Vis. Bligh sailed in daylight in 662, taking MGBs 659 (Barlow), 674 (Bowyer) and MTBs 637 (Davidson), 638 (Lummis).

As the five boats headed northwards they suddenly sighted a convoy of four I-boats. In a short space of time two were sunk and two were captured, along with ninety-two prisoners. It was eventually discovered the convoy was an attempted German evacuation from Dubrovnik. It was a somewhat ill-fated one: the fifth I-boat was captured off Vis, the sixth in open sea off Ancona, and prisoners said the seventh had scuttled itself.

Vospers of the 20th Flotilla also joined Giles' force from Ancona, and on the 22nd Landing Craft Horse 282 arrived at Ist and Giles established his headquarters aboard, while ML 240 sailed with the German officers and wounded from Bligh's haul of prisoners the previous day.

The same night the first patrols went out: V 57, Tim Bligh, sailed with five boats to patrol fifteen miles west of Dugi to intercept a small convoy reported by the Senior Naval Officer, Northern Adriatic (Snona), and two LCGs sailed to a position close inshore off Veli Rat in case the convoy tried to creep along the coast. But both forces were unlucky.

Some enemy destroyers (a term loosely used to describe old destroyers, new-construction torpedo-boats and corvettes) had been causing a lot of trouble among the islands. They had a brush with the LCGs and "Dog" boats on the 23rd but escaped undamaged.

On the same day—this fact is mentioned merely because it has not been possible to fully describe the co-operation which existed between the British and the Partisans—the two I-boats captured by Tim Bligh were handed over to the Partisans. These replaced a "Tiger"[1] accidentally sunk by a South African Beaufighter in Olib Harbour two days earlier.

Life aboard LCH 282 was anything but peaceful. Apart from the need to be forever changing anchorages to avoid providing a sitting "horse" for an E-boat, German destroyer or one-man submarine, Morgan Giles had the task of operating the MTBs, MGBs, MLs and landing-craft working from the islands; arranging the agents who cheerfully sat on enemy-held islands and radioed sighting reports if they saw ships passing; co-operating with the R.A.F. regarding targets; and generally working with the Partisans. This was, of course, in addition to the pile of administrative detail such a job entailed.

But although the "Tigers" had little idea about time or navigation, although friendly vessels were shot up by friendly aircraft, although— at this particular time—the German destroyers could not be caught, it was an interesting job.

On 26th October, four days after LCH 282 arrived, a Croat arrived in Ist and said he had been aboard two German destroyers which for two days had been lying up during daytime in a cove on the south coast of Rab Island under camouflaged netting.

Giles suggested to Fotali (Flag Officer, Taranto) that we should send destroyers into the Adriatic to deal with the enemy vessels, although, as will be seen later, this was not approved.

To give some idea of the tempo of life aboard LCH 282 it is proposed to give extracts from the rough log[2] for 28th October.

0400. *Sailed MFV 2017 to Vis.*

0905. *Message received from ML 494 in Mulat that enemy vessel*

---

[1] A Partisan schooner.   [2] For various reasons times are approximate.

R

(destroyer or above) had been sighted and reported by Partisans in Olib. Shortly after that an observation post party on another island reported an unknown vessel, probably a destroyer, moving north.

0922. ML 494 reports ship now identified and has been seen at 0920 at Seleva, moving down Silba Channel.

Partisan 2 Sektor H.Q. states the ship is a hospital ship painted black and flying a Red Cross flag.

1300. Vosper MTBs 287 (S.O.), 371 and 295 arrive from Ancona.

1650. Signal received from Fotali that hospital ship Bonn operating in this area is not accepted by British Government and must be taken prize.

1535. Signal from Fotali not approving that destroyers should operate in the area.

1630. LCH 282 and MTBs 297, 287, 371 and ML 240 sailed to operate north of Olib.

2000. Two enemy destroyers sighted at 1958, course south, speed 20 knots plus. Lost by radar at 2006.

2110. Vospers despatched to Pag.

2115. Recalled Vospers in receipt of (radar) echo 198 degrees five and a half miles.

2115. Loud German R/T (heard)—"Achtung, Achtung" etc. Echo for which Vospers recalled later proved false.

2121. Echo again detected.

2155. Echo faded.

2201. Loud German R/T (heard) giving series of numbers . . . then "Achtung von Otto ——", "In direction of ——", "south-west corner of ——".

2235. Echo having appearance of several craft at first appeared to be going south-east down Maon Channel, then towards Novalja Harbour, where it faded.

2240. Vospers detached to Skerda Channel to intercept.

2246. German R/T cipher "Otto" was calling "Richard".

2326. Very loud German R/T in cipher—"Otto" to "Richard".

2332. Merchant vessel making smoke sighted to seaward.

2340. M/V passed close to Radovan Point. Vospers recalled.

2350. Course of M/V by radar (plotting) north-north-east.

2355. Vospers rejoining. Despatched to position fifteen miles north. M/V was too large to enter Lussingrande Harbour and known that Lussino Channel impassable owing to broken bridge. It was known

German shipping did not pass between Krk and Cherso, therefore it was considered it would pass fairly close to Dolfin Island.

0010. *Radar placed M/V in position ——.*

0015. *Position by radar ——. It appeared the ship was heading for Pag to run up close inshore as was their usual practice.*

0130–0135. *Echoes detected. From the (radar) plot it appeared that the target consisted of two ships in line abreast eight to ten cables apart, course 012 degrees, speed 20 knots.*

    Information of these echoes passed to Vospers by R/T.

0142. *Echo lost at eight and a half miles.*

0200. *Wash felt.*

0207. *Second wash felt, confirming radar theory of two destroyers.*

0306. *Signal received from Vospers: "Have fired four at two destroyers and one M/V. No hits."*

    Vospers rejoining.

0415. *Vospers rejoined.*

0420. *Fleet sailed on reverse route to Ist. . . .*

   .   .   .   .   .

The German destroyers were soon severely shaken. The shaking lasted only a short while, as will be seen later. On 1st November two Hunt-class destroyers, H.M.S. *Wheatland* (Lt. H. A. Corbett, R.N.) and H.M.S. *Avonvale* (Lt. Ivan Hall, R.N.) arrived and, at 1700, sailed with MTBs 295, 287, 274, MGBs 642, 638, 633 and ML 494.

All the vessels were under the orders of Morgan Giles in *Wheatland*, and the plan (Operation "Exterminate") was that first of all the destroyers would land a South African shore-watching party on the north side of Pag and then patrol west of the island. The MTBs were to patrol west of Rab, while the MGBs were to cover the passage between Premuda and Asinello.

At about 1950, while the destroyers were still landing the shore party by whaler, the MTBs signalled that they had sighted two German destroyers on a southerly course.

Giles steamed the two destroyers out on a south-westerly course, and in less than twenty minutes after the MTBs' warning *Wheatland* signalled: "Am engaging two enemy destroyers, position ——".

Wheatland and *Avonvale* took a target each. The first salvoes hit both the enemy ships and set them on fire. Within minutes *Wheatland* and *Avonvale* were circling the targets and engaging with pom-pom and other close-range weapons until they sank.

Both the Hunts closed to pick up survivors, and while they were doing this their radar picked up yet another enemy destroyer coming down from the north. This was the *Audace* and both the Hunts engaged it, their first salvoes hitting the bridge, killing all the officers and wrecking the fire-control system. Soon she followed her former compatriots. Before midnight Morgan Giles, in *Wheatland*, was able to signal: "Three enemy destroyers sunk. Am returning to base now. MGBs proceed to position —— and search for survivors."

However, the weather worsened and the search was not very successful. The two Hunts returned to Komiza Harbour, at Vis, with no ammunition left. Somewhat pleased with themselves, the two vessels sailed in with a near-Partisan flag flying and with a Viennese waltz being played over the loud-hailer.

The touchy Partisans were quick to spot that there was no red star on the flag and that the waltz bore little or no resemblance to their national anthem. It took Giles a long time to explain away the situation. The wrong side of the record had, of course, been played, and there had not been time to make a red star to put on the flag.

The enemy destroyers sunk were, in addition to the *Audace*, the DD. 202 and DD. 208. About ninety survivors were picked up, and E-boats were sighted in the area of the action next morning.

The action had started when the *Wheatland's* motor-boat and whaler were still landing the shore party. When they saw the gunfire and burning ships they were a little perturbed, and as neither of the destroyers returned to pick them up they presumed the day had gone against the British and they were, so to speak, orphans.

They hauled their craft up the beach and hid them and waited throughout the night. Next morning a signaller saw MTBs searching close inshore for survivors and promptly called them up with an Aldis signalling lamp. He was stopped in a matter of seconds by an officer, who correctly identified them as E-boats.

Later in the day the weather worsened, and soon a bora was blowing. The redoubtable ML 494, under Lt. Dennis Romain, stood by in hiding for four days to pick up the men who were having the uncomfortable experience of being pin-pointed by German direction-finders every time they used their radio. They were taken off after four days.

LCH 282's log is not all blood, boras and thunder. On the 6th November it records: "D.A.F. [Dalmatian Air Force] asked permission through Snovis to bomb us in Solinc Bay. Request not granted."

Three days later, however, there is this entry:

2130. *Wind veering to north-west, strength 5–6. . . .*

2135. *Six Coastal Forces craft lying alongside sent to another and better berth.*

2230. *BORA.*

2235. *"To ALL: Strong north or east wind will probably continue. All craft set anchor watch and if necessary get under way to Mulat Island.*

2300. *CHAOS—all is confusion.*

.   .   .   .   .

The bad weather continued for several days, but the night it cleared MTBs and MGBs raided Cigale Cove, on Lussin Island, where Partisan reports and aerial reconnaissance had shown there was a concentration of MAS-boats, explosive motor-boats (these craft did not belie their name: they were headed straight for the target vessel and the crew "bailed out" at the last minute. The craft was then supposed to hit the target and explode), and one-man submarines.

At the end of the month a couple of Vospers came to a sticky end. Some "Dogs" under Cornelius Burke were at Mulat one day, when, just before breakfast, 658's first lieutenant was woken by the quartermaster, who said that a Vosper was alongside and the C.O. wanted to see him urgently.

He writes: "It was Frank Dowrick. 'Is Corny aboard?' he asked. 'I think you'll have to do a rescue act—I left 371 and 287 three hours ago stuck on the putty way up north, well behind the German lines. I could not get them off, so came down for help—I couldn't get any joy on the radio.'

"Corny was soon informed, and permission was obtained for us to sail north at speed with Ted Smyth (642) and Dickie Bird (643) on our 'errand of mercy'. The prospect was interesting, as the possibility of contacting the enemy in a daylight action, or of air attack, could not be ruled out. . . .

"We made about 20 knots northward. . . . We cut in towards Unie Island and then round the corner until suddenly, high and dry on a low, deserted island, we spotted the two Vospers. They had been making 10 knots in pitch darkness. Their dead reckoning must have been a little out, and they had run straight on to the very low island without any warning or slackening at all.

"Corny nosed up to the second one. We rigged towing gear on to her after gun turret and carefully took the strain and began to increase until we were pulling at about 1,200 revs, the boat shaking like a leaf, but with no change in the position of the Vosper.

"Ted Smyth came up and yelled through his megaphone: 'Say, Corny, do you think it would help if I created a bit of a wash? It might lift her a few inches, and if you pull at the same time she might come off.'

" 'O.K.,' said Corny. 'Let's try it.'

"So we stood by to heave and Ted disappeared to gather speed for his run past. A minute or two later he came thundering by only fifty yards offshore, doing full revs, and as he passed a great wave steamed out from each quarter and from the bow.

"We had taken the strain and begun to increase revs as the wave crashed in. We watched it reach the Vosper. It lifted and then, instead of responding to our pull, wafted ten feet farther up the beach and settled down with a groan.

" 'I think that's that, don't you?' said Corny. 'Now I reckon they're there for good.' "

They were. It was impossible to move them. All secret equipment was removed, along with other equipment and gear, and the two "Dogs" took off the crews and then opened fire on them until they were destroyed. (See picture facing page 241.)

* * * * *

By December Tirana, the capital of Albania, had been captured by Partisans; farther north Split and Sibenik had been cleared of the Germans and were in Partisan hands. The boats moved up to be based on Zara and most of their operations were in co-operation with other vessels.

By 3rd December most of the boats of the 60th Flotilla had returned to the Adriatic from the Aegean, although MGBs 661, 645, and 646 stayed in Greek waters. Civil war had by this time broken out in that sorely-tried country, and British troops, after being feted as liberators, came in for their share of attacks from the rebels. Someone has noted earlier the adage: "Beware of Greeks when they come bearing gifts. . . ."

At the end of the year various administrative changes were made, and these also affected officers. Lt. A. C. B. Blomfield, D.S.C.*, S.O. of the 7th Flotilla, was given command of a destroyer and Lt. A. H. Moore, D.S.C., took over as S.O.

A new flotilla of Vospers, the 28th, had arrived in the Mediterranean, and Charles Jerram, a veteran "Dog" C.O., was appointed S.O. Among the MLs there were also some changes. Lt. K. M. Horlock, O.B.E., took over from Lt.-Cdr. Whillingham as S.O. of the 29th, and Lt. E. G. Friend took over from Lt. G. W. Whittam, D.S.C., as S.O. of the 43rd ML Flotilla.

CHAPTER XXXVII

" FIRE WHEN YOUR SIGHTS ARE ON "

THE year 1945, the last of the war, saw the Germans retreating on almost every front, with the wilier of them preparing their alibis for the day of surrender. But they still fought tenaciously.

Off the west coast of Italy the weather during January—as it had been the previous month—was still adverse, and patrols were only possible on five nights. On the first of these, 10th/11th, Bullwinkle, in 422, made a single-handed torpedo attack on an F-lighter convoy, hitting and sinking two of them. A PT-boat had been on patrol with him.

Five nights later PT 313, MGB 177 (Lt. Smith) and MTB 378 (S/Lt. G. P. H. James) found another convoy of five F-lighters. The unit was illuminated by star-shells from shore batteries and James was able to use their light to close to visual range, 700 yards, and attack, sinking one and possibly sinking a second F-lighter.

On both these attacks, commented C.C.F., "accompanying U.S. PT-boats fired their torpedoes independently and somewhat early by radar".

February brought rather better weather, allowing operations on 50 per cent of the nights. However, targets were scarce and on three nights in the middle of the month full-scale operations in co-operation with Hunt-class destroyers and LCGs drew blank.

The outstanding action of the month was on the 7th/8th, when Bullwinkle, in 422, shared with two PT-boats the destruction of two merchant ships off Savona. Bullwinkle pressed home his attack so close that his torpedoes hit the target when the ship was practically stopped in the harbour entrance.

March, too, was an unproductive month, with only one success recorded. This was an F-lighter sunk by a unit of the 7th Flotilla under Steve Moore, embarked in 377 (Aitchison), with 378 (James). The two boats were part of an LCG-MTB force under Bobby Allan doing a sweep east of the Gulf of Genoa, and shortly after Aitchison hit with two torpedoes the boat came under heavy fire from the F-lighters. Shrapnel spattered the water close to the boats, and an irate gunner in Aitchison's boat complained of some hot fragments down his neck. The last month of the war, April, was a busy one with the boats operating off the Italian Riviera.

. . . . .

In the Adriatic 1945 opened somewhat disastrously with the loss of HDML 1163 on the 4th/5th January. She was last heard of making an enemy report of four unidentified vessels at 2130.

MTBs and MGBs were out in patrols every night of the month except two, although they did not have much success. However, three "Dogs" under a newcomer to the Adriatic, Lt.-Cdr. J. A. Montgomerie, most thoroughly destroyed three E-boats. With his own 699, 706 (Lt. M. H. Shapcott-Hume) and 698 (Lt. P. G. Wrate) they were patrolling off Unie Island in daylight when they found the three E-boats stranded. Two were destroyed by fire and the third damaged beyond repair by torpedo and gunfire. (See picture facing p. 241.)

Vospers operating from Ancona were hampered by the weather, and the only action was on the 4th/5th January, when MTBs 374 and 298 attacked a small convoy just entering Parenzo Harbour. The visibility was bad and no hits were scored.

In February Jerram's 28th MTB Flotilla, all new Vospers fitted with effective S.O. radar, made its debut. He had spent some time in Malta working up, and then moved to Ancona to begin operations.

On their second patrol they had a success. This was on the 7th/8th February, when Jerram took three boats on patrol west of Parenzo. He embarked in 406 (S/Lt. J. Collins, M.B.E.), and the other two were 404 (Lt. E. Lassen) and 407 (Lt. H. C. du Boulay).

The unit stopped a mile offshore south of Port Daila and at 2000 two small echoes were picked up on the radar at 2,000 yards range. Believing them to be fishing boats, Jerram ordered the three MTBs to close on one silenced engine and gave preparative Flag 5[1] over the R/T.

Almost immediately an aircraft, with navigation lights on, was seen coming up astern. Considering it was a reconnaissance air-craft, Jerram immediately stopped the boats so that they should not be spotted.

---

[1] Prepare to attack with guns.

His radar then reported a further echo, this time much larger, closing from the north at two miles range. Almost immediately Jerram sighted a large ship in the direction of the radar bearing. It appeared to be an escort vessel of the corvette type, making about 10 knots.

Jerram writes in his action report: "I considered that an attack should be made without plot, as our wake would have given us away and we were in an ideal firing position.

"The target opened fire with a large-calibre gun but did not seem to be very sure of our bearing, as she missed about forty or fifty yards to the right of 407, and she turned abruptly to port towards the coast.

"I ordered the boats to fire when they had their sights on it and to disengage to port. At 2014 all boats fired and disengaged at 12 knots. Two hits were observed to register on target, one forward and one aft. A loud explosion and sparks and a red glow were heard and seen. . . .

"The unit was immediately subjected to heavy and accurate fire from at least four points, consisting of quadruple Oerlikon and 88-mm. Some of the 88-mm. was anti-personnel."

Jerram considered that Lassen, a New Zealander, had scored the two hits, as Collins had had (fortunately, as will be seen later) a misfire and du Boulay had not fired until just before the target was hit.

The three boats headed westwards at high speed, and after covering two miles the radar picked up another echo proceeding on the same course as the corvette which had just been sunk.

Jerram had already stopped the boats and shouted to them to report damage, and, so the story goes, du Boulay's rather high-pitched voice had come across the still night: "My dear Charles, I think I'm sinking."

"Well, you'd better —— well find out!"

"I've sent the First Lieutenant to check up."

The First Lieutenant, S/Lt. Hudson, quickly reported that the boat had been hit below the waterline forward. When the boat was under way the hole was out of the water because of the lift of the bows, but when stopped water poured in.

This was relayed to Jerram, who recommended that, for the time being, a certain portion of the First Lieutenant's anatomy should block the hole until a tingle (patch) could be put over it, rather on the lines of the Dutch boy and the hole in the canal wall. This was done, and du Boulay was ordered off to a rendezvous position while Jerram returned to attack the new echo with Collins' remaining torpedo——the misfire having been rectified by A. B. Heritage.

With Lassen in company, 406 closed the target at 6 knots and sighted it ahead. 2035 Collins fired his torpedo. It hit and there were two distinct explosions and a large red glow.

Jerram and Lassen then returned to the rendezvous to find du Boulay and learnt that his boat had made three feet of water forward. Du Boulay was ordered to take the lead to keep clear of the other boats' wash, and the unit headed back to Ancona at high speed to keep 407's bow out of the water.

Jerram then writes: "As we withdrew a terrific battle was seen to be taking place between the remaining enemy ships . . . the last target did not sink, as it was held on radar for twenty-five miles, proving it to be a very large ship, but it remained stationary from the time it was torpedoed."

As soon as the three boats arrived in Ancona it was decided to send two "Dogs" to finish off the merchantman. Jerram went with them, and when they arrived off Parenzo in daylight they passed through a good deal of wreckage and sighted a merchant ship in Parenzo Harbour.

This news was signalled back to base and the R.A.F. sent over some planes which hit her in No. 4 hold. She took on a list and blocked the jetty. The ship was the 6,300-ton ex-British *Dalesman*.

This successful operation by the 28th Flotilla was followed up by another five nights later, when Jerram, in 404 (Lassen), with 405 (Lt. F. Scoble) and 407 (du Boulay), patrolled off Caorle and sank the Italian steamer *Mediceo*, of 5,083 tons.

.   .   .   .   .

The "Dogs" based on Zara had, during February, probably never worked so hard for less spectacular results. They did sixty-four patrols —a record for the Mediterranean, and the only definite success was on the 13th/14th, when Walter Blount, S.O. in 634, took out 710 (Lt. A. W. Bone) and MGB 660 (Lt. A. Robinson).

Taking advantage of their new S.O. (P.P.I. screen) radar and their inshore position, the boats attacked three large craft, sinking one immediately by gunfire, torpedoing another after aiming by radar, and destroying a third with gunfire.

Bone's boat was badly damaged, two men being killed and two wounded. A direct hit by an 88-mm. shell just abaft the bridge, on the engine-room coach-roof, flung shrapnel into the engine-room. This pierced three main engines and both auxiliaries, killing the leading stoker and an A.B.

Two nights later three "Dogs" bombarded Cherso town, and on the next night other "Dogs" patrolling the Planinski Channel—more generally known as the "Plan Chan"—illuminated Karlobag with star-shell.

This reconnaissance was followed up the night after, the 17th/18th, with a gun and torpedo attack by four "Dogs" under Lt.-Cdr. J. Montgomerie—MTBs 699, 703, 655 and MGB 660. Two torpedoes were fired into the harbour, and a machine-gun post and a large building were destroyed.

In March the Vospers of the first division of Jerram's 28th Flotilla continued their successes, starting off with an attack on 9th/10th by MTBs 406 (Collins), 405 (Scoble) and 407 (Du Boulay), Jerram being embarked in Collins' boat. They sank a merchant ship off Umago.

The next night the most successful radar attack to date was made by Jerram. He was embarked in 406 (Collins), and the other boats were 404 (Lassen) and 407 (du Boulay). The three craft left Ancona for a patrol between Caorle and Tagliamento on a fine night with no moon and visibility about three miles, although there was mist about.

After lying offshore for a while, an echo came up on the radar screens and Jerram shadowed with the three boats, finally getting into a firing position close to the entrance to the Venice swept channel.

In his action report Jerram writes: "At 2342 I sighted one ship at 1,500 yards on the port bow and ordered Lt. du Boulay to try to attack it, as he was in the best tactical position. I recognised it to be an F-lighter and gave preparative Flag 4[1] over the T.C.S.[2]

"Lt. du Boulay, however, had not at that time actually seen the ship, so although the tactical position was bad for him I ordered S/Lt. Collins, who actually had it in his sights, to try with one torpedo.

"He fired his starboard torpedo at 2345 at a range of 1,300 yards. At this moment the radar reported, and I saw, more F-lighters in close formation astern of the first one. I ordered the boats to turn to starboard and fire when their sights were on. . . .

"Lt. Lassen fired his torpedoes together at the fourth in line and Lt. du Boulay fired singly at the second and third. S/Lt. Collins fired at the last in the line with his port torpedo.

"All boats turned to starboard and disengaged at 12 knots on a southerly course. Almost instantaneously there were six explosions

---

[1] Order to prepare for a torpedo attack, passed by R/T.
[2] Bridge-to-bridge radio-telephone.

starting with the leading lighter. Columns of water rose about 200 feet in the air. . . ."

They watched the echoes disappearing off the radar screen and Jerram concludes: "All five lighters were sunk, and of these two were sunk by S/Lt. Collins, two by Lt. du Boulay, and one by Lt. Lassen."

. . . . .

The "Dogs" had their first encounter of the month off the Arsa Channel on the 6th/7th, when three boats under Lt.-Cdr. Basil Bourne, 656 (Masson, with the S.O. embarked), 703 (Taylor) and 705 (Davies), attacked a convoy, sinking one ship and damaging two others.

Montgomerie in 699 took out 703 (Taylor) and 710 (Bone) on the 12th/13th and fought a prolonged action with a series of enemy units.

Two F-lighters and a tug were first seen entering the Arsa Channel from the south, and they opened heavy fire, forcing the "Dogs" to retire under smoke. Then more enemy vessels tried to leave the channel, but thought better of it when illuminated by Montgomerie's boats.

An hour later the enemy tried again, but Montgomerie's call for more star-shell, and four torpedoes, kept them somewhat hesitant. By a strange chance two of the torpedoes either hit a mine or detonated each other ahead of the three "Dogs" and shook them up considerably.

Finally, after two hours, the enemy tried to leave the channel at the same time as five more enemy vessels approached from the north. Montgomerie immediately attacked with the remaining torpedoes, and one F-lighter was hit.

In the middle of the month Coastal Forces ran into an unlucky period of losses from enemy mines. On 15th March ML 179 detonated a mine west of Premuda, but damage was not extensive. But MTB 710 was less fortunate the next day when a mine damaged her shafts and propellers north-west of Premuda. She was towed into Mulat.

This was followed by a disastrous thirty-six hours on the 22nd/23rd. Three "Dogs", MGB 674 (with Lt.-Cdr. Bourne embarked as S.O.), MTB 655 (Lt. Derrick Brown) and MGB 643 (Lt. Hill), had been operating from Zara around the entrance to the Arsa Channel. It had been an uneventful night and at about 0300 the boats left to return to Zara at 10 knots.

Lt. Brown continues the story: "655 was second in line. The weather was clear, the sea calm, with just a light breeze from the south-west. Visibility was good—in fact it was one of those fine Mediterranean nights which made operations almost a pleasure.

"On clearing the coast I handed over the watch to my First Lieutenant, S/Lt. John R. Mudd, and settled back on my doormat, which had been placed in its usual position at the after end of the bridge. A doormat is very useful—a great deal more comfortable than the floorboards, and even when wet it still creates a lot of warmth. I drifted into a semi-sleep.

"Almost immediately, it seemed, I came to full consciousness on top of a tremendous upheaval under the bridge.

"Everything was disintegrating—one felt it rather than heard it—and it all rapidly became a bad dream of a peculiar world where everything was topsy-turvy and confusion, until even the unreality of that faded out too.

"When I came round again—it must have been some minutes later—I was lying face down on a piece of decking which was rapidly disappearing beneath me, and almost immediately left me no alternative but to swim. There was plenty of incentive—our 100-octane petrol, released by the burst tanks, had caught fire and was spreading across the water.

"At that moment I was right on the edge of it, and realised immediately that the only hope lay in getting to windward of it, as the light breeze was sending the flames along at an alarming rate.

"I struck out as strongly as I could, now conscious of a broken thigh and infinitely grateful for the buoyancy of my protective clothing—a kapok suit under oilskin overalls: I had often wondered how effective these were, and now found myself floating like an advertisement for Michelin tyres.

"The area was really well lit up, much of the wreckage was visible and a number of heads near me became recognisable. I felt we were a ship's company again and some guidance was necessary.

"We must keep together and make for the bows of 655, which floated drunkenly some way off, clear of the flames, and which would at least provide us with something to hang on to. We splashed along, making various remarks of encouragement to the laggards.

"It was then that 643 appeared in the flickering light, nosing in gently some fifty yards ahead of us, scrambling nets down and the port side lined with figures eager to help. Good old Joe Hill. It seemed by a miracle that 643 had avoided the wreckage in the first place, keeping as she was close station astern of 655.

"In fact the miracle was Joe's instant reaction in ordering 'Hard a'starboard, full astern starboard engines', thereby scraping past us with only slight under-water damage on his port side.

"One by one we reached 643 and were hauled out of the water. They found room in every corner—dry clothes and rum for the uninjured, first aid and attention for the less lucky ones.

"With particular gratitude I remember an Englishman, Tom Coles, a man of genuine conscience who had joined an American Medical Service Group rather than a combatant unit. He did wonderful work and yet was only on board as a passenger at his own request.

"Passengers were never popular in our boats, as there was little enough room anyway, especially on the bridge, so before we left Zara Joe and I had spun a coin, the loser to have Tom Coles on board! I now felt ashamed of my reluctance to embark such a dependable character.

"Basil Bourne, in 674, had decided to remain in position until first light, not only to be certain that no survivors remained to be picked up, but also to have a better chance to avoid any more shallow-depth mines there might be.

"At dawn, then, having vainly searched for more survivors, the two boats set off towards Zara at slow speed, on account of damage done to 643's propeller. We were met halfway by a Vosper MTB which had been despatched with the Base M.O. on board.

"Among the missing were the navigating officer, S/Lt. Terry Murphy, a very promising young officer not long out from the United Kingdom, and the coxswain, Petty Officer L. Nicholl, D.S.M. and Bar. He had survived the mining of MGB 663 five months before with injuries which would have kept him permanently ashore had he not volunteered to rejoin me in 655. Now this was his reward for loyal service, and I felt his loss very deeply."

That same afternoon MTB 705, on passage from Ancona to Zadar, had her stern blown off by a mine and sank in fifteen minutes. Three ratings were lost. The mine losses continued into April. On the 10th, MTB 710, which had escaped less than a month earlier, was blown up. The midships section of the boat disintegrated and the C.O., First Lieutenant and thirteen ratings were lost.

Chapter XXXIII

THE WHITE FLAG

APRIL 1945. By the end of the month the Swastika, the crooked cross that Germany demanded the world should worship, had tumbled in the dust; and in its place were white flags, dead men of all nations, and the excuse that the Nazi Party had been to blame.

In Germany and Italy the last days of the Second World War were like an opera spawned by Wagner and Franz Kafka. In Italy Gen. Alexander opened his offensive along the uneven front line from Ravenna, in the Adriatic, to between Spezia and Pisa on the west coast, on the 9th. Soon the Axis forces were driven back; and within three weeks, on the 29th, they surrendered: nearly a million men with arms and equipment.

On the same day Milan and Venice were entered by the Allies; but two days earlier at Lecce, a small village on the hillside above Lake Como, a sordid drama had been enacted. Benito Mussolini, his mistress and a dozen of his Cabinet were captured. The mob, well versed in violence by Il Duce and his Fascists in earlier days, summarily executed him and his mistress.

Radio Belgrade, freed of the sickly-sweet tune of "Lili Marlene", reported on the 30th that Partisans had entered Trieste, and on 2nd May Gen. Sir Bernard Freyberg accepted the surrender.

In the Dodecanese the German commandant, Gen. Wagener, signed the surrender at Symi on 8th May; and in the Cyclades the garrisons surrendered on the 9th, followed on the same day by men holding Crete.

But April—"April is the cruellest month," wrote Eliot—brought some hard and bitter fighting in the Adriatic. Within sight of victory men were yet to die.

·   ·   ·   ·   ·

Apart from the boats lost by mines, described earlier, there were many gun and torpedo attacks by "Dogs" and Vospers. On the 9th/

10th Charles Jerram, embarked in 410 (Woodhouse), went on patrol in the Gulf of Venice with 411 (Syrett) and 408 (Tonkin).

Again it was a fine night—a light breeze rippling the sea, a slight haze to seaward, and little or no swell. Visibility was about 3,000 yards when the three boats sighted a small sailing vessel. Jerram writes in his action report that it was manned "by six Italian deserters from Parenzo who for the past few minutes had busied themselves with the satisfactory manipulation of a large white flag.

"After the usual exclamations of joy and surprise at their interception by some of H.M. ships had abated they were divided between the three boats, their own craft destroyed by MTB 410, and the unit resumed course and speed for the patrol."

Five miles off Caorle the boats stopped and a radar watch started. Within a few minutes Woodhouse's set picked up an echo thirteen and a half miles to the westward, and for the next forty minutes the target's course and speed was carefully plotted.

When the range was down to 11,500 yards Jerram ordered the boats to close on silenced engines. Soon the targets were sighted and identified as F-lighters. Preparative Flag 4 was given over the R/T, and then all three boats fired. Each had a misfire and had to disengage with a torpedo left in the tube.

"At 2309," writes Jerram, "there was a large explosion; speculation on the soft promise of a Triestian night had ceased for the crew of one F-lighter."

The three boats regrouped and Jerram prepared to re-engage. The other F-lighters showed a remarkable indifference to the fate of their late sister-ship and appeared to have made no effort either to inquire into her situation or to antagonise the people responsible for it.

Once in position, Woodhouse fired his remaining torpedo, but a misfire caused a delay and it left the tube ten seconds late, missing astern. This was followed by Syrett, who also had a misfire. Tonkin was luckier and his torpedo hit the leading F-lighter.

Woodhouse, having used up all his impulse charges (three of which were defective), came alongside Tonkin's boat, collected another one, and prepared to re-engage. But his radar broke down and an attempt was made to guide him towards the targets, using radar in another boat. This failed when the R/T broke down. He searched, but could not find the targets. The unit, defeated by defective impulse charges, defective radar, and defective R/T, returned to Ancona.

Meanwhile four "Dogs", on the same night, were fighting a bitter battle off the Arsa Channel against the same enemy, F-lighters. Tim Bligh was in his own boat, 662, and with him were three MTBs, 634 (Blount), 638 (Lummis) and 633 (Golding). 638 and 633 had been equipped with the new 6-pounders.

Bligh picked up four F-lighters by radar at 8,000 yards, and after plotting them for some time attacked from inshore, but the "Dogs" had obviously been seen by the heavily-armed enemy. They fired torpedoes, but the Germans stopped (an old F-lighter dodge), causing them to miss ahead. The F-lighters then opened intense and accurate 88-mm. and 20-mm. fire.

Almost at once 633 (Golding) and 638 (Lummis) were hit and stopped. Golding, severely wounded and his coxswain killed. Lummis tried to go ahead, but found his boat had a gaping hole in the bows, and she started to dive as soon as she had way on.

Meanwhile Bligh and Walter Blount immediately closed and engaged the F-lighters with gunfire. After ascertaining the position on the other two boats they made another run on them. Bligh's boat was hit by three 88-mm. shells and three men were killed and five severely wounded.

But the odds were too heavy and the F-lighters reached the entrance to the channel. The other three "Dogs" closed 638 to help her. The foredeck was under water and it seemed she would have to be abandoned and sunk, but Blount took her in tow, stern first, and managed to get her back to Ancona.

The next night two MGBs, 647 and 643, met three F-lighters escorted by two E-boats in the Planinski Channel. They closed for a gun attack but again were met with heavy fire, 647 having most of her stern blown off by an 88-mm. shell.

Jerram was out again on the 11th/12th with two boats, 409 and 408 (411 having developed engine trouble), to patrol off Caorle. After picking up one convoy by radar and moving into an attacking position, a second convoy was sighted. This was followed by a third. Jerram, finding himself about to be caught in the midst of an embarrassingly large number of enemy ships, attacked; but the guardian angel of impulse charges was again on the side of the Germans, because two of the four torpedoes misfired.

After disengaging he attacked again to use up the remaining torpedoes, after the impulse charges were replaced; but, like the first two, they missed. Although Jerram's luck was out that night, he spent an instructive couple of minutes watching the three enemy convoys engage each other.

Jerram made up for this somewhat abortive night on the 12th/13th, when, with three boats—410 (Woodhouse), 409 (Holloway) and 408 (Tonkin)—he went for yet another patrol off Caorle. The action is best described in the signals he sent back to Ancona:

> *Investigating unidentified radar plot in position* 180 *degrees Caorle five miles.*

Then, half an hour later:

> *Am engaging enemy in position* 180 *degrees Caorle five miles.*

Twenty minutes later:

> *Have disengaged. Five F-lighters sunk.*

And finally:

> *Heavy enemy fire. No damage or casualties.* E.T.A. 0500.

The next night it was the turn of the "Dogs". The invasion of Rab Island was under way and there was a shortage of boats—some of Bligh's boats had been damaged on the 9th/10th action, and 710, one of Montgomerie's flotilla, had been mined the day after.

So on the 12th/13th Montgomerie, in MTB 670 (Eric Hewitt), took out MTB 697 (Booth) and MGBs 643 (Hill) and 658 (Reynolds) for a patrol at the northern end of the "Plan Chan" to stop reinforcements reaching Rab from Fiume.

Reynolds—who had joined Montgomerie for the first time earlier that day—describes the action: "All was very quiet and at about 0130 we lay cut, close to the coast. I went down to the radar to inspect the outlook and satisfied myself that nothing was about.

"At about 0215, though, an excited radar operator called the bridge and reported two large targets just entering the channel from the north, at about four-miles range.

"I immediately called Monty on the R/T and passed him the news, and there was rapid reaction. All boats started up, and we got into line abreast.

"Every minute the radar operator passed up more information. By this time Joe's (Hill in MGB 643) set was warmed up and he was confirming the echoes.

"At last a little patch of denser blackness in my binoculars told me that the leading ship was in sight, and at the same time we heard from Monty that he had seen her too.

"'Preparative Flag 4,' he ordered. 'Range will be 1,500 yards.'

"I could imagine Eric and Dennis (Booth) fiddling with the sight bar on their torpedo sights. . . . Still, they would have an accurate idea of the speed from the previous reports, and that was the most common error in firing torpedoes.

"A few moments later Monty ordered 'Flag 4!', and we heard first Erics', then Dennis' fish leave the tubes. Immediately after our loud-speaker yelled: 'Come on, Rover, Flag 4!'

"I was completely taken aback, and suddenly realised that Monty, who had probably never seen 658 before, was under the misappre-hension that she was an MTB. I grabbed the microphone and replied: 'Hello, Monty, this is Rover. Sorry I can't oblige—I wasn't made that way!'

"There was no time for Monty to reply, as the inky blackness was split by a most colossal explosion and followed rapidly by two more. The radar operator shouted up the voice-pipe: 'Bridge, sir, the leading target has disappeared. The other is stopping.'"

As the "Dogs" disengaged it was seen that the second ship had not in fact stopped after her companion[1] had been sunk but was moving off fast.

Next day the R.A.F. reported a great deal of wreckage and survivors on rafts at the point of attack, and also a Partenope-class warship heading for Pola. Intelligence reports later showed that the destroyer they had sunk was on its way to evacuate the Rab garrison. (See picture facing p. 241.)

Two nights later Montgomerie was taking three "Dogs" to patrol off Krk Island, which was in the process of being invaded by Partisans, to prevent German reinforcements reaching the island from Fiume—the same type of operation which had been successful off Rab. He was embarked in 658 (Reynolds), and astern of him was 697 (Booth) and then 633.

They had been told that Partisans had swept the area for mines, although no one was very reassured by that news, since sweeping to

---

[1] A Partenope torpedo-boat (destroyer) armed with two 100-mm., one 40-mm., three twin 37-mm., three 13.2-mm., a twin 37-mm., and ten 20-mm. guns.

them meant towing a wire between two small boats, and Reynolds writes: "We had negotiated the gap between the islands and were sailing along the coast closer than I had ever conceived to be possible before when there was a colossal explosion, which seemed to engulf us, and a lurid flash.

"We turned, aghast, and there, only thirty yards astern, was 697—split in two and bows burning furiously. 633, illuminated brightly in the glare, had just managed to stop in time. I began to turn short round—I had no desire to career about in such deadly waters—and we edged towards the wreckage and the men we could see in the water. Tony launched our dinghy, and he and Monty went rowing round for survivors. We had already picked up George Heard, 697's pilot, and three other injured survivors.

"In the glare of the burning hull, about twenty yards from us, was the gleaming, polished and spiky surface of a very large mine, which had presumably been released from its moorings by the force of the explosion.

"As I watched from the bridge, it struck me that the scene was similar to an Impressionist's painting of Death and Hell-fire—a ravaged ship burning, a ghostly flickering light on the oily sea surface, the horns of that mine, and a dinghy moving silently across the scene like the boatman on the Styx.

"Suddenly George Heard, dripping wet from his own immersion, and pale with tension and shock, pointed into the darkness and in a flash was diving into the sea and swimming strongly towards a man he had seen. He brought him back, and we helped to bring the rescued man inboard. It was a very gallant act and he was later awarded the Albert Medal."

In the dinghy Tony Brydon and Montgomerie were having to paddle Red Indian fashion because the rowlocks could not be found. They reached the flaming wreckage, and Montgomerie writes: "We carefully skirted the worst spot and headed to where we were sure we could hear cries of someone in the water.

"As we drew near we saw in the light of the flames a cork life-jacket from which merged the head of a man surrounded by wreckage. He was screaming in a most piteous fashion, and his oil-and-blood-covered face made him look scarcely human. He appeared at first glance to have half his jaw missing (it was found afterwards to have been broken in three places), while one of his arms appeared to be badly injured.

"To get him into our dinghy was the next problem, and in our first two attempts we nearly succeeded in joining him. He was so completely covered in oil that our hands kept slipping as we tried to get a grip. He must have been in considerable pain and we tried somewhat unsuccessfully to reassure him with cries of: 'Take it easy, old boy; we'll have you back on board with a nice tot of rum inside you in no time'—a sentiment, at the time, we were far from believing ourselves.

"I, personally, was most apprehensive, as we were fairly close to the now abandoned remains of 697's bows, which were blazing fiercely with her ammunition blowing up in great style, fortunately mostly in the air and over our heads.

"After what seemed an eternity we finally dragged the man on board, nearly drowning the poor fellow in our waterlogged dinghy as his head got jammed under one of the thwarts. At last we started off . . . and that return journey was a nightmare I am sure Tony and I will never forget."

Soon the boats started the throat-tightening job of getting out of the minefield. They did it without incident and returned to Zara to hand over the wounded.

For Montgomerie there was still one unpleasant task—setting out in cold official language a string of typewritten words which began: "Sir, I have the honour to report on the loss of H.M. MTB 697 by striking a mine . . ."; and concluded: ". . . It is regretted that no sign could be found of the ten missing ratings. . . ." This was one of the last patrols of the war, and, but for the final chapter on the surrender, the last to be described here.

Chapter XXXIX

THE FINAL TASK

BY the end of April there was little scope for enemy shipping and the possibility of MTB operations had become very limited.

Most of the boats' crews were beginning to recognise that the war in Europe was nearly over. It was generally felt to be unlikely that many of them would be sent out to the Far East. And there was a common but unspoken thought uppermost in many minds—they had survived World War II. Fears withdrew and imaginations were stilled. It became sensible to hope.

But on the morning of Tuesday, 1st May aircraft reported a number of enemy ships (mostly F-lighters) moving along the west coast of the Istrian Peninsula. Discussions were held on the possibility of staging a grandstand finish by sending a considerable number of boats to attack this large convoy during the latter part of the afternoon. But the Senior Naval Officer, Northern Adriatic, decided against such a plan, probably on the grounds that a daylight attack on F-lighters would have resulted in heavy damage and casualties to our own forces with little possibility of commensurate harm to the enemy.

Later in the day there were reports of a large number of enemy ships leaving Trieste and steering westwards. As a result ten MTBs were ordered to leave for a rendezvous some ten miles south of Tagliamento Point (right at the top of the Adriatic), with sailing orders on the following lines:

"Proceed to intercept an enemy convoy reported as twenty-plus F-lighters accompanied by tugs and E-boats with other small craft who left Trieste on Tuesday morning and were last reported to be making for Grado between Trieste and Tagliamento. It is believed that these vessels are willing to surrender and that their original intention was to make for Ancona. Use your best effort to bring these craft to Ancona. Three MLs will stand by immediately south of the rendezvous to assist the escorting of any vessels in your charge. Spitfire reconnaissance aircraft will be over the enemy at dawn and a striking force of aircraft will be available if called for."

V.57 (Bligh) was in charge of the MTBs. He sailed in 634 (Blount), with 651 (Ennis) and 670 (Hewitt) in company. V.28 (Jerram), with seven Vospers, sailed independently to the rendezvous. The "Dogs" left Ancona at 2230 on Tuesday night.

There were some reservations in the minds of many of the officers and men on board the boats as to the intentions of the enemy. The general view was that the whole operation might well end in tears. These unquiet thoughts were in no way allayed on the "Dogs" when they received a signal at 0345 on Wednesday morning from Jerram, saying that the weather conditions were unsuitable for his unit and that the Vospers were returning to harbour. The "Dogs" continued at 18 knots and reached the rendezvous after seven.

As the sun rose the north-west wind dropped and the May morning dawned calm and clear. Spitfires could be seen over Tagliamento. They reported that there were about forty ships, including two destroyers, off the river mouth and that they were being fired on from time to time as they flew overhead. They could not distinguish any white flags on the enemy ships.

At the same time the "Dogs" could see columns of smoke and explosions off Tagliamento, and it seemed fairly certain that the enemy were not intending to surrender but were blowing themselves up; and it was probable that they would resent any suspected interference with their arrangements.

This was all rather dismal, but after waiting at the rendezvous until the light had got really bright the three "Dogs" moved northwards at 6 knots in open arrowhead formation and flying white flags. When the enemy was within signalling distance the "Dogs" fired flares and rockets and the Senior Officer flashed the largest enemy ships in turn, but no reply of any sort was made.

This was very discouraging, because it seemed at the time to be desperately important not to get too close to the enemy until some sort of contact had been made. But their indifference was one degree better than hostility openly declared and the "Dogs" continued to approach the river mouth.

The forty-five minutes of the slow approach was a time of great tension. Most of the officers agreed afterwards that in many ways it was the most unpleasant period which they had spent during the whole war. In looking back Bligh says, "Past a doubt, there was not one man on the three 'Dogs' who was not thinking that this was an unhappy way of finishing the war. For us there was nothing to gain—the war was as good as won—and one's life to lose.

"For them, as we saw it, their whole way of life had come to an end and they could only look forward to captivity: to the fanatics among them death might seem preferable. Further, they had two destroyers, faster than us, who might well enjoy a last fling before scuttling themselves in honour. Moreover, their ships were aground or nearly aground and could not be sunk (not that the Germans would have cared very much if they were), whereas the 'Dogs' were not so indifferent.

"Besides, they probably hated us. Nor was there reason to believe that they would respect our white flags. It is easy, now, to discount all these fears; but it wasn't at the time."

Support for these cautious thoughts came to light when subsequent examination of the German craft showed that all their guns (including those not suitable for anti-aircraft fire) were found to be loaded with the safety-catch set to fire. No large measure of imagined provocation would have been needed to have set the whole situation ablaze, as the Senior Officer pointed out in his report, and this would have been regrettable if only because it would have defeated the object of the operation as set out in the sailing orders.

When the "Dogs" were about a mile off the river mouth the largest vessel in sight flashed some unreadable Morse, a not unfriendly sign, and towards eleven o'clock the boats were right in the midst of the enemy ships, which, for the most part, paid no attention but went on entering the harbour over the shallow-looking bar.

Some of them seemed to be aground just inside the harbour and others were several cables inland up the river. At the least they did not appear to be positively offensive. That was a help. But it was a difficult situation to grip. There was nothing to show which German was in charge.

A unit of R-boats was seen to seaward of the larger part of the German assembly. They had an organised look about them which caused Bligh to wave the leading boat alongside 634. Two young German naval officers came on board at five past eleven with enthusiastic observance of ceremonial. A parley was held in the charthouse, V.57 being assisted by Lt. M. Strnjshek, R.Y.N., as interpreter.

One of the Germans was the Senior Officer of the Sixth Raumsboote Flotille and the other was an R-boat commanding officer. They were surprised to see English boats north of the minefield (did they use the clear channel?). They had no intention of surrendering. Neither of them wished to appear to have any idea of the imminence of the armistice in Europe. They purported to have no conception of what they themselves were meant to be doing at that time.

They were not, they said, engaged on an offshore patrol to prevent interference with the performance going on inside the harbour. They did not add that they were merely waiting their turn to be ordered to go up the river and blow themselves up in peace without getting their feet wet, but went on to say that there were some 2,000 troops ashore, that all the senior German naval officers were ashore, that no move could be made without prior authority of the senior officer ashore; and that they could not leave the chaps on the beach without food or protection. What, they implied, did the English propose to do about it?

Bligh had reasoned that they had left Trieste (where they could quite well have blown themselves up and kept dry in the process) because they did not wish to become the prisoners of the Partisans, so he mentioned that the Allied armies had not yet reached Tagliamento, but that the Partisans would probably be occupying the coastline in the course of the day. He added that there were good facilities for looking after all the Germans at Ancona and then went back to the bridge of 634 to reassess the position.

There were about thirty German craft within a few hundred yards of the "Dogs". They all appeared to have guns manned and showed no white flags of any description. It is true that no destroyers were in the immediate neighbourhood, but the boats were in no position to dictate terms. As the report says, "The British unit was under a flag of truce and any attempt at a show of force would have been foolish, illegal and contrary to paragraph four of the sailing orders."

Bligh accordingly sent off a signal for all available "Dog"-boat reinforcements to be sent as soon as possible and returned to the parley to suggest a conference with all the German coastal force captains on board one of the R-boats. Just before leaving 634 "an unkempt and more than normally unshaven individual approached in a small craft flying the Croatian flag and said that he was in charge of the Croatian forces, whom he wished to give up, but all his ships were on the beach and could his 500 troops be given safe passage? No action was taken on this matter".

The conference on the R-boat was not very fruitful. Most of the young German officers disbelieved what they were told about the general state of the war. They wished to fight on. Bligh suggested that before reaching a final decision they ought to consult their crews, who might well have different views.

He repeated that the territory on which their compatriots were beaching themselves was not occupied by any army but that it would soon be infiltrated by Partisans, who would undoubtedly treat any German prisoners whom they might care to take very stringently indeed, and who would certainly not be in a position to give them much, if any, food. And how could they fight without access to fuel, ammunition and stores? Why did they not surrender honourably and sail to an established naval base with proper facilities for looking after their ships' companies?

Some of the commanding officers appeared to weaken and they all agreed to talk to their crews except for one blond-haired lad, who just slumped in his bunk saying over and over again, "Krieg ist krieg." Meanwhile two small transport craft, the *Condor* and the *Lugia*, and a schooner began circling round the "Dogs" (sometimes passing very close) and indicated that they were prepared to sail to Ancona if escorted. 670 was told to look after these "defectors".

At this point a new arrival appeared on the scene from the direction of Trieste, an F-lighter of recent construction with ten guns and nine white flags. The captain of this craft was quite prepared to go to Ancona, or anywhere else he was told, as the English had won the war, God-damn-them (but with a cheerful grin).

At the same time the three MLs under Lt. D. Romain had appeared from the opposite direction. They were asked to round up the willing starters and take them back to Ancona; it was hoped that the sailing of a few German ships would persuade the waverers to be sensible. Romain got the beflagged "F", the *Condor*, which had just tried to ram 634 (probably playfully), the *Lugia* and one other, all in the mood at the same time and two small convoys left for Ancona—alas, unfollowed.

Bad news then came from the beach. At half-past three a message was flashed to the "Dogs" from the land, "We are New Zealanders", to be followed a little later by, "The port is captured". An Army officer came out to 670 (where V.57 had gone aboard) in a small German boat with the S.O. of the 6th R-boat Flotilla and a conference was held over tea and toast.

The Germans had, as feared, persuaded the New Zealanders to accept responsibility for them as prisoners of war, thereby removing the only weapon of persuasion left to the "Dogs" to get the Germans to leave the harbour by sea under their own steam, i.e. the threat of being captured by the Partisans. The New Zealanders could not very well help it, but the timing of their advance was not at all suitable to the Navy.

It was very irritating for Bligh (who knew the facts perfectly well) to be told by the Army officer over the tea-table that Tagliamento village was very small, that the number of Germans ashore was very large, and that it would be better if the prisoners could be taken away by sea, which should be arranged by the Navy because the German ships could not, unfortunately, be used.

Bligh pointed out, with commendable restraint, that the whole harbour was full of sea-worthy F-lighters. The German at once denied this. He said that the ships had all been damaged by the morning air attacks (*sic*) and by weather, and that he had been told by the senior captain of all the boats that there was only one F-lighter working.

Bligh suggested that if that were the case (which he doubted) there were a number of R-boats in good running order which could be used to ferry the troops down to Ancona in batches. Very soon after this the German went away in such a hurry that he left a piece of toast half-eaten, and almost at once the R-boats, which had been lying outside the harbour aimlessly sniffing the "Dogs", began to enter Tagliamento and started running themselves aground. 670 at once went into the harbour to try and stop this, but she went aground herself, inadvertently, and had to leave them to it.

Welcome reinforcements in the shape of five "Dogs", MGBs 662, 642, 643, 645 and 659, arrived from Ancona at half-past seven that evening. They were met to the south of the harbour by V.57, who transferred to 662, and led the force back to the scene of operations. The weather had begun to deteriorate and the eight boats had to anchor in unsheltered water off the harbour. They were disposed in a rough semicircle and warned to be prepared for some private-enterprise gunnery from Germans who might have overfortified themselves against the onset of peace. 662 kept her American radar set going through the dark hours and was able to plot the course of three ships which drifted out of the port during the night, borne along the coast by the north-west wind.

At eleven o'clock that night V.57 permitted himself the modest luxury of sending a "situation report" to Snona by plain-language W/T, in which he outlined the main features of the day and commended the "studied dignity of the 'Dogs' " as having contributed towards the calm which largely prevailed. He also suggested that the situation "though not in hand completely is not uncontrolled".

At five o'clock the next morning the "Dogs" took the initiative. The Germans had failed to yield to persuasion; their ships would have to be towed to Ancona. The weather, although unpleasant, would permit this. V.57 told all the boats that this was the general intention and 642 (Lt. E. F. Smyth) and 643 (Lt. D. Hill) were sent off to the eastwards to find and tow back the three craft which had drifted out of the harbour and took in tow a lightly manned F-lighter that was only slightly aground near the harbour entrance.

This test case provoked no reaction other than angry words from the men on board, and the "F" was taken outside to the area designated as the collecting point, where she was anchored with a small prize crew on board. Throughout the rest of the morning "Dogs" were going in and out of Tagliamento towing craft to the collecting point, putting prize crews on board and making their prizes as ready as possible for the journey to Ancona. This gave rise to irritation and annoyance amongst the Germans, but nothing further.

In his report V.57 said: "Throughout the whole forenoon there was a heavy swell which made going alongside a good feat of seamanship in itself, and the difficulties in handling and towing heavier craft in down to six feet of water added considerably to the times taken for what might appear simple tasks."

During the morning Bligh had another interview with the authorities ashore. The N.Z. Army said that they were very short of food for the prisoners, that the Germans had said that some of the F-lighters were loaded with food and that they would like to unload these up the river; unfortunately, said the Germans, it so happened that all the particular "Fs" which had the food on board had been towed outside the harbour by the English boats, and if the Army would arrange for the Navy to tow them back again it would be much better for all concerned.

Bligh pointed up the river to the twelve "Fs", which the "Dogs" had been unable to move, and mentioned that some craft had been allowed to drift overnight; nevertheless he undertook to examine all the captured "Fs" and to return, temporarily, any which were loaded with significant amounts of food. The Army said that the Navy was setting too much store on "what was, after all, a lot of worthless junk". This made Bligh angry, and it gave him pleasure to learn from all the "Dogs" that none of the prizes had any food on board, except a few tins.

On the way back from this conference Bligh called in on the *Fasana*, a coaster of about 1,000 tons and the second largest ship in the harbour. Although Bligh was correctly dressed in regulation No. 5 uniform, the captain received him with hands in pockets and cigar in mouth. When asked if he were ready to proceed to Ancona, the German said that he was not, "because he was aground, because his main engines were out of action, because he had hit a mine, because he had no fuel, because he had orders, because he had to provide food, clothing, and shelter for all the troops who were ashore and anyhow he liked it how he was". There did not seem to be anything more to be said.

The "Dogs" had by then bitten off as much as they could chew. V.57 sent a signal to Snona suggesting that there was still scope for three MLs and saying that the "Dogs" were returning. At half-past twelve the first convoy, under Ted Smyth, left Tagliamento for Ancona. It comprised:

MGB 642 towing an "F"
     643 towing an "F"
     659 towing the barge *Karl* and a small caïque
Adria, *Sigismund*, and a small craft under their own power
MGB 645 to act as rover and picker-up of lost boats

As night fell the weather became worse. At a quarter to seven 645 took in tow *Sigismund* and the small craft. An hour later 642's tow parted for the fourth time and F.619 was sunk by gunfire at ten to nine. During the rest of the night 645's tow parted twice, 659's once and 643's once. This convoy reached Ancona at midday on Friday, 4th May.

The second convoy left Tagliamento at a quarter to three on Thursday afternoon. It was made up as follows:

MGB 662
MTB 634 towing an "F"
     651 towing *Edda* and a small boat
     670 towing an "F"
Tow "Fs" under their own power
Small hospital ship

This group met with an early setback, as F.1156D was unable to make good enough speed to steer. She was abandoned at anchor about eight miles south of Tagliamento, a signal being sent to Snona. MTBs 651 and 670 were sent on at 8 knots, while 662 took S/Lt. Finlay's F-lighter in tow and, with 634, made good about 5 knots. At half-past nine the wind was blowing a good Force 6, and 662 parted her tow.

The prize crew were unable to haul a new tow inboard (incidentally 662 fished up a large mine from the bottom of the Adriatic while this was going on). However, Finlay signalled that he had two engines and was happy to proceed under his own power, but that he had no means at all of lighting the compass and could not see to steer. 634 was sent on at her best speed and 662 stayed with the prize, switching on her navigation lights to full brilliancy and steering a series of reciprocal courses in the grain of the "F".

In this manner a speed of just over 2 knots was maintained until four o'clock, when the customary morning moderation of the weather made it possible to pass a fresh tow. At nine o'clock the "F's" bridle parted, but a new one was rigged and the prize was eventually anchored in Ancona at a quarter past four on Friday, 4th May, the return journey having taken twenty-five and a half hours and V.57 having been three nights without sleep.

In forwarding the report of the operation to the C.-in-C., Mediterranean, Rear-Admiral Morgan wrote: "This was probably one of the strangest operations of the war, and I consider that Lt.-Cdr. Bligh's handling of a situation almost without precedent is deserving of the highest praise." (Bligh was subsequently awarded the O.B.E.)

It was a strange operation. It did not result in the anchoring of all German ships from Trieste in Ancona. But it did show Coastal Forces in the Mediterranean right up to the end of the war, and beyond, doing a job of work—a job that no other ships could have done, and a job for which they manifestly were not designed. It showed them ready to tackle any tasks from the most exciting to the most pedestrian. And it is, perhaps, permissible to say that it showed that during the war not only had they identified themselves with all the splendid traditions of the Royal Navy but they had written another chapter in those richly-coloured annals.

EPILOGUE

BEFORE leaving Vis, Brig. Tom Churchill had a memorial erected at the Old Naval Cemetery. The wording, given here, also provides a fitting tribute to those men of Coastal Forces who perished in the Mediterranean theatre of war:

AFTER MORE THAN ONE HUNDRED YEARS
BRITISH SOLDIERS AND SAILORS
WHO FOUGHT AND DIED FOR THEIR COUNTRY'S HONOUR
ON THE SEAS AND ISLANDS OF DALMATIA
HAVE AGAIN BEEN LAID TO REST
IN THIS ISLAND CEMETERY
1944

HERE DEAD LIE WE BECAUSE WE DID NOT CHOOSE
TO LIVE AND SHAME THE LAND FROM WHICH WE SPRUNG
LIFE TO BE SURE IS NOTHING MUCH TO LOSE
BUT YOUNG MEN THINK IT IS AND WE WERE YOUNG

They shall be mine, saith the Lord of Hosts,
In that day when I make up my jewels.

APPENDIX A

Ships	Number fired	Hits and probables	Percentage of hits
Battleships	12	1	8.3
Cruisers	91	20	22.0
Destroyers	537	84	15.6
Coastal Forces	1,279	352	27.5
Submarines	4,967	1,105	22.2
Naval aircraft	615	224	36.4

TABLE OF TORPEDOES FIRED AND HITS REGISTERED BY ALL BRITISH
WARSHIPS BETWEEN 3RD SEPTEMBER 1939–1ST MAY 1945

NOTE: It will be seen that, despite their extremely limited sphere of operations—the coasts of the North Sea, Channel, Mediterranean and certain parts in the Far East—the Coastal Forces' percentage of torpedo hits is far higher than any other type of warship.

In addition, cruisers and destroyers frequently used torpedoes to give the coup de grace to enemy warships already crippled and possibly stopped by gunfire. Those sinkings are included in this table.

Naval aircraft have to jettison unused torpedoes before landing.

The Coastal Forces' torpedo expenditure figures in the above table are for all areas; but to give a fair picture, the Mediterranean figures for 1st January 1945–1st May 1945 are given below because they are considerably higher than the above average.

Number fired	Hits	Probables	Misfires	Percentage of hits
110	44	7	7	40.0

TABLE OF TORPEDOES FIRED AND HITS REGISTERED BY MTBs IN THE
MEDITERRANEAN 1ST JANUARY–1ST MAY 1945

APPENDIX B

Type	Sunk or destroyed by gun or torpedo	Probably sunk or destroyed	Damaged	Captured
Merchant vessels	25	6	6	—
F-lighters and Siebels	58	11	13	6
I-boats	12	—	4	2
Schooners and caiques	32	3	2	14
Warships	12	1	10	—
E- or R-boats	25	2	23	—
Pil-boats	12	—	1	—
Miscellaneous vessels	14	7	4	14
Unknown craft	6	1	5	—
TOTAL	202	34	68	36
Aircraft	16	3	4	—

TABLE OF ENEMY VESSELS SUNK, DAMAGED OR CAPTURED
BETWEEN 1ST JANUARY 1943–1ST MAY 1945
(Compiled from action reports and not necessarily complete,
especially where reports were not made or lost.)

Of the 158 successful reported actions during this period, 121 British boats
and 15 or more PT were involved.

Sixty-eight were fought by Fairmile "D" MTBs or MGBs; 73 by Vosper
and Higgins type MTBs; 14 by MLs and 3 by HDMLs. Four actions were
by mixed "Ds", Vospers and MLs.

This table does not include inconclusive engagements; and "sunk" means
seen to have sunk or confirmed by Intelligence.

Appendix C

REVIEW OF THE YEAR 1944

WEST COAST OF ITALY

Nights	Nights on which ops carried out	Nights of no ops	Total number of patrols	Actions
366	182	184	203	60

Sinkings

32 F-lighters   2 E-boats
2 torpedo-boats   3 large barges
2 K.T. ships   1 tug
1 tanker   1 small craft
Total: 44

Probable sinkings

6 F-lighters
3 merchant ships
2 E-boats
1 large barge
Total: 12

Possible sinkings

3 F-lighters
1 torpedo-boat
1 large barge
Total: 5

Damaged

5 F-lighters
3 E-boats
4 torpedo-boats
2 trawlers
Total: 14

Mines swept: 3rd ML Flotilla (in year) 177; 31st ML Flotilla (in eight months) 143.

ADRIATIC (for eight months)

Nights	Nights on which ops carried out	Nights of no ops	Total number patrols	Actions
244	177	67	249	41

(Losses below are for twelve months.)

Sinkings

1 cruiser	2 motor-boats	
1 torpedo-boat	3 E.M.B.s	
1 coast-defence ship	1 pinnace	
2 tankers	9 F-lighters	
4 merchant ships	5 lighters	
2 tugs	1 barge	
1 Siebel ferry	17 schooners	
6 E-boats	8 Pil-boats	
16 I-boats	2 caïques	
1 R-boat	1 landing-craft	

Total: 84

Captured

10 schooners
2 I-boats
1 lighter
1 motor-boat

Total: 14

Probably sunk

1 E-boat
1 I-boat

Possibly sunk

1 E-boat
1 I-boat

Damaged

6 E-boats	1 torpedo-boat
2 schooners	1 Siebel ferry
1 E.M.B.	1 I-boat
1 M.S. boat	

Total: 13

Mines swept: 8th ML Flotilla (since Aug.) 16; 24th ML Flotilla (since Oct.) 28; 41st ML Flotilla (since Aug.) 63.

AEGEAN

(The following table does not include HDML operations.)

Sinkings

2 tankers	1 E.M.S. boat
1 merchant ship	1 schooner
1 E-boat	6 caïques
1 R-boat	
1 large barge	

Total: 14

Damaged

4 merchant ships
1 tanker
3 R-boats

Total: 8

Appendix D

REVIEW OF 1945 (JAN.–APRIL)

WEST COAST OF ITALY

Nights	Nights on which ops carried out	Nights of no ops	Total number of patrols	Actions
120	56	64	90	9

Sinkings
2 merchant ships
1 K.T. ship
1 F-lighter
      Total: 4

Possible sinkings
1 K.T. ship
1 escort vessel
1 F-lighter
2 unknown ships
      Total: 5

Probable sinkings
2 F-lighters

Damaged
1 F-lighter
1 unknown ship

ADRIATIC

Nights	Nights on which ops carried out	Nights of no ops	Total number of patrols	Actions
120	105	15	154	29

Sinkings
3 merchant ships   3 armed barges
1 torpedo-boat   1 schooner
1 escort vessel   1 small T.B.
15 F-lighters   3 E-boats
            Total: 28

Damaged
1 K.T. ship
1 merchant ship
2 E-boats
4 F-lighters
1 R-boat
      Total: 9

Possible sinkings
3 F-lighters

INDEX